Ignatius Brown

Logan's History of Indianapolis from 1818

Giving a carefully compiled record of events of the city from the organization of the

state government;its mercantile, manufacturing, political and social progress,

course of development, present importance

Ignatius Brown

Logan's History of Indianapolis from 1818
Giving a carefully compiled record of events of the city from the organization of the state government;its mercantile, manufacturing, political and social progress, course of development, present importance

ISBN/EAN: 9783337289232

Printed in Europe, USA, Canada, Australia, Japan

Cover: Foto ©ninafisch / pixelio.de

More available books at **www.hansebooks.com**

LOGAN'S

HISTORY OF INDIANAPOLIS

· FROM 1818

by

Ignatius Brown

LOGAN'S
HISTORY OF INDIANAPOLIS,
FROM 1818.

GIVING A CAREFULLY COMPILED RECORD OF EVENTS OF THE CITY FROM THE ORGA-
NIZATION OF THE STATE GOVERNMENT; ITS MERCANTILE, MANUFACTURING,
POLITICAL AND SOCIAL PROGRESS; COURSE OF DEVELOPMENT, PRES-
ENT IMPORTANCE AND FUTURE PROSPERITY; AS SEEN BY
A NATIVE BORN RESIDENT AND WORTHY CITIZEN.

Indianapolis, the political and commer- cial capital of Indiana, is situated on the west fork of white river, latitude 39° 55', longitude 86° 5', and about 527 feet above the sea. It is two miles northwest of the centre of the State, and one mile south-west of the centre of Marion county. It occu- pies the midst of a shallow basin, the ground rising gradually for miles in all directions. The soil is a clayey loam, sub-soil clay, on thick beds of drift gravel and sand, resting on silurian clays, limestones and shales.

The gravel beds are great natural filters, producing thorough drainage and holding ample supplies of the purest water. The whole country was once densely covered with large hard wood trees, and in many places on the city site were extensive thick- ets of prickly ash and spicewood. The thick undergrowth afforded safe covert for all kinds of game, and for a number of years after the settlement bears and deer were readily found in the neighborhood. Hun- ters seldom returned unsuccessful from the chase, and, as late as 1842, saddles of veni- son sold at from 25 to 50 cents, turkeys at 10 and 12 cents, and a bushel of pigeons for 25 cents. The river was so fully stocked with fish that an old settler declared "a stone thrown in it anywhere, from the grave yard ford to the mouth of Fall creek, would strike a shoal of fish." The Indians reluctantly yielded the country on account of the abundance of fish and game, and many of them lingered in the vicinity long after the treaty. Though they had no per- manent village here, their hunting and fish- ing camps were numerous on and north of the city site, and a traveller who passed up the river several years before the settlement says the banks were then dotted with wig- wams and the river often parted by their canoes. The scene was very striking at night when the savages were fire hunting or fishing. The Shawnees and Delawares had moved to this section sometime between

1790 and 1795, and had built several vil- lages along the river, the nearest being about twelve miles above this point. An old white woman, the wife of a French trader, lived there after the rest of the tribe had left. She had been taken prisoner, when nine years old, at Martin's Station in Kentucky, had married an Indian and rais- ed a half breed family, and after the death of her Indian husband married the French- man.

1818 By treaty at St. Marys, Ohio, Oc- tober 2, between the Delaware Indians and the Lewis Cass, Johnathan Jennings and Ben- jamin Parke, United States commissioners, the former ceded all their lands in central Indiana, agreeing to give possession in 1821. The reported fertility and beauty of "the new purchase," as it was afterward called, excited the frontiersmen, and, without wait- ing for possession to be given under the treaty, they entered it at various points. William Conner, an Indian trader, had set- tled at a Delaware village on White river, four miles this side of Noblesville, several years before this date. His location drew the attention of others to that stream, and several persons from Fayette and Wayne counties, visited this section just before and after the treaty. In the Spring of 1819, two brothers, named Jacob and Cyrus Whit- zel, having got permission of the old Dela- ware chief, blazed a trace from the White- water river to the bluffs of White river. They remained and raised a crop there during the Summer, and moved their fami- lies out in October. (Jacob Whitzel died there July 2, 1827.) Lewis Whitzel, the noted Indian scout, celebrated in border annals, was a brother of these men and visited them there shortly after, while on his way to Louisiana. Late in the Fall of 1818, Dr. Douglas had ascended the river from the lower settlements, stopping awhile at the bluffs; and James Paxton descended

it from the headwaters, reaching this point in January, 1820. These exploring trips were attended with some risk, for the Indians were in full possession and not well disposed toward the intruders.

1819 According to most authorities, the honor due to the first settler belongs to George Pogue, a blacksmith from Whitewater, who reached this point from that section March 2, 1819. After reaching the river he turned back and built his cabin on the high ground east of the creek which now bears his name, close to a large spring, and near the present eastern end of Michigan street. The ruins of this cabin were

(George Pogue's Residence, the First Cabin Built on the Donation.)

visible for many years afterward. Pogue was killed by Indians about daybreak one morning in April, 1821. His horses had been disturbed during the night, he declared the Indians were stealing them, and taking his rifle set out in pursuit. When last seen he was near their camp, gunshots were heard, and as his horses and clothes were afterward seen in their possession little doubt remained as to his fate. His death greatly excited the settlers, but their numerical weakness prevented any effort to avenge it. The creek on which he settled, which then pursued a very winding course through the south-east part of the plat, alarming the inhabitants by its floods, received his name and remains a lasting memorial of the first inhabitant of the present city.

Pogue's claim as the first settler has been contested, and in a published article by Dr. S. G. Mitchell, in the Indianapolis Gazette, in the Summer of 1822, it is stated that the McCormicks were the first emigrants in February, 1820, and that Pogue arrived with others in March, 1820, a month later. It is singular that this statement, if ill-founded, should not have been contradicted publicly in the paper at the time, but the weight of tradition is against it and concurs in fixing Pogue's arrival in 1819.

1820 Pogue seems to have been the only inhabitant from March, 1819, to February 27, 1820, when John and James McCormick arrived and built their cabins on the river bank, just below the mouth of Fall creek and near the present bridge. John Maxwell and John Cowan followed shortly after, building cabins early in March, in the north-west corner of the donation on Fall creek, near the present Crawfordsville road bridge. In March, April and May, other families arrived following the trace left by Cowan and Maxwell, and by the first of June there were perhaps fifteen families on the present donation. Among them were those of Henry and Samuel Davis, Corbaley, Barnhill, VanBlaricum, Harding and Wilson. The first cabin on the old town plat was built in May, by Isaac Wilson, near the north-west corner of the state house square. Other emigrants arrived during the Summer and Fall, and the settlement grew slowly for a year afterward. The government surveys in this section were made in 1819 and 1820.

The congressional act of April 19, 1816, authorizing a state government for Indiana, had donated (with the privilege of selection,) four sections of unsold lands for a permanent capital. The assembly, on January 11, 1820, appointed George Hunt, John Conner, John Gilliland, Stephen Ludlow, Joseph Bartholomew, John Tipton, Jesse B. Durham, Frederick Rapp, William Prince and Thomas Emerson, commissioners to make the selection, directing them to meet at Conner's house, on White river, early in the Spring. A part of them only served. Ascending the valley on horseback and making examinations, they met as directed at Conner's, where, after very serious disputes between them as to sites at the bluffs, or the mouth of Fall creek and at Conner's, the present location was chosen by three votes against two for the bluffs. On the 7th of June, 1820, they reported the choice of sections one and twelve, east fractional section two and eleven, and enough of west fractional section three, in township fifteen, range three east, to make the four sections granted. The location gave the place important reputation, and assisted in bringing emigrants to it during the Summer and Fall of 1820, and Spring of 1821. Among those who then came were Morris Morris, Dr. S. G. Mitchell, John and James Given, Matthias Nowland, James M. Ray, Nathaniel Cox, Thomas Anderson, John Hawkins, Dr. Livingston Dunlap, David Wood, Daniel Yandes, Alexander Ralston, Dr. Isaac Coe, Douglas Maguire and others, and the cabins clustered closely along the river bank, on and near which almost the whole settlement was located. Most of the above

named parties came in the Spring of 1821.
In the north-west part of the donation, and west of the present blind asylum, a tract of one hundred and fifty or two hundred acres was found where the heavy timber had been killed years before by locusts or worms. The undergrowth was cut off, brush fences enclosed portions of the "caterpillar deadning," and during this and following years it was cultivated in corn and vegetables by the settlers as a common field. Its existence was a great benefit, for it saved much heavy labor in cutting off dense timber and was immediately available for cultivation. It yielded abundantly, game was readily procured, and though considerable sickness occurred during the Summer and Fall, the people got along with comparative comfort during the Fall and Winter of 1820.

1821 The legislature confirmed the choice of site January 6, 1821, named the town Indianapolis, and appointed Christopher Harrison, James Jones and Samuel P. Booker, commissioners to lay it off, directing them to meet on the site first Monday in April, appoint surveyors and clerk, make a survey, prepare two maps, and advertise and sell the alternate lots as soon as possible, the money received from the sales to be set apart as a public building fund. At the appointed time Judge Harrison was the only commissioner here and the only one who acted. Elias P. Fordham and Alexander Ralston had been selected as the surveyors, and Benjamin I. Blythe clerk. Mr. Blyth became a resident of the town and was subsequently the agent. Of Fordham little is known. Ralston was an old bachelor, a talented Scotchman, and when young had assisted in surveying Washington city. He was afterward connected with Burr's expedition and on its failure remained in the West. We are indebted to him for the regular plan, large squares, wide streets and diagonal avenues of the old plat. He afterward settled here, highly esteemed for his virtues and mental powers, and dying January 5, 1827, lies somewhere in the old cemetery in an unmarked grave.

The surveying party having been organized in April, the plan was determined on, the plat made and the survey begun. The lines and corners of the four sections were traced out, with a fraction on the west bank to complete the 2,560 acres granted. A town plat one mile square was marked out near the middle of the donation. A circle lot of nearly four acres in extent surrounded by a street eighty feet wide occupied the centre, and from the outside corners of the blocks next to it avenues ninety feet wide were drawn to the corners of the plat. The other streets ran north and south and east

and west, and were ninety feet wide except Washington which was one hundred and twenty. There were eighty-nine squares of four acres in extent, each four hundred and twenty feet front, divided by two alleys fifteen and thirty feet wide crossing at right angles. There were also six fractional squares and three large irregular tracts in the valley of Pogue's run. The present North, South, East and West streets, were not included in the original design, the plat abutting directly against the undivided donation lands, but were added afterward by Judge Harrison at the suggestion of James Blake, who said that fifty years afterward they would afford a fine four mile drive around the town and a half mile from its centre. The donation outside the plat was not laid off or divided, for no one supposed the town would ever extend beyond the plat, and no provision was made for it. It was afterward divided by the agent, under direction of the assembly, into large out-blocks, with few and narrow roads or streets, and sold for farms. The "sub-divisions" are properly in the squares of the old plat and in these out-blocks, and the "additions" are properly outside of the donation limits. Unfortunately no rule has ever been adopted by the legislature or city council requiring sub-divisions, and especially additions, to conform generally to the city plat. Each owner has been left free to regulate the size and shape of blocks and lots, and the width and direction of streets and alleys, to suit his own interest or convenience, and as a natural consequence the newest portions of our city are the most irregular and unsightly portions shown on its map. A rule on this subject should be at once adopted for the future, and large sums will have to be expended some day on account of the failure to adopt it in the past. The city long since covered the donation, and its suburbs extend in most directions from a half mile to a mile beyond, but the municipal government and revenues are still restricted to the original donation limits. The old town plat was not located in the center of the donation. The joint corner of the four sections is in the alley ten feet west and five feet south of the southeast corner of the Palmer House lot. The surveyors found that if the centre of the plat was fixed there too much of the plat would be thrown in Pogue's run valley, then a most unpromising locality. In searching for a better point the natural elevation in the present circle was found and at once chosen. It was then covered with a fine grove of tall, straight sugar trees, which should have been preserved. The surveyors were much embarrassed in their work by the bayous which then crossed the

donation in a north-east and south-west di- in September, 1822. The people were direction, and by the dense thickets through satisfied with him and with his successor,
which they had to cut their way. In some James Milroy, (who held the office a few
places these bayou channels are not yet en- months and then resigned, because they did
tirely obliterated, and portions of the old not become permanent residents of the town.
thickets were found in protected spots till Bethuel F. Morris was appointed December
1850. 24, 1822; Benjamin I. Blythe February 1,

The surveys and maps being completed, 1825; Ebenezer Sharpe April 8, 1828,
the lot sale was duly advertised and held by dying September, 1835; John G. Brown
Gen. John Carr, (the first State agent, who then held it a few months, being succeeded
had reached here shortly before,) on the January or February, 1835, by Thomas H.
10th of October, at a cabin on Washington Sharpe; John Cook, state librarian, held it
street just west of the present canal. The a short time in 1843-4, and the office was
sale lasted nearly a week. The first day then transferred to the auditor of State Jan-
was cold and raw with a high wind, and a uary, 1844, and the business closed up by
man at the sale came near being killed by him.
a falling limb. There were many buyers Until 1821 the centre and north part of
present both citizens and strangers, and the State was included in Delaware county
Carter's, Hawkins' and Nowland's taverns, yet unorganized but attached, for judicial
as well as many of the private houses, were purposes, to Fayette and Wayne counties,
thronged with guests; competition was brisk whose courts had concurrent jurisdiction.
and high prices were obtained. The main The people in the new purchase were sued
settlement was near the river, but lots to and indicted in the courts at Connersville and
the east and north sold best, for the unusual other points on Whitewater, and the cross
sickness during the summer and Fall (here often exceeded the debt, damages or fines,
after mentioned) had convinced the people Conflicts of jurisdiction also occurred, (li-
they must leave the river neighborhood. feeling was aroused, and the people here
Each four acre block was divided into 12 finally rebelled against it. To prevent
lots 67½ by 195 feet, and the alternate lots trouble the assembly, January 9, 1821, au-
were reserved beginning with number one. thorized the appointment of two justices of
Three hundred and fourteen lots in the cen- the peace for the new settlements, appeals
tral and northern parts of the old plat were lying from them to the Bartholomew circuit
sold for $85,506,25, one-fifth or $7,119,25 court. In April Governor Jennings ap-
down and the balance in four equal annual pointed John Maxwell, of this place, a ju-
installments. The lot west of court square tice of the peace, the first judicial officer
on Washington street sold highest, $500, in the new purchase, but he resigned in
and the similar lot west of state square June, and the citizens elected James Mcll-
brought $500. Intervening lots on the vain, who was duly commissioned in Octo-
street sold from $100 to $300. One hun- ber. His twelve foot cabin stood on the
dred and sixty-nine lots sold at this time north-west corner of Pennsylvania and
were afterward forfeited or exchanged by Michigan streets, where he held court, pipe
the buyers for others. The reserved and in mouth, in his cabin door, the jury ranged
forfeited lots were repeatedly offered at sub- in front on a fallen tree, and the first con-
sequent periods, both at public and private stable, Corbaley, standing guard over the
sale; but money was scarce. the town im- culprits, who nevertheless often escaped
proved slowly, prices declined and for sev- through the woods. Calvin Fletcher was
eral years few sales were made. Nineteen then the only lawyer, and the last judge in
hundred acres of lots and lands remained all the knotty cases, the justice privately
unsold as late as 1831, but were mostly dis- taking his advice as to their disposal.
posed of in that year by order of the legis- There was no jail nearer than Connersville,
lature, the minimum price being ten dollars and it being expensive and troublesome to
per acre. The amount received up to 1842, send culprits there in charge of the consta-
when the sales were ended and closed, was ble and posse, the plan was adopted of
about $125,000, and from this fund the frightening them away. A case of this kind
state house, court house, Governor's circle, occurred on Christmas, 1821. Four Ken-
clerk's office and treasurer's house and office tucky boatmen, who had "whipped their
were built. General Carr received the weight in wild cats" on the Kanawha and
money and made the deeds at the first sale. elsewhere, came from the bluffs to "Napli-"
His cabin stood on Delaware street where to have a Christmas spree. It began early,
Hereth's block now stands, and the elections for the citizens were roused before dawn by
were held and the courts began there till a great uproar at Daniel Larkins clapboard
the court house was built. He was appoint- grocery, which contained a barrel of whisky.
ed in 1821 at a salary of $600, but it was The four heroes were discovered busily em-
reduced next year to $300, and he resigned ployed in tearing it down. A request to

desist produced a volley of oaths, a display of big knives, and an advance on the citi- zens, most of whom immediately found pres- sing business elsewhere. They were inter- ested, however, in the existence of the gro- cery, and furthermore such defiance of law and order could not be tolerated. A con- sultation was held, resulting in the determi- nation to take the rioters at all hazards. James Blake volunteered to grapple the leader, a man of great size and strength, if the rest would take the three others. The attack was made, the party captured and marched under guard through the woods to justice McIlvaine's cabin, where they were at once tried, heavily fined and ordered to jail at Connersville in default of payment or bail. Payment was out of the question, and they could not be taken to Connersville at that season of the year. Ostentatious pre- parations were made, however, for the trip, the posse was selected for the journey next day, a guard was placed over them with secret instructions, and during the night the doughty heroes fled to more congenial climes.

But the Fayette and Wayne county courts still claimed jurisdiction, and the annoyance therefrom continued. Doubts existed as to the legality of Maxwell and McIlvain's ap- pointments, and a meeting was held at Hawkins' log tavern, late in the Fall, to de- vise some remedy for the difficulty. It was resolved to demand the organization of a new county, and James Blake and Dr. S. G. Mitchell were selected as lobby members to attend at Corydon and secure it.

The Summer of 1821 was noted for con- tinuous and heavy rains. There is little doubt that much more water fell forty years ago than now. Storms of wind, rain and thunder, were more frequent and violent; streams rose higher and remained full longer; sections now dry were then very swampy; and bayous ran bank full that are now unknown. To travel even a few miles was sometimes a desperate undertaking, and teams were often stopped for weeks by high water. The whole country was wooded and wet; the air was damper, modifying the Winter cold and Summer heat; the wind generally came from the south and west, and the climate was milder and more uni- form than now. As the timber and swamps disappeared the air grew dryer, fogs were less frequent, winds had more sweep and came oftener from the north, variations of heat and cold increased, till at present the cultivation of peaches,—formerly a certain crop,—has been abandoned; and if the change continues with the deforesting of the country, it is questionable whether other crops besides peaches will not be lost.

In consequence of the wet condition of the country and the want of roads the set- tlement was almost entirely isolated. The national road had been designed to run fif- teen miles south of this point before the site was chosen, but the assembly, January 8, 1821, memorialized congress, stating the lo- cation of the capital, and asking that it be made a point on the line. This was after- ward conceded, to the great joy of the peo- ple, but the road was not commenced in this State till 1830, and was abandoned in 1839 before its completion, leaving the town still in the mud. It is impossible, at present, with our railroads and good common roads, to realize the situation of the early settlers after a Spring thaw or a long wet spell, separated from civilization by sixty miles of mud and slush, with unbridged streams, floating corduroys and fathomless mud holes. Horse-back travel over the so called roads was often a serious business, and with a team an impossibility. Until a compara- tively late period a "stage" often consisted of the four wheels and axles, on which balanced a crate containing one or two wet, muddy, half-frozen passengers, dragged wearily into town by four or six horses looking like animated masses of mud.

The Summer of 1821 was distinguished by the general sickness resulting, it was thought, from the heavy fall of rain. It is said that storms occurred every day in June, July and August. Clouds would suddenly gather and send a deluge of water, then as quickly break away, while the sun's rays fairly scorched the drenched herbage, gen- erating miasmatic vapors with no wind to carry them off. Sickness began in July but did not become general till after the 10th of August, on which day Matthias Nowland had a raising, all the men in the settlement assisting. Remittant and intermittant fe- vers, of a peculiar type, then began, and in three weeks the community was prostrated. Thomas Chinn, Enoch Banks and Nancey Hendricks, were the only persons who es- caped. Though so general the disease was not deadly, about twenty-five only, mostly children who had been too much exposed, dying out of several hundred cases. The few who could go about devoted their time to the sick, and many instances of generous devoted friendship occurred. Their mutual suffering at this time bound the early sett- lers together in after life, and none recur to this period without emotion. New comers were disheartened at the prospect, and some left the country circulating extravagant re- ports about the health of the town, greatly retarding its subsequent growth. Disease that year was general in the West. It was little greater here than elsewhere, and the relative mortality was scarcely so great. It abated here by the end of October, the gen-

eral health was soon after entirely restored. The people busily engaged in preparations for the winter.

The sickness having prevented proper cultivation of the common field, and the throng of strangers at the lot sale having consumed all surplus food, absolute starvation impended over the settlement. No roads or mills whatever existed, and all provisions and goods had to be packed on horses sixty miles through the wilderness from Whitewater. Regular expeditions were organized for procuring food. Flour and meal were brought on horseback from Goodlander's mill on Whitewater, then the nearest one, and corn was bought and boated down in canoes and rafts from the Indian villages up the river. The arrival of supplies from either of these points excited general joy among the half sick and half starved people. They aided each other in this new distress as in the former one, and many pecks of meal, pounds of flour, bacon, fish and other articles of food, were given more destitute neighbors.

Emigrants were constantly arriving during the year ending August 1. 1821, by which time there were fifty or sixty resident families. The October sales attracted others and by the end of the year the population was estimated at four or five hundred. Many, however, were only waiting till their cabins were built in the country to move out. Obed Foote, Calvin Fletcher, James Blake, Alexander W. Russel, Caleb Scudder, Nicholas McCarty, George Smith, Nathaniel Bolton, Wilkes Reagan and others, arrived during the Summer and Fall of 1821. The wet and sickly Summer was succeeded in October by a long and beautiful Indian Summer. The sick recovered health and spirits, business improved, new and better cabins were built further from the river, for the settlement left the river after the sickness, though it was still mainly west of the canal, where a cluster of cabins was dignified with the title of Wilmot's row, Wilmot keeping a little store there. During the Fall the timber on the streets was offered to any one who would cut it, and as it was largely composed of splendid ash, walnut and oak trees, Lismund Basye accepted the grant as a chance for fortune, and labored zealously in felling the trees on Washington street. After cutting a large part of the timber down the question arose "What will he do with it?" and as there were no mills to cut it into lumber, Basye was unequal to the answer. He had drawn the elephant and having done so abandoned it. The street was so blocked with standing and felled timber and undergrowth that it was impossible to get through it, and the citizens burned it where it lay during the Winter and Spring. John Hawkins had built a log tavern early in the Fall, where the Sentinel office now stands, using logs cut from the site and the street, and so dense was the timber and undergrowth that a person at that tavern could not see Isaac Lynch's house and shoe shop where 5 and No 7 west Washington now are, and it took nearly a half mile travel to go from one point to the other. The work of clearing and burning steadily progressed, and by the close of the Spring of 1822 the people rejoiced at being able to take a wagon along a zig zag path on and near the street for a considerable part of its length. The first marriage, first birth and first death, occurred during the Summer of 1821. The first marriage was that of Jeremiah Johnson to Miss Jane Reagan. He walked to Connersville and back, one hundred and twenty miles, for the license, and had to wait several weeks for a preacher to come along and marry them. He died at his residence near the city April 5, 1857. Mordecai Harding (still living,) was the first person born on the donation, and James Morrow, the first in the old town plat. The first death was that of Daniel Shaffer, the first merchant of the place, who had come in January, 1821, and kept a few goods and groceries at his cabin on the high ground south of Pogue's run, near Pennsylvania street. He died in May or June and was buried in Pogue's run valley, near Pennsylvania street, but was taken up and reburied in the old graveyard August 25th. The first woman who died was Mrs. Maxwell, wife of John Maxwell, dying July 3d, and buried on the 4th on the high ground near the Crawfordsville road bridge over Fall creek. Eight persons were buried there during the Summer and Fall. No cemetery had been set apart in the original survey, but Judge Harrison, at the request of the people, assigned the lot on the river afterward known as the old burying ground, and on December 31, 1822, the assembly confirmed the grant. In the meantime twenty-five or thirty persons had been buried there. It was covered with heavy timber and undergrowth, but at a citizens' meeting March 10, 1824, it was resolved to clear and enclose it. Nearly fifty persons had then been laid in it.

It may be interesting to give here the names and dates of arrival of the pioneers in the different trades and professions. John McClung, a new light minister, came in the Spring of 1821, and preached the first sermon here shortly after, in the grove on the circle, the audience sitting around him on the grass and logs in Indian style. Services continued there during the Summer and Fall whenever the weather per-

mitted. He died north of town August 18, 1823. Other authorities say the first sermon was preached during the Summer, at the state house square, by Rev. Resin Hammond. James Scott, first Methodist preacher, was sent by the St. Louis conference, and reached here October, 1821, after much difficulty in finding the place. O. P. Gaines, first Presbyterian minister, came August, 1821. John Waters, first Baptist preacher, came October, 1823. Isaac Coe, physician, May, 1820. Calvin Fletcher, lawyer, September, 1821. Daniel Shaffer, merchant, January, 1821, died May, 1821. James B. Hall, carpenter, Winter of 1820. Matthias Nowland, brick-maker and mason, November, 1820, died November 11, 1822. Andrew Byrne, tailor, November, 1820. Isaac Lynch, shoemaker, Fall of 1821. William Holmes, tinner, Spring of 1822. Michael Ingals, teamster, Fall of 1820. Kenneth A. Scudder, Summer of 1820, died March 5, 1820, opened first drug store in 1823. Wilkes Reagan, butcher and auctioneer, Summer of 1821. John Shunk, hatter, October, 1821, died September 2, 1824. Amos Hanway, cooper, came up the river in a keelboat, June, 1821. Conrad Brussel, baker, Fall of 1820. Milo R. Davis, plasterer, Winter of 1820. George Norwood, wagon maker, Spring of 1822. John McCormack, tavern keeper, February 27, 1823, died August 27, 1825. George Myers, potter, Fall of 1821. Caleb Scudder, cabinet maker, October, 1821. Henry and Samuel Davis, chair makers, April or May, 1820. Isaac Wilson, miller, March, 1820. He built the first cabin on the old plat, on the north-west corner of the state house square, in March, 1820, and the first grist mill on Fall creek, north-west of Blackford's addition, in the Summer of 1821, and died November 4, 1823. George Pogue, first settler and blacksmith, March 2, 1819, killed by Indians April, 1821. James Linton, sawyer and mill-wright, Summer of 1821, built the first saw mill on Fall creek, near the Crawfordsville road bridge, in September and October, 1821. Nathaniel Bolton, editor and printer, September, 1821. George Smith, printer and book-binder, August, 1821, began book-binding 1823. Joseph C. Reed, teacher and county recorder, Spring of 1821. Samuel Walton, spinning wheel maker, October, 1826. A. McPherson, first foundry, July, 1832. Samuel S. Rooker, house and sign painter, Fall of 1821. Daniel Yandes, tanner, January, 1821. John Ambrozene, watch and clock maker, February, 1825. James Paxton, militia colonel, October, 1821. Samuel Morrow, lieut. colonel, Spring or Summer of 1820. Alexander W. Russell, major, Spring of 1821.

John Maxwell, justice of the peace, March, 1820. William W. Wick, circuit judge, February, 1822. Harvey Bates, sheriff, February, 1822. James J. McIlvain and Eliakim Harding, associate judges. Summer of 1820. James M. Ray. county clerk, Spring of 1821. Joseph C. Reed, county recorder, Spring of 1821. John McCormack, county commissioner, February 27, 1820. John T. Osborn, county commissioner, Spring of 1821. Samuel Henderson, postmaster, Fall of 1821. William P. Murphy, dentist, November, 1820. Elizabeth Nowland, first boarding house, November, 1820, began 1823. Samuel Beck began gunsmithing July, 1833, still at it, 1868. . Hubbard, Edmunds & Co., book-store, began May, 1833. David Mallory, colored barber, in Spring of 1821.

Daniel Shaffer had opened the first store in February or March, 1821, at his cabin on the high ground south of Pogue's run, but dying in May or June, stores were shortly afterward opened by John and James Given and John T. Osborn, near the river bank, and by Wilmot, at Wilmot's row, near the present site of the old Carlisle house. Luke Walpole began in the Fall or Winter, on the south-west corner of the state house square, and Jacob Landis on the south-east corner. Jeremiah Johnson also began on the north-west corner of Market and Pennsylvania streets. The first log school house, Joseph C. Reed teacher, was built in 1821, near a large pond just west of the Palmer house. Reed taught a short time being succeeded temporarily by two or three others, but no permanent school existed till after June 20, 1822, when trustees were chosen, and Mr. and Mrs. Lawrence selected as teachers by a meeting held for the purpose at the school house. After the Presbyterian church was finished and the school opened there, Mr. and Mrs. Lawrance taught there for several years. The first frame and also the first plastered house was built in the Fall of 1821, by James Blake, on the lot east of Masonic hall. It stood till 1852, and was occupied as the *Sentinel* office from 1841 to 1844. During the same Winter Thomas Carter built a two story ceiled frame tavern, (the first two story house,) eighteen by twenty feet, at 40 west Washington street. It was long known as the Rosebush tavern from its sign. It was afterward moved to the vicinity of the canal, and again to a point near the soldier's home, where it is yet standing. James Linton built the first saw mill in September and October, 1821, on Fall creek, above the Crawfordsville bridge; and about the same time he built the first grist mill, for Isaac Wilson, on Fall creek bayou north-west of Blackford's addition. Until this mill was

finished the people sent sixty miles to healthier and better housed and acquainted, Goodlander's for flour and meal, or hulled became sociable and merry. Dances, quiltings and weddings were frequent. Canditerward built here had no bolting cloths, dates were numerous and busily canvassing and fine flour was not made here until the for the county offices. Christmas brought steam mill was built in 1832. Linton also its round of festivities, and the Winter passbuilt the first two story frame dwelling in sed pleasantly in spite of past sickness, the Spring of 1822, at 76 west Washington threatened famine and cold, which was both street. It was burned during the Winter of severe and protracted. The snow was deep 1847. The first market house was built in and large logs were hauled on the ice in the maple grove on the circle, in May, the river, but fuel at least was plenty, and 1822, and Wilkes Reagan first sold meat with large chimneys, great back-logs and there in June. The first brick house was roaring fires, the inmates of the rude cabins bid defiance to the weather.

1822. The assembly, on the 3d of January, ordered the unsold lots to be leased, the lessees to clear them in four months. Two acres were to be sold for a brick-yard, and a three year lease given of the ferry. Lands in west Indianapolis were leased in lots of five to twenty acres. Improvements on unsold lots could be removed in forty days after sale. One hundred thousand dollars were soon after appropriated to cut roads through the wilderness.

(The First Brick House.)

built for John Johnson, begun in 1822 and finished in the Fall of 1823, on the lot east of Robert's chapel and is yet standing.

Doubts having arisen as to the validity of the survey and sales, Harrison only having acted, the assembly confirmed them November 28th, and on the 31st of December passed an act organizing Marion county. The organization to be complete April 1, 1822. Square fifty-eight,—court square,— was made the permanent seat of justice. Eight thousand dollars was appropriated to build a two story brick court house, fifty feet square, to be completed in three years, and used by the State, federal and county courts forever, and by the assembly for fifty years or till a State house was built. Two per cent. of the lot fund was devoted to county library. The sessions of the courts were to be held at Carr's house. Johnson, Hamilton, and most of Boone, Madison and Hancock counties, were attached to Marion for judicial purposes. Marion, Lawrence, Monroe, Morgan, Greene, Owen, Hendricks, Rush, Decatur, Bartholomew, Shelby and Jennings counties, constituted the fifth judicial circuit. William W. Wick was elected judge and Harvey Bates was commissioned sheriff by Governor Jennings. Both gentlemen were from Whitewater, and arrived here in February or March, 1822.

During the Winter, the people being

The Indianapolis *Gazette*, the first journal in the new purchase, edited printed and published by George Smith and Nathaniel Bolton, was first issued January 28th, from a cabin south-west of the intersection of the canal and Maryland street. The office was moved to the present theatre corner the next year, and a few years afterward to east Washington street near Glenn's block. The ink used on the first numbers was a tar composition. The paper appeared irregularly, the mails being so infrequent that news matter could not be obtained to fill the columns, but several mail routes were opened in April and May and that difficulty was measureably obviated. The second number appeared February 11th, third the 25th, fourth March 6th, fifth the 18th, sixth April 3d, seventh, May 4th, after which date it appeared weekly till discontinued in 1831. Heavy rains fell in April flooding the country, and as the editors happened to be absent when the flood came, they were stopped by high water for a month, suspending publication from April 3d to May 4th. B. F. Morris became editor May 3, 1821. Smith & Bolton dissolved April 27, 1823, Bolton continued the paper about a year, when they rejoined and published together till July 23, 1829, when they again dissolved. Bolton continued it till after the *Indiana Democrat* was issued, when the list of subscribers was transferred to that paper.

The *Gazette* of February 25, 1822, stated that much improvement was going on. Forty dwellings and several workshops had been built, a grist and two saw mills were running and others being built near town.

There were thirteen carpenters, four cabinet makers, eight blacksmiths, four shoemakers, two tailors, one hatter, two tanners, one saddler, one cooper, four brick-layers, two merchants, three grocers, four physicians, three lawyers, one preacher, one teacher, and seven tavern keepers. This list gives, perhaps, half the adult population of the place.

Harvey Bates, sheriff, by proclamation February 22, directed an election on April 1st, for two associate judges, a clerk, recorder, and three county commissioners. The voting precincts were at Carr's house, John Finch's, near Conner's station, John Page's, Strawtown, John Berry's, Andersontown, and William McCartney's on Fall creek near Pendleton. Returns were to be forwarded by the 3d of April. James Page, Robert Patterson, James McIlvain, Eliakin Harding, John Smock and Rev. John McClung were candidates for associate judges. James M. Ray, Ahio E. Davis, Morris Morris, Thomas Anderson and John W. Redding for clerk. Alexander Ralston, James Linton, Joseph C. Reed, Aaron Drake, John Givans, John Hawkins, William Vandegrift and William Townsend, for recorder, and twelve or fifteen candidates for county commissioners. Nearly half the population were candidates for some office, and all were busily canvassing. Nominating conventions were unknown and each ran on his personal merit. The Whitewater and Kentucky emigrants had brought their local prejudices and candidates with them. James M. Ray represented the first, and Morris Morris the last party. The canvass was thorough and the excitement culminated at the election.—Whisky flowed freely. Persons usually sober, excited by victory or grieved at defeat, joined in the spree and the whole community got drunk. Many Kentuckians had lived here less than a year and had no vote, and the Whitewater party being ably managed defeated them. The Kentuckians, however, afterward outvoted and outgeneralled their opponents. James McIlvain and Eliakin Harding were chosen associate judges; James M. Ray, clerk; Joseph C. Reed, recorder; and John T. Osborn, John McCormack and William McCartney, county commissioners. Two hundred and twenty-four votes were cast here, nearly half being from residents on the donation, and 336 votes were cast in the county, which then included most of the present adjoining counties. James M. Ray got 217 votes, the highest for any candidate. The county board organized and held their first session April 15, at the corner of Ohio and Meridian streets, and divided the county into Fall creek, Anderson, White river, Dela-

ware, Lawrence, Washington, Pike, Warren, Centre, Wayne, Franklin, Perry and Decatur townships, but several of these were united for township purposes for want of population.

No post routes or office was opened here till March, 1822. The mails had been brought, until that date, from Connersville at different intervals, by private hands. A citizens' meeting was held at Hawkins' tavern, January 30, to take measures for a regular private mail. Aaron Drake was chosen postmaster. He issued a circular to postmasters stating the fact and asking that letters for this point be sent to Connersville. He returned from the first trip after nightfall, his horn sounding far through the woods, arousing the people who turned out in the bright moonlight to greet him and learn the news. This effort aroused the government, and in February President Monroe appointed Samuel Henderson postmaster. He opened the office March 7th or 8th, and on the 3d of April published the first letter list of five letters to old residents. Henderson continued in office till removed by Jackson in February, 1831, being succeeded by John Cain, who resigned in 1841. Joseph M. Moore then held it till 1845. John Cain again held it until 1849. Alexander W. Russell succeeded in 1849, and his son, James N. Russell, was appointed for the balance of his term. William W. Wick held it from 1853 to 1857; John M. Talbott till 1861; Alexander H. Conner till 1866; and D. G. Rose till the present time. The office was first kept near the canal, then at Henderson's tavern, then on the north side of Washington west of Meridian street, then in the present Hubbard's block on south Meridian street, then in Blackford's old building opposite, from which it was moved in 1861 to the government building on north Pennsylvania street.

Plans for a court house were called for by the commissioners May 22. That of John E. Baker and James Paxton was chosen, and the contract given them in September. The house was begun the next Summer and finished in the Fall of 1824 at a cost of $14,000. Wilkes Reagan, Obed Foote, and Lismund Basye, were elected justices May 23. The sheriff was directed in May to obtain proposals for building a jail and clearing the court house square, both to be completed by the first of August. James Blake induced the board to save two hundred of the young maples growing on the square, but no specific instructions being given the contractor left two hundred of the largest trees on the tract, and when the surrounding forest was cut away the storms so damaged them that all had to be cut

down. The jail was a two story hewed log can September 26, 1822, at Carr's cabin, house, built in July and August, in the William W. Wick presiding judge, James north-west corner of the square, and was McIlvain and Eliakim Harding associates, used till 1858 when it was turned by a James M. Ray, clerk, Harvey Bates Shernegro prisoner, who was nearly suffocated in. After organizing the court adjourned before being rescued. Its foundations were to Crumbaugh's house west of the canal, visible till filled over in 1852. After its Calvin Fletcher was appointed prosecuting attorney for the first three terms, being succeeded by Harvey Gregg, Hiram Brown, William Quarles and others. There were thirteen civil causes on the docket at the first term. The first case tried was Daniel Bowman vs. Moridy Edwards, action on the case. The grand jury, Joseph C. Reed foreman, returned twenty-two indictments, six of which were non pros-ed. The first criminal case tried was the State vs. John Wyant for selling whisky without license, and nearly all the rest were like unto it. The term lasted three days and eleven attorneys were present, five of them being residents. Richard Good, an Irishman, was naturalized on the first day. John Hawkins was licensed to keep tavern and sell

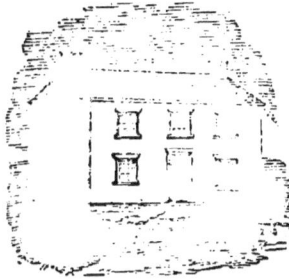

(The First Jail.)

destruction the old brick jail was built east in whisky. "Prison bounds," beyond which of the court house and used till 1845, when no debtor under arrest could go, were estaba hewed log jail was added just north of it. lished along certain streets the first day. These were torn away on the completion of The first divorce case was brought at the the present stone jail began in 1852, finish- May term, 1823, Elias Stalcup vs. Ruth ed in 1854, and since enlarged at a total Stalcup. The second session of the court cost of $60,000. began at Carr's May 5, 1823, and adjourn-

Arrangements for the first Fourth of July ed to Henderson's tavern where Glenn's celebration were made at a meeting June block now is. The third session began at 17th, at Hawkins' tavern. The celebration Carr's November 3, 1823, and adjourned to occurred at the corner of West and Wash- Carr's November 3, 1823, and adjourned to ington streets. The Rev. John McClung Harvey Gregg's, lot 11, square 46. The preached from Proverbs XIV, 34. Judge fourth began at Carr's April 12, 1824, adWick read the declaration, prefacing it with journed to John Johnson's, lot 8, square 44; remarks on revolutionary events and men. the fifth began at Carr's Oct. 11, 1824, and Obed Foote read Washington's inaugural adjourned to the court house, then nearly address, with remarks on sectional issues finished. The first sessions were attended and parties. John Hawkins read Washing- by several prominent lawyers from abroad, ton's farewell address, with appropriate re- who talked of locating here; but the sickmarks. Rev. Robert Brenton closed with ness, isolation of the place and dullness, prayer and benediction. A barbecue then deterred them. The early local bar comsucceeded. A deer killed on the north part prised a number of talented men, including of the donation the preceding evening by William W. Wick, James Morrison, Hiram Robert Harding, was roasted in a pit under Brown, Calvin Fletcher, Philip Sweetser, a large elm tree close by. An ample supper William Quarles, Harvey Gregg and othwas served on long tables under the trees. ers, and held a high rank in the State. Speeches were made by Dr. S. G. Mitchell Many amusing anecdotes are related showand Major John W. Redding, toasts were ing the peculiarities of the bench and bar offered and the festivities closed with a ball at that period. at Jacob R. Crumbaugh's house near the A meeting held at Crumbaugh's Septemcanal. ber 26, petitioned the assembly for repre-

William Hendricks received 315 out of sentation therein, for the improvement of 317 votes cast here at the August election White river, and for opening roads. A for Governor. Harvey Bates was elected committee made and published a long sheriff and George Smith coroner, the first report on the improvement of the river. elected incumbents. The first militia elec- Several roads to Whitewater and the South tion was held September 7. James Paxton were located and partly opened in Septemwas chosen colonel of the fortieth regiment, ber and October, by commissioners who Samuel Morrow lieutenant colonel, and Al- directed the work and expenditures; but exander W. Russell major. years elapsed before the roads were really

The first session of the circuit court be- passable, and not until a recent period,

when gravelled or planked, have they been 1835, when Maguire sold his interest to S.
firm in wet or thawing weather. V. B. Noel. Douglass & Noel (Mr. Noel
A westward migration of gray squirrels editor, continued till February, 1842, when
was noticed in the Fall, these animals cros- Douglass became sole proprietor, and T. J.
sing the river at several places in almost Barnett editor. Mr. Noel bought the es-
countless numbers. These movements have tablishment in March, 1843, Barnett remain-
occurred several times since, and in one in ing as editor. Kent succeeded him, and in
1845 they came into the town. The first March, 1845, John D. Defrees became edi-
camp meeting began September 12, east of tor. He also became proprietor in Febcn-
town, lasting three days, under charge of ary, 1846, and edited and published it till
Rev. James Scott, the first Methodist Min- October 20, 1854, when the Journal Co. was
ister, but no facts can now be given regard- formed (he being a large stockholder), by
ing it. A meeting was held December 1st, which it was published till 1863. John D.
at Carter's tavern, to get a weekly mail to Defrees and B. R. Sulgrove being editors
and from Vernon during the session. The for part of the time, and B. R. Sulgrove
first tax sale occurred December 7th, the and Barton D. Jones for the remainder.
long delinquent list and the amounts due Wm. R. Holloway & Co. then purchased
generally ranging from twenty-five cents to the establishment. Holloway becoming chief
one dollar, the highest being $2,871, showed manager and editor. Shortly afterward
the existence of hard times. A petition James G. Douglass and Alexander H. Con-
was sent to the assembly in December to ner became partners, and in 1865 Samuel
incorporate the town, but the project was M. Douglass purchased Holloway's share,
strongly opposed and abandoned. No mu- and the paper has since been published by
nicipal government existed till 1832. The Douglass & Conner, with H. C. Newcomb
year closed with better prospects than the and W. R. Holloway as editors. During its
last. The adjacent country was being set- existence the Journal has been published
tled, the sickness had not been so general as from several different offices on Washington
in 1821. People were becoming acclimated street, being located for long periods oppo-
and were better fixed, and Christmas was site Washington Hall, and also over the
greeted with the usual festivities. present Gem billiard room, and in the

1823. The people had clamored for a three-story brick just opposite. From 1853
year for representation in the Assembly, to 1860 it was located in Sharpe's building
and that body yielded it January 7th. Can- on Pennsylvania street, opposite the old
didates were numerous and busy till the Branch Bank. It was then removed to the
August election, and their merits were duly Journal building, erected for it by the com-
set forth in the papers; for, in addition to pany on the corner of Circle and Meridian
the Gazette, a second journal, The Western streets, and issued there till January, 1867,
Censor and Emigrants' Guide, was now pub- when it was transferred to the present five-
lished. The first number appeared March story building on Market and Circle streets,
7th, 1823, from an office opposite Hender- erected in 1866 by the company. The
son's tavern, edited and printed by Harvey weekly edition of the paper has borne the
Gregg and Douglass Maguire. The second same name ever since January 11, 1825.
number appeared March 19, third, March Semi-weekly editions were published for
26, fourth, April 2, fifth, April 19, sixth, many years during the sessions, the first ap-
April 23, after which it appeared regularly. pearing December 10, 1828; the first Tri-
Much difficulty was experienced in getting Weekly December 12, 1838. Daily editions
the press and material over the bad roads were at first only issued during the sessions,
from Cincinnati, and for ten years afterward the first appearing December 12, 1842, and
all the papers frequently passed a publica- ending February 15, 1843. The present
tion day on account of failure in the arrival daily began October 7, 1850, and with suc-
of their paper. The Censor started with cessive changes in size, shape and in name,
the motto, "He is a freeman whom the October 20, 1854, to Indianapolis Daily Jour-
truth makes free." Mr. Gregg was chief nal, has regularly appeared to the present
editor, but retired from the paper October time. Since January, 1866, it has appeared
29, 1824, and was succeeded November 16 as an eight-page sheet. The Journal carn-
by John Douglass. Mr. Maguire acting as estly supported the Whig party during its
editor. January 11, 1825, the paper was existence, and aided the organization of the
enlarged to super-royal size and called the Republican party, to which it has since de-
Indiana Journal. It was enlarged to impe- voted its energies. It has always been the
rial size October 29, 1831. Mr. Maguire State organ of its party, is the leading jour-
left the paper November 7, 1829, S. Merrill nal of the State, and holds high rank among
taking his place as editor; but in the fall of western newspapers.
1829 Douglass and Maguire resumed their There was no church edifice except the
partnership and continued till October 17. Methodist, no regular minister till 1823. A

Methodist camp-meeting was held east of town in September, 1822, and union meetings were occasionally held at the circle grove and in private houses. The Presbyterians met February 23d and March 6th at the schoolhouse, to organize and build a church. Subscription and building committees were appointed, and March 22 trustees appointed. The church was formally constituted in July. A lot was bought on Pennsylvania street, and the building raised in the summer and finished in 1824, at a cost for house and lot of $1200. It was used till 1842 or 3, then used as a carriage shop, and finally torn down in 1859. A

(The First Presbyterian Church.)

new brick church was built in 1841-2, on Market and Circle streets, at a cost of $8,000, and used till 1866, when sold to the Journal Co. and torn away. The present edifice on New York and Pennsylvania streets was built in 1865-6-7, at a cost of $75,000, and occupied in December, 1867. Rev. O. P. Gaines was the first Presbyterian minister, acting as a missionary in 1821-2, but David C. Proctor, a missionary here in 1822, was first pastor of the church from 1823 to August, 1824. George Bush—widely known afterward as a theologian—was pastor from September, 1824, to June, 1828, and left here March 20, 1829. Differences had arisen between him and the church on church government, and after severing his relation with them he preached for some time in the Court House. The average attendance during his ministry was seventy-five to one hundred persons. Moreley was called May or June, 1829, remaining until 1832. Wm. A. Holliday was called in the fall of 1832. James W. McKennon was called February, 1835, remaining till 1840. Phineas D. Gurley was called November, 1840, and remained till the fall of 1819. The church was without a pastor till October, 1851, when John A. McClung was called. T. L. Cunningham was called October, 1855, leaving in 1858.

Then ensued two years without a pastor, and in 1860 J. H. Nixon was called and still remains with the society. After the division in the church on the slavery question a portion of the members left, forming the Second church in the summer of 1838, and in September, 1851, a further division formed the Third church. These in turn have colonized until at present seven or eight prosperous bodies look to the First church as a common mother. It would be interesting to mention their history in detail, but the limits allowed in this sketch forbid it. Beside these, other branches of the great Presbyterian family exist here, and movements have lately been made to unite them as one common body.

The first Sabbath School was organized April 6, 1823, in Caleb Scudder's cabinet shop, on the south side of the State House square. It was a union school, very successful for the time, seventy scholars being in attendance the third Sunday; but was discontinued in the fall. It was revived on its anniversary, and continued steadily from that time, the First Presbyterian being its present representative. After the Presbyterian church was finished the school met there. The average attendance at the union school was forty the first year, fifty the second, seventy-five the third, one hundred and six the fourth, and fifty the fifth. 150 volumes were in the library bought in 1827. Successive colonies formed schools for other churches, the first forming the Methodist school April 24, 1829, and the third the Baptist in 1832. Want of space forbids fuller mention of this important enterprise, but it may be stated here that Dr. Isaac Coe was the founder and most active supporter of the movement. Nearly every church now has a school, and a number of mission schools originated by associations or individuals also exist.—Thousands of scholars and teachers are enrolled, and thousands of books and papers are circulated each week from the libraries. A Sabbath School Union was started shortly after the first school, with visiting committees to solicit the attendance of scholars and keep up the interest of parents in the enterprise.

Israel Mitchell, Stephen Howard, and John Martin Smith, three resident young men, left March 21st for Russian America via the Pembina settlement. They reached Fort Armstrong on the Mississippi May 4th, and Fever river August 15th, having seen no white men for twenty-three days after leaving the Vermillion salt works, and being robbed by the Indians and nearly starved for food. Their ultimate fate was unknown. The Indiana Central Medical Society was formed in the spring, with Dr. S. G. Mitch-

ell, President, and Livingston Dunlap, Secretary. It licensed physicians to practice, and the law at that time, and continued this year, in existence for years, being the forerunner and of the present medical society of the city.

The first woolen machinery in the county, was started at Wilson's mill June 20, by Wm. Townsend and Earl Pierce.

The celebration of the 4th of July occurred at Wilkes Reagan's cabin on Pogue's run and Market street. D. C. Proctor was chaplain, Daniel B. Wick reader, Morris orator, and Rev. Isaac Reed closed with benediction. Reagan gave the barbecue and fed the crowd and Capt. Curry's rifle company, closing with toasts and speeches. Political feeling grew warm as the August election approached. Two hundred and seventy votes were cast in the county, James Gregory, of Shelby, being elected first senator, and James Paxton first representative. The population was estimated at six hundred in September by the Censor, and the health was better than had been reported. The paper denounced the jealousy manifested toward the capital by other towns — a jealousy which lasted through subsequent years, and until the growth and superiority of the city rendered such a feeling ludicrous. Instead of aiding to build a city here of which the State could be proud, every town long labored to prevent its growth and build up cities in other States.

During this summer Thomas Carter built a frame tavern on Washington street opposite the court house, and opened it October 6th, and on the 26th the first sermon by a Baptist preacher was delivered there. This house was burned January 17, 1825, during the first session of the Assembly; and between the fire and the efforts of excited citizens to save property, Carter lost nearly all he had. Several persons desirous of saving the new sign on a tall post in front of the house chopped it down, and were much astonished when the fall crushed it into splinters. James Blake and Samuel Henderson had also built a tavern during the summer, the Washington Hall, a two-story frame, where Glenn's block now is, and opened it with a ball January 12, 1824. Henderson had kept there before in a log house. Blake & Henderson dissolved in March, 1826, and for a few months after November, 1832, Town & Pullian succeeded Henderson, but he resumed in March, and kept it till June, 1836, when the house was removed to the lot east of its former site, and the new Washington Hall built in its stead. A part of the old frame house was standing, occupied as a clothing store, till February, 1866, when it was torn down and Gramling's block afterward built on its site.

The clearing of lots along Washington and the cross streets progressed during scattered farms on the plat donation were opened, connected by foot-paths winding through the dense thicket, in which it was easy to miss the way and get lost.

The Gazette in December surprised the citizens by stating that Mr. and Mrs. Smith, late of the New York theatre, would appear at Carter's tavern, Wednesday night, December 31st, in the "Doctor's Courtship, or the Indulgent Father," to be followed by the "Jealous Lovers;" tickets 37½ cents. The town was excited and considerable opposition aroused. Carter insisted that the orchestra — one poor fiddle — should only play solemn music. A curtain was drawn across one end of the room for the players. The orchestra occupied a stool at one side, and the audience were seated at the other end of the room. Several performances were given. Such was the origin of the drama here. Mr. and Mrs. Smith returned in June, 1824, and gave several performances, the first on the 21st, but the experiment was not repeated for many years. The editor of the Censor in announcing the show in 1824, said he did not oppose the representation of tragedies and comedies as many did, but he thought that company would not do. In the next issue he announced that they had absconded without taking any of his money.

1821. The first military school here was opened January 13, by Major Sullinger, for the instruction of militia officers and soldiers. The first real estate agency was opened early in the same month by Wm. C. McDougal.

The Assembly had hitherto declined to move to the new Capital, and the southern counties delayed action as long as possible, but the new purchase members having taken their seats the subject was pressed, and on the 25th of January an act passed making Indianapolis the permanent seat of government, directing the State offices and archives to be moved here by January 10, 1825, and the Assembly to meet in our court house on that day. Samuel Merrill, State Treasurer, was charged with the removal and effected it in the following November, being ten days in making one hundred and twenty-five miles over the rough roads then over the rough roads then between Corydon and here, and received a complimentary supper February 21st, at Washington Hall, in approval of their services. The toasts and speeches evinced great joy at the removal of the government to this point. Many Indians still lingered in this country, and an event occurred March 22d

which caused much fear of a border war. Two men, three women, two girls and two boys of the Shawnee tribe were murdered at their camp, eight miles above Pendleton, by four white men and two boys. The whites were Bridges and his son, Sawyer and his son, Hudson and Harper. The Indians had hunted and trapped on Fall Creek during the winter, obtaining so many furs that Harper determined to secure them. He got his party drunk, told them the Shawnees were horse-thieves, and proposed to kill them. They went to the camp, asked the three men, Logan, Stephen Ludlow and another to help hunt cattle, and after going a short distance fired on them, killing the first two, but the third escaped. Returning to camp the women and children were killed, the children's brains knocked out against trees, and the bodies mutilated as if Indians had killed them, and the bodies thrown in a pond where they were found next day, one of the women still breathing. The wretches divided the property between them, and its possession betrayed them. They were arrested, confessed the crime, but being assisted by friends soon after escaped. All were retaken but Harper, the leader, who traveled on foot to Ohio, eighty miles through the woods, in twenty-four hours, and escaped. They again escaped in July, but were recaptured. Hudson was tried at Anderson in November before Judge Wick, was convicted, and hung in the winter. The rest were tried in May, 1825. Young Sawyer was convicted of manslaughter, the rest of murder. Old Bridges and old Sawyer were hung June 3d. Young Bridges was brought under the rope where his father had just died, his coffin by his side, when Governor Ray mounted the platform and announced his pardon in a speech to the people. These executions quieted the Indians and no retaliatory measures were taken; but at first the settlers in the vicinity were much alarmed and fled to the Pendleton mills for protection, and there was a general uneasiness here.

A census taken by Sunday school visitors in April showed one hundred families on the donation, comprising one hundred and seventy-two voters, forty-five single women between fifteen and forty-five; number of children not stated. There had been but little increase since November, 1821, but many persons then here had moved to the country. For a number of years the town increased very slowly. The want of roads, and of a market for surplus products cut off travel or trade, and prevented any rapid progress. Improvements, however, were made. The court house, school house, Presbyterian church, and State offices

were being erected, the trees on the streets felled and the plat gradually cleared. A series of great storms in April and May deluged the country with water, bayous, ponds and creeks everywhere overflowed, White river attained a height never equaled, unless by the floods of 1828 and 1847. The boats took advantage of the high water, and the keel-boat "Dandy," twenty-eight tons, arrived May 22d with the new purchase staples, salt and whisky.

The Methodist quarterly meeting began May 15th in the Presbyterian church, then nearly finished. James Scott was the first minister here, sent by the St. Louis conference, and arriving October, 1821, after much difficulty in finding the town. Services had been held at private houses, and camp meetings held, the first September 12th, 1822, on James Givens' farm east of town, and the second began there May 23d of this year, lasting one week. These meetings were held in or near the town for ten or fifteen years, not only by the Methodists, but other denominations; but as church accommodations increased they were abandoned, and none have been held in the immediate vicinity for nearly twenty years. The Methodists had no church edifice till the summer of 1825, when they bought a lot and hewed log house for $20, on the south side of Maryland street east of Meridian, which was used till 1829, when a brick church, built in 1828-9, at a cost (with lot) of $3000, was opened on Circle and Meridian streets.

(First Methodist Church.)

This was used till 1843, when the walls becoming cracked and unsafe, it was torn down and Wesley Chapel built on its site at a cost of $10,000. This chapel has been used till the present time, but preparations are now on foot for its sale, and the erection elsewhere of a new and more expensive edifice. In 1842 the church was divided into the eastern and western charges, but in 1843-4 Roberts Chapel was built at a cost of $10,000, on Market and Pennsylvania streets, by the eastern charge. This church also will soon be sold and a new and more expensive edifice erected for the

congregation. By the division of confer- mileage over the terrible roads. They ar-
ences and charges, Strange, Asbury and rived on horseback, singly or in groups,
Trinity, with several Mission, German and muddy and weary, at the different taverns,
African Methodist churches have since been for several days before the session. The
built, and the denomination is perhaps the influx of strangers, with new topics of
strongest in the city unless the Catholics thought and conversation, excited the quiet
outnumber it. Further mention of the villagers; and after the session opened
church or of the many talented ministers crowds of gaping natives witnessed the pro-
who have been stationed here is prevented ceedings with unsated curiosity. For years
by limited space. afterward the annual session was anxiously
The 4th of July being Sunday, the cele- awaited. The money then disbursed was
bration took place at Wilkes Reagan's on an important item; trade then revived, and
the 3d. Gabriel J. Johnson addressed the business of all kinds improved. Property
citizens and Major J. W. Reding the mili- which had formerly declined was held more
tia. Obed Foote was reader, and Reagan firmly, though no marked advance took
furnished the barbecue, the affair ending place in it till 1835, when it suddenly
with the usual toasts and speeches. The reached extravagant figures, only to fall
August election was hotly contested, the back and leave the people poorer than be-
contest being on sheriff, Morris Morris and fore.
A. W. Russell being candidates. Four On the 23d of January, 1824, the Assem-
hundred and thirty votes were cast, one bly ordered the agent to lay off twenty out-
hundred and sixty more than in 1823, Rus- lots of four acres each on the north and
sell having two hundred and sixty-five and south sides of the old plat, and sell them by
Morris one hundred and forty-eight votes. auction January 24th, 1825. The lots had
At the November election Clay received been laid off during the following summer,
two hundred and thirteen, Jackson ninety- and were sold as directed, the highest bring-
nine, Adams sixteen. Clay always received ing nine, the lowest $63, the average being
a heavy vote here afterward, and his sup- about $100 for each four-acre block. After
porters had held the first meeting and or- this sale, the Assembly on the 12th of Feb-
ganized July 17th, James Paxton, Presi- ruary ordered the agent to lay off and sell,
dent, and Hiram Brown, Secretary. on the 2d of May, twenty additional lots on

A large number of emigrants passed the north and south of those already sold;
through the town during the fall on their also the reserved lots on Washington street
way to the Wabash country. and elsewhere; to have Pogue's run valley

The Indianapolis Legislature was organ- cleared if the expense did not exceed $50;
ized during the fall by the lawyers and and to lease the ferry for five years. Mr.
leading citizens, and sessions were held dur- Blythe complied with these directions, ex-
ing the winter for ten or fifteen successive cept clearing the valley, part of which was
years. Its rules, and the pending measures heavily timbered till 1845. Two of the old
and subjects for debate, were similar to trees are still standing south of the Central
those in the body it copied. Talented men depot; others south of the old Bellefontaine
were assigned as members from the several depot were cut down in April of this
counties, and the mock representative often year. He held the sale of reserved and
had far more ability than the real one. The other lots on the 2d of May; $360 was the
Governor's messages were often witty and highest price obtained for reserved lots on
able documents, and sometimes published. Washington street, and $134 the lowest.
The Governor was elected whenever the Seventeen lots on Washington street, equiv-
members wanted a new message or inaugu- alent to a frontage of nearly three squares,
ral. After the General Assembly met here, sold for $3,328. The twenty additional out-
its leading members joined the Indianapolis lots sold for $1,467, averaging a little over
organization, and the debates and proceed- $18 per acre.
ings in the law, frequently guided and con- This year was distinguished for the form-
trolled legislation in the first-named body. ation of various societies. The Indianapo-
1825. The State officers having arrived lis Bible Society was formed on the 15th of
with the archives in November, 1824, the April, and has continued in active operation
State government was formally and perma- ever since. Mrs. George Bush was among
nently located here January 10th, 1825. the most earnest supporters of the society,
The Assembly met in the court house (still and for many years past Mrs. Margaret
unfinished)—the Senate in the upper, the Givan has been the President of the society.
House in the lower room—and the session The Marion County Bible Society, an aux-
continued there till December, 1835, when iliary of the American Bible Society, was
the State house was finished, and the Legis- organized November 13th, 1825. B. F. Mor-
lature met there for the first time. The ris, President. J. M. Ray, Secretary. The
members at that time fully earned their Indianapolis Tract Society was formed in

the spring of this year and continued its operations for many years. In July and August meetings were held at the court house to organize an agricultural society, and it was completed September 3d, Calvin Fletcher, Henry Bradley, Henry Burton, and others being leaders in it, but no permanent effect resulted from the effort, and it is notable only as the first attempt in that direction.

In September the land office was removed from Brookville to this point, and in September and October an unusual number of emigrants passed through the town on their way to the Wabash and the Illinois prairies.

1826. On the 13th of January the Assembly directed the agent to contract with Ashael Dunning to build a two-story brick ferry house 18 x 30 feet, on the river bank. It was built the following summer, and though partially burned November 27th, 1855, was repaired, and is standing in good repair near the mill-race on Washington street. Sickness, and lack of trade and money, had prevented many lot buyers from meeting deferred payments on their lots, and they were liable to forfeiture at any time. The Assembly, January 20th, allowed further time, and permitted buyers of several lots to surrender part, and transfer the cash payments on the lots surrendered to meet deferred payments on others. This act was followed by similar ones at subsequent dates, greatly relieving embarrassed buyers. Western lots were surrendered and the settlement went still further east. The centre of population and business has shifted considerably at different periods. At first the town was on the river. The sickness in 1821 drove it eastward, and the lot-relief act carried it still further to the east. 1836 the town was on and near Washington street, between West and New Jersey streets. It then tended westward to the canal, under the internal improvement excitement. After the abandonment of the public works it moved eastward to the square on which the Palmer House stands, and for a long time was nearly stationary, for there was little change in the size and business of the place. In 1848 it moved southward, tending to the Madison depot; the construction of other lines arrested it and it moved north-east, till the war suddenly scattered business and population in every direction. At present it is probable the centre of population is not far from the east market house, and the centre of business near the north-west corner of Pennsylvania and Washington streets.

A census in February showed seven hundred and sixty inhabitants, two hundred and nine of them being children of school age, and one hundred and sixty-one of them in the Sabbath school. In March the influenza prevailed here as an epidemic, attacking nearly every person in the town. Great rains fell for two weeks in March and April, four inches of water falling in one night. The streams rose very high, and all mills were stopped.

A cannon having been sent here an artillery company was formed under Captain James Blake, and thereafter at 4th of July and other celebrations, the artillery squad became an important though dangerous adjunct, for several men were afterward maimed for life by that gun. On the 20th of June the Indianapolis Fire Company was formed, John Hawkins, President, J. M. Ray, Secretary. The company used buckets and ladders, and turned out at the call of the church bell. It maintained its organization (being incorporated January, 1830,) till February, 1855, when it was merged in the Marion fire engine company. The usual military and civic parade occurred on the 4th of July, with exercises at the court house. Rev. George Bush was chaplain, L. Dunlap, reader, C. Fletcher, orator, and John Hays furnished the dinner. On the 12th of August public funeral services were held for Adams and Jefferson. A military and civic procession marched to the court house, where B. F. Morris and D. Maguire delivered eulogies on the illustrious dead.

There was the usual great westward emigration in the fall. The town was unusually healthy, although the summer was hot and dry. Lorenzo Dow, the noted revivalist, visited the town in June and preached to the people in a grove near the present Madison depot, and the next evening at the court house steps. He attracted large audiences, more by eccentricities of speech and dress than by eloquence.

A treaty was concluded with the Indians at Fort Wayne in the fall, by which more territory was ceded, and the government agreed to deliver certain cattle, hogs, wagons, &c., the next spring. In January, 1827, John Tipton, Indian agent, advertised for proposals for the delivery of two hundred hogs, two hundred cattle, ten wagons, and the building of eight brick houses in the Indian country under the treaty. The heavy rains the following spring prevented the delivery of the wagons and stock, and the savages were somewhat dissatisfied thereat.

1827. The Assembly, on the 26th of January, directed the agent to survey and sell seven acres near the river for a steam mill site, and on the 28th of January, 1828, incorporated the Steam Mill Company with $20,000 capital, in $50 shares. The company—the first one incorporated here—organized shortly after, Nicholas McCarty,

James Blake and J. M. Ray being the leaders in it. Subscriptions were slowly obtained during 1829-30, materials were collected in 1830-1, the building raised in September and finished in December, 1831. The saw mill had been finished before. The grist mill began work in January, 1832, and was the first in this section that had

(Old Steam Mill.)

bolting cloths or made fine flour. The wool-carding apparatus was put in motion in June, 1832. The mill ran irregularly, for there was difficulty in getting good wood at seventy-five cents per cord; the demand for flour was not equal to the supply, and shipments were out of the question. The mill stood north-east of the present bridge, and was the largest building in the place, being a heavily framed structure of three full stories with a high gambrel roof, allowing two additional stories. The boilers and engines—the first ones ever used here—were to have been brought up on a steamboat, but were wagoned out from Cincinnati with great difficulty in 1831. The mill was unprofitable, and was abandoned and the machinery offered for sale in 1835. It remained vacant till 1847, when it was refitted and used till 1852 by Geisendorff as a woolen mill. It again became vacant, and was fired and totally destroyed with the neighboring toll house, on the night of November 16, 1853, endangering the White river bridge, which was only saved by great exertions on the part of the firemen. One hundred men worked two days in raising its heavy frame, and no liquor was used, a fact which excited much comment at the time, for serious doubts had been entertained whether so large a building could be raised without the aid of whisky.

The Assembly appropriated five hundred dollars January 20th, to build a Supreme Court clerk's office, eighteen by thirty-six feet, on the west side of court square. It was built by S. and J. Patterson during

(2)

the summer, and stood there till 1855.

(Clerk's Office.)

Four thousand dollars were also appropriated for a two-story brick house on the Circle for the Governor, and the Circle was to be enclosed by a rail fence by the first of May. The house contract was signed March 17th, and it was built at a cost of six thousand five hundred dollars during the summer by Smith, Culbertson, Bishop and Speaks. It was a solidly-built, square, two-story, hipped-roofed brick house, with lookout, large windows, doors and chimneys, two cross halls, and four large rooms on each floor, and dark, damp basement under the whole structure. These vaults were a

(Governor's House.)

source of terror to all small boys, for they fully credited the legend that they were tenanted by a headless ghost whose appetite for youngsters was insatiable. The house was totally unfit for a residence and was never occupied as such. At the session of 1829 it was proposed to add wings to the east and west ends and use it as a State house, but the proposition failed. The rooms were successively occupied by the State officers, State library, State Bank, State engineers, Supreme Judges, old bachelors, debating societies, and Supreme Court clerk. At the session of 1856-7 it was ordered to be sold, and was disposed of by auction April 16th, 1857, for six hundred and sixty-five dollars, and torn down April 25-30. Its material was partly used in the Macy house and the dwelling adjoining it. The Circle has since been used for political

and other open air meetings. In the fall of 1867 the city council ordered it graded, planted, fenced, and surrounded with a decent sidewalk, for the first time in its history.

The Assembly, January 26th, directed the agent to offer at public sale, with certain exceptions, all reserved, forfeited and unsold lots. Several alleys and squares were vacated. Square 22 was reserved for a State Hospital and square 25 for a State University. This square has since been claimed by the Bloomington College, which was then a "State Seminary," so designated in the act creating it, and with funds and lands specially set apart for it; and though afterward made a college, no act ever recognized it as the "University" for which square 25 was reserved as a site, nor has the Assembly ever at any time in any manner given it any claim on that square. The Assembly, January 26th, 1852, authorized the agent to lease square 25 for thirty years to the trustees of the Marion County Seminary, who might build on the south-east or south-west corner thereof, and if the square was needed for a university before the lease expired, a half-acre where the seminary stood was to be sold or deeded to the trustees. The trustees took possession under the lease, and in 1833-4 built on the

(Marion County Seminary.)

south-west corner and opened the school September 1st, 1834, with E. Dumont as principal. W. J. Hill succeeded January, 1835; Thomas D. Gregg, May, 1836; Wm. Sullivan, December, 1836; Wm. A. Holliday, August, 1837; James S. Kemper, October, 1838; J. P. Safford, 1843; Benjamin L. Lang, 1844. The seminary was long the leading school in Central Indiana, and under Kemper, Safford and Lang had a high reputation. Many of the present business men of the city were wholly or partially educated in it. After the city free

school system was adopted the building was used from Sept., 1853, to 1859, as a high school, but was torn down in August and September, 1860. After the lease to the seminary trustees, the Assembly directed the agent, February 6th, 1837, to lease the north-west corner for twenty years to the Lutheran church, the lease to be given up if the square was needed for a University. The church, however, was built elsewhere. On the 17th of February, 1838, the agent was directed to lease the north-west corner for twenty years to the trustees of the Indianapolis Female Institute, first getting a release from the Lutheran church, but the institute also was afterward built elsewhere. On the 21st of January, 1850, the Governor and State officers were directed to sell one acre of the square at its appraised value, to the Indiana Asbury University for the use of its medical department, the Central Medical College. The acre was accordingly selected, and appraised at $3,566, but the appraisement being thought too high, and opposition arising to the sale, it was never completed, and the college was discontinued. In 1865-6 the city took possession of the square, fenced, graded and planted it at an expense of over $2,000, and in future it will probably be used as a park. Hitherto it has been used as a pasture, as a lumber and stone yard, and as a parade and play ground. In June, 1860, a large part of it was covered with a frame structure called a "Coliseum," built by Mr. Perine, and intended for shows and monster meetings. The edifice was about three hundred feet square, consisted of a board wall twenty-five feet high, with battlemented towers at the entrances and corners. The interior contained a large pit or open space at the south side, with a tall flag-staff, from which seats ranging from four feet at the front to twenty feet high near the walls, were arranged on the east, west and north sides, making an amphitheatre capable of seating fifteen or twenty thousand persons. Wide aisles led to the several tiers of seats. By great efforts it was got ready and opened July 4th with a military parade, band concert, and balloon ascension by J. C. Bellman, closing at night with the finest display of fireworks ever seen here. The enterprise was not pecuniarily successful, but deserved to be so, if only for its magnitude and boldness. No auditorium as large has ever been built elsewhere in the West, and perhaps not in the country. After standing some weeks it was torn away. The vacant square was subsequently used for military parades, especially during the Morgan raid, when the City Regiment, twelve hundred strong, was daily and nightly mustered there at stroke of bell, to go through agonizing partings

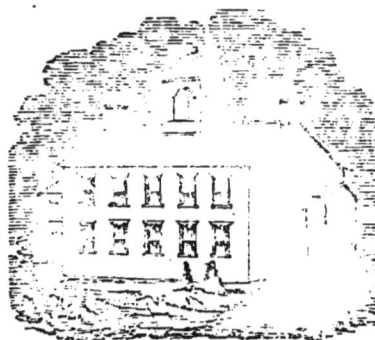

with mothers, wives and sweathearts, while their twelve hundred martial bosoms throbbed, doubtless, with strong desires to meet the foe.

The *Journal* in February, 1827, said the town then contained a court house, a Presbyterian church with thirty members; a Baptist church with thirty-six members, worshiping in a small cabin; a Methodist church with ninety-three members, worshiping in a small cabin, but building a new brick church, the walls of which were completed and enclosed during the fall. A Sabbath school had also existed for five years, and now contained twenty teachers and one hundred and fifty scholars. There were twenty-five brick, sixty frame, and eighty hewed and rough log houses in the town. In the fall it stated that rents were high and houses in demand. The Governor's Circle was being built. Six two-story and five one-story brick houses, with a large number of frame houses, had been built. It called for the introduction of steam engines and home manufacturing, and said nearly $10,000 worth of goods and provisions had been brought to the town and sold during the past year. Among the articles were seventy-six kegs tobacco, two hundred barrels flour, one hundred kegs powder, four thousand five hundred pounds spun yarn, and two hundred and thirteen barrels of whisky. Seventy-one additional barrels of whisky had also been made here and sold. A Sunday school census taken November 25th showed five hundred and twenty-nine white, and thirty-four colored males; four hundred and seventy-nine white, and twenty-four colored females; total, one thousand and sixty-six inhabitants in the town. Two hundred and eighty-four barrels of whisky seems a large allowance for this number of people, but the water then was doubtless very impure, from the vast quantity of decaying vegetable matter.

A tornado passed a few miles south of town on the 5th of April, destroying the timber but injuring no person.

The sale of lots ordered by the Assembly took place May 7th and 8th. One hundred and fifty-three lots (twenty-four of them on Washington street,) and thirty or forty squares of four acres each, were offered. One hundred and six lots sold at $189 per acre, and thirty-eight outlots and squares at $23 per acre. Mr. Knight, commissioner in charge of the National road survey, located the line to this point July 8th, and went on westward next day. The Fourth of July was ushered in with twenty-four rounds by the new artillery company. The procession included citizens and the rifle and artillery companies, and marched to the court house. Ebenezer Sharpe was reader. N. Bolton orator. John Hays provided the dinner, which closed with the usual toasts and speeches. The first public school examination and exhibition took place at the court house October 5th. During the fall squirrels and other animals were migrating in great numbers, and several bears were killed close to town.

Hitherto the ladies of the place had been compelled to make their own bonnets and clothes in backwoods fashion, but in October opened by Mrs. Matilda Sharpe, and thereafter style began to be assumed in the new town.

The town improved but slowly from this date to 1834. The settlement was mainly on Washington street and one or two squares north and south, with detached dwellings on other parts of the plat. The timber had been cut from the greater portion of the plat, but the outlots were still in the woods. Large trees stood in places within two squares of Washington street, and the greater part of the ninth ward was a forest till 1846. All the territory south of Maryland and east of Meridian streets was unimproved except as farms till 1845, and most of it till 1855. A fine walnut grove existed in the first and second wards north of North street, and Drake's addition was a good hunting ground till 1848. Squirrels, rabbits and turkeys were killed in sections now thickly peopled. No grading whatever had been done, and few sidewalks existed, even on Washington street. Ponds along the bayous afforded skating in winter, and in summer were covered by green scum and tenanted by countless frogs. The streets were semi-fluid in thawing weather, but the drainage in many places was better than since the engineers changed it. The town was a dull country village, with no excitement beyond the annual sessions, when a little animation was given to society and to trade. It seemed to have attained its growth. Few expected a brighter future, nor was there any prospect of it till the internal improvement scheme was originated.

1828. The spring was very wet with heavy rains, and in May a flood occurred in White river, rivaling that of 1824, and those of 1847 and 1858. Less damage was done then than since, there being fewer settlements along the bottoms. There is no doubt that White river then had a greater average depth of water than now, and was better fitted for navigation. Repeated attempts were made to navigate it, and boats of good size used. In May, 1822, the keel-boat Eagle, fifteen tons, with salt and whisky, arrived from the Kanawha, and the Boxer, thirty-three tons, with merchandise, from Zanesville; and the Dandy, twenty-

eight tons, in May, 1824, with salt and river falling rapidly they returned. In whisky, and many other boats arrived from 1829–30 General Hanna and others took the lower river, and departed loaded with contracts on the National road, and resolved produce. Large flatboats also were built to bring up a boat to haul stone and timber and ran to the southern market, and the from the binds for the abutments and trade was kept up till the dams on the river bridges. A medium-sized boat, the "Rob interfered with its navigation. The Assem- ert Hanna," was bought, and after some bly and the people regarded White river as trouble arrived here loaded and towing a a very important channel for heavy freights. loaded barge, on the 11th of April, 1831. Alexander Ralston was appointed commis- She was greeted by the entire community, sioner February 12th, 1829, to survey and and by Captain Blythe's artillery squad fir- report the expense of removing obstructions ing a National salute. A meeting was in it from drift, snags and leaning trees. called on the 12th, Isaac Blackford, presi- He made the survey during the summer, dent, and James Morrison, secretary, which and reported that from Sample's Mills in passed resolutions of welcome, asked for the Randolph county to Indianapolis was one improvement of the river, and extended an hundred and thirty miles, from here to the invitation to the boat owners and officers forks two hundred and eighty-five miles, for a public dinner. Two excursion trips and from thence to the Wabash forty miles; were made up the river on the 12th with a total four hundred and fifteen miles; and great crowd of passengers. During the sec- that for that distance the river might be ond one she ran into the trees on the bank, made navigable for three months in the knocking down her pilot-house and chim- year by expending $1,500. There were two ners, and injuring the wheel-house. The falls, one of eighteen inches, eight miles passengers were terribly frightened, and slid above Martinsville, and one of nine feet in off in great numbers. The boat was too one hundred yards, ten miles above the high and large for so narrow a river with forks. There was also a great drift at the overhanging trees, and unfit for the purpose Daviess and Greene county line. After this for which she was designed. She started report the Assembly repeatedly memorial- down on the 13th, grounded for six weeks ized Congress, asking for the improvement on a bar at Hog Island, where the captain's of the river, and considerable sums were child was drowned, and did not get out of appropriated from the State treasury for the river till the fall. No subsequent effort that object, the county commissioners along at steam navigation was made till 1865, the river governing the expenditure. In when the Indianapolis and Waverly packet, 1830–35, John Matthews and others pro- Governor Morton, built by a company at a posed slackwater navigation, building lev- cost of $11,000, ran a few trips several miles ees, dams and locks, and using steamboats up and down the river during the summer and tugboats for barges, to carry passengers and fall, and following spring. From want and freight from this point to the lower of water, leakiness, defective construction, river. Mills would be built at the dams, and distrust by the community, she failed to and serve as feeders to the trade, and the realize the hopes of her builders, and was stone, timber, iron ore, coal and produce of wrecked just below the bridge in the sum- the river valley, could be brought more near of 1866, after a brief but glorious ca- cheaply to our town than by any other reer. mode. Matthews pressed this plan for The first stage line from Indianapolis was years, and the Assembly in February, 1851, started to Madison by Mr. Johnson, in June chartered the White River Navigation or July, 1828. In July the Indianapolis Company for twenty years, but nothing was Library Society was formed, the members done, not even a survey, to test the practi- donating the books, and continued its ex- cability of the plan. If at all feasible it istence for six or eight years. The Fourth certainly deserves attention and a survey at of July was celebrated with more display least to test its practicability, for our manu- than usual. The artillery and rifle com- facturers and builders would derive advan- panies, the citizens, and the Sabbath school, tages from it they can never get from any which now participated for the first time, other work. In 1828 or 9, Governor Noble formed in procession and marched to the becoming convinced that steamboats of a court house. Hiram Brown acted as presi- small size could be used on the river, en- dent, Henry Brenton vice president. Rev. deavored to get some captain to bring a Geo. Bush was chaplain, A. Ingram reader, boat to this point, and offered $200 reward B. F. Morris orator. The Handelian Soci- to the first one who succeeded, and to sell ety (formed in the spring,) furnished the the cargo free of charge. In April, 1830, music. After the exercises closed the Sab- Captain Saunders with the "Traveller" bath school returned to the school house, reached Spencer, and the "Victory" came and the military and citizens marched to within fifty-five miles of this point, but the Bates' grove, east of town, where a dinner

was eaten, with the usual toasts and speeches. A military ball at Vigus' tavern, opposite the court house, closed the festivities.
Nine hundred and thirteen votes were
cast at the August election, and nine hundred and sixty-one at the November election,
Adams receiving five hundred and eighty-
two, Jackson three hundred and seventy-
nine. The first cavalry company, David
Buchanan, captain, was organized in August. A heavy emigration westward occurred this fall, and also during several following years, fifty teams per day often passing through town. A similar movement
occurred in 1839-40. In December, twenty-eight blocks and seventy-two lots in the
old plat were yet unsold, and nearly all the
donation land outside the plat. The winter
was colder than usual, with much snow in
February.

1829. The Methodist Sabbath school,
the second one in the town, was organized
April 24th with eleven teachers and forty-
six scholars, and at the end of the year had
twenty-seven teachers and one hundred and
forty-six scholars. Wesley Chapel school
is its present representative, but eight or
nine colonies have left it since its origin.
The Fourth of July hitherto had been celebrated by the civic and military procession,
the schools participating for the first time
in 1828, but this year the school display
was the only one. The two town, with five
country schools, formed on the Circle, and
accompanied by eight hundred adults,
marched to Bates' woods, on East, between
Ohio and Market streets, where the children
were seated, a hymn sung, and bread and
water distributed. Reverend Jamison
Hawkins prayed, Ebenezer Sharpe was
reader, James Morrison, orator, and Rev.
Henry Brenton closed with benediction, and
the procession returned to town. James
Blake acted as marshal, and continued,
with but few exceptions, to act in that capacity for nearly thirty years afterward.
The Sabbath school celebration continued a
leading feature till 1858, but the number of
schools and scholars became so great that
the general celebration was abandoned. The
exercises were always of the same character.
During the war the military displays were
the chief attraction. Since that date the
firemen's processions and picnics have been
the chief features of the day.

There was much sickness during the summer and fall, and many deaths, an unusual
proportion being young married people.
The Indiana Colonization Society, Isaac
Blackford, president, was organized in November, and continued its operations for
many years afterward. In September and
October contracts were let on the National
road. The people were much rejoiced, for
it promised a direct route to the East, and
its early completion was confidently expected. It was begun in 1830, but from defi-
cient appropriations, and the fact that work
was carried on simultaneously across the
whole State, it progressed slowly, and was
abandoned in 1839 before its completion.
The bridge here was contracted for July
26th, 1831, by Wm. H. Wernweg and Wal-
ter Blake, at $18,000, and finished in the
spring of 1834.

1830. The winter was very severe, the
thermometer marking five or six deg. below zero, and much snow fell. The Legislature celebrated the 8th of January, A. F.
Morrison delivering an address. For eight
or ten years afterward this celebration continued regularly. A theological debate—the
first one here—on the future punishment of
the wicked, began January 21st, between
Jonathan Kidwell, Universalist, and Rev.
Edwin Ray, Methodist. Like all such discussions it settled nothing and roused bad
feelings.

The Indiana Democrat, an administration
paper, was first issued by A. F. Morrison in
the spring. The Gazette, which had been
published since January, 1822, was discontinued in the fall, and the Democrat furnished to its subscribers. The paper was
published till 1841, the office being most of
the time in a one-story brick building at 32
West Washington street, and was owned
successively by Morrison, Morrison & Bolton, Bolton & Livingston, and John Livingston. It was sold to the Chapmans July
21st, 1841, who moved the office to a frame
house where Blake's Commercial Row now
stands, and changed the name to Indiana
Sentinel. The second number of the Sentinel
was issued August 4th, 1841, and weekly
afterward. In November, 1841, the office
was moved to a brick built for it on North
Illinois street. In November, 1846, John
S. Spann became a partner. Chapman &
Spann dissolved May 20th, 1850, and June
1st W. J. Brown bought the paper and
moved it to 8 West Washington street, Ellis
& Spann retaining the old job office. In
August, 1852, the office was moved to Tom-
linson's new building, and published by A.
H. Brown (Wm. J. Brown, editor,) till
March 2d, 1855, when Walker & Cottam
became proprietors, Walker and Holcombe
editors. Spann & Norman bought it December 4th, 1855, and sold to Larrabee &
Cottam January 24th, 1856, A. F. Morrison
and W. C. Larrabee being editors. Larrabee, Bingham & Co. became proprietors
August 25th, 1856. Bingham & Doughty
bought it January 13th, 1857, and moved
the office to the old Capital House. On the
7th of April, 1857, the office was nearly destroyed by a boiler explosion, which killed

a boy and badly injured one or two others, and the paper was suspended till April 21st. The office had just been completed and the engine put in motion for the first time, and the explosion entailed a heavy loss. The paper was then published by the *Sentinel Company* till July 31st, 1861, when it was moved to the old *Locomotive* office in Hubbard's block, the *Locomotive* discontinued and merged with the *Sentinel*, which was then published by Elder, Harkness & Bingham. A new three-story brick office was built for it in 1863, on Pearl and Meridian streets, where it was issued till 1865, when the paper was bought by C. W. Hall and moved to the old office, 16 East Washington street, where it has since been located. The name was changed to the *Indianapolis Herald*, and published by Hall & Hutchinson till October, 1866, when it passed into a receiver's hands and was bought by Lafe Develin in January, 1867, and published by him till April, 1868, when K. J. Bright became the owner and changed the name to *Indianapolis Sentinel*. Joseph J. Bingham has been the chief editor for over ten years.

The Chapmans issued the first daily paper in the place, the *Daily Sentinel* first appearing December 6th, 1841, and continuing during the session. The second volume began December 6th, 1842, for the session, and the third began December 6th, 1843. Semi-weekly editions had been issued during the sessions before and after these dates. The present daily began April 28th, 1851, and appeared regularly till April 7th, 1857, when the boiler explosion destroyed the office and suspended the paper till April 21st. It has since appeared regularly, under the names of the *Sentinel* and *Herald*.

The Fourth of July was separately celebrated by the schools and citizens. Considerable rivalry existed. Demas McFarland and James Blake, the respective marshals, addressed the crowds on the street corners, calling for adherents. Rain being threatened the schools went to the Methodist church, where the usual exercises took place. The citizens went to a grove near the present central engine house. Isaac Blackford was president. W. W. Wick, orator, and A. St. Clair reader. A dinner was spread and the usual toasts given. The cannon was taken to fire salutes, but the artillery officers being with the schools, inexperienced men were handling the gun, and at the third fire Andrew Smith lost his arm. The accident put an end to the exercises and threw a damper on such celebrations for several years afterward.

McComber & Co.'s menagerie, the first show here, exhibited at Henderson's tavern July 26-7th, and on the 23d-4th of August another exhibited at the same place.—

Among its animals was a "Pompo," doubtless a relative of the "Guyascutas." The summer was hot and dry, with considerable sickness and many deaths. The Indiana Historical Society, Benjamin Parke, president, B. F. Morris, secretary, was organized December 11th, at the court house, and continued its existence for many years. The first gift enterprize was started in the fall by T. J. Langdon, who offered the Indianapolis Hotel, opposite the court house, as the first prize, to be drawn December 30th.

The winter of 1830-1 was steadily and severely cold. The snow fell twelve to eighteen inches deep in February, and the thermometer fell to 18 and 20° below zero, by far the coldest weather since the settlement.

1831. M. G. Rogers, the first portrait painter here, announced his arrival in February for a few weeks' stay, at Henderson's tavern. In the same month, Samuel Henderson, who had been postmaster since February, 1822, was removed and John Cain appointed.

Several railways had been projected in 1830, and the Assembly on the 2d and 3d of February chartered the Madison & Indianapolis, Lawrenceburgh & Indianapolis, Harrison & Indianapolis, Lafayette & Indianapolis, New Albany, Salem & Indianapolis, and Ohio & Indianapolis railways. Surveys were made on them in following years, being completed on the Madison, Lawrenceburgh, Jeffersonville and Lafayette roads in 1835. Several were rechartered in 1834-5, and some work done on them. They were revived in 1835-6, and State aid given them, but stopped with the State work and were not built until 1849-53.

The agent was directed, February 9th, to divide the donation into outlots, fix a minimum price, and sell them publicly in May. The subdivision was accordingly made, and nearly nineteen hundred acres in and out of the plat offered in lots of two to fifty acres at a minimum price of ten dollars per acre, but a part only was sold. The Assembly on the 10th of February resolved to build a State house. A committee had reported in its favor at the last session, estimating the cost at $56,000, and estimating the value of the unsold donation at $58,000. James Blake was appointed commissioner to superintend it and procure materials, and $3,000 was appropriated therefor. He was to offer $150 for a plan (to be reported at the next session) comprising a Senate hall for fifty members, Representatives' hall for one hundred members, Supreme Court and Library rooms, twelve committee rooms, &c. The building was not to cost over $45,000. Blake bought some stone and other materials, and re-

ceived a plan from Ithiel Town and I. J. Davis, of New York City, which was adopted by the Assembly January 20th, 1832, Noah Noble, Morris Morris and Samuel Merrill were appointed commissioners Feb. ruary 2d, 1832, to superintend the building according to the plan, to employ an archi- tect, and use the material already bought. The house was to be completed by Novem- ber, 1833, and examined and approved by a committee of five from each House before being accepted. They contracted February 19th with Ithiel Town for its erection, at $58,000. It was begun in the spring of 1832, and by great exertion finished in De- cember, 1835, in time for the annual session beginning on the 7th. It is generally Doric in style, but contains a large rotunda and dome, surmounted by a cap ornament mod- eled after the tomb of Lycidas. The brick work was well done, but the stone used in the foundation was not durable. The house was stuccoed inside and out in imitation of sandstone, and though well done such work is not durable in this climate, and always looks ragged. The building cost about $60,000, and was regarded with great pride as the finest in the West. The feeling has since diminished. The roof has several times been partly stripped off by winds, and in December, 1867, the ceiling of Repre- sentatives' Hall was thrown down in a storm, crushing the desks and injuring the building. A new structure is needed, one in which the materials and construction will defy time and bad usage. The square was filled to a depth of nine feet in 1834, and the trees now growing on it were planted in 1835-6.

On the 11th of April the steamboat Rob- ert Hanna arrived and was greeted as here- tofore stated. On the 17th of May Sophia Overall, a colored woman, was declared by all the physicians as having the small pox, the first case here. A panic ensued, and a citizens' meeting was called. Dr. S. G. Mitchell, Isaac Coe, L. Dunlap, J. E. Mc- Clure, C. McDougal, J. L. Mothershead, Wm. Ticknor, and John H. Sanders, were appointed the first board of health, and au- thorized to take all necessary measures to prevent the spread of the disease. No other cases occurred, however, and the pan- ic subsided.

The first soda fountain in the place was put up July 2d in Dunlap & McDougal's drug store, and largely patronized. The Fourth of July was celebrated in the usual way by the schools and young men. Nine hundred and fifty votes were cast in the township at the August election. A full- grown elephant and calf elephant, the first here, were shown as "natural curiosities," at Henderson's tavern August 12th. The

first three-story brick house in town was erected at 4 and 6 West Washington street, during the summer, and is still standing. The Methodist conference held its first ses- sion here October 4th, with a full attend- ance. The summer and fall were the healthiest since the settlement of the place. The Indianapolis Lyceum or Atheneum was organized in the fall, giving lectures and scientific discussions, and continued its existence for several years. The winter was cold and snowy. 1832. News of the Indian outbreak under Black Hawk was received June 3d, and one hundred and fifty mounted volun- teers from the fortieth regiment were called for on the 4th, by Colonel A. W. Russell, the same number from adjoining coun- ties. They rendezvoused here June 9th, armed with rifles, tomahawks, knives, a pound of powder each, and balls in propor- tion, and were organized in three compan- ies, under Captains J. P. Drake, J. W. Red- ing and Henry Brenton, and marched for Chicago the same day under Colonel Rus- sell. The cannon was fired on the day of rendezvous, and by a premature explosion William Warren, an Irishman, lost both arms, shedding the only blood here during that war. After reaching Chicago the bat- talion marched round the south end of the lake to St. Joseph, and returned home with- out accident July 3d, participating in the celebration and dinner of the 4th as veter- ans. They were paid off by Major Larned, January, 1833. Wm. Conner, a merchant here, and formerly an old Indian trader and scout, piloted the expedition.

Meetings had been held and subscriptions made in August and September, 1832, to build a market house, C. J. Hand, John Givans and others being prominent in the movement, and after some difficulty as to location, it was contracted for in May, 1833, and finished in August, on the square north of the court house, and regulations agreed on for holding the markets. Josiah Davis, Thomas McOuatt and John Walton were the committee in charge of the work. L. Dunlap, J. S. Hall and D. McFarland were elected the first seminary trustees in Aug- ust. The Indianapolis Foundry, the first in the place, was started in August west of the river, by R. A. McPherson & Co., and continued several years. The cholera swept many places in the West this year, being diffused by the troops from the Indian war. The people here held meetings, organized a board of health, and adopted sanitary mea- sures, but no cases occurred and the panic passed off.

Until this time no municipal government had existed, the township and county offi- cers enforcing the State laws; but at a

meeting held September 3d, at the court house, it was resolved to incorporate the town under the general law. The election of five trustees was held in September, and the board organized shortly after, electing Samuel Henderson, president, I. P. Griffith, clerk, Samuel Jenison, marshal and collector. The town was divided into five wards, inside the old plat: all east of Alabama, 1st; thence west to Pennsylvania, 2d; thence to Meridian, 3d; thence to Tennessee, 4th; thence west, 5th. A general "ordinance" No. 1, in thirty-seven sections, "established by the board of trustees of the town of Indianapolis for their own government and for the regulation of the town," was probably adopted in November, and published December 1st, signed by S. Henderson as president. At the same time a market ordinance in seventeen sections was adopted and published. The general ordinance or charter provided for the election by the board of a clerk to keep records, issue warrants, &c.; a treasurer, who was to report annually in December; an assessor, who was to make an annual assessment in January; a marshal, who also acted as collector, and enforced ordinances, abated nuisances, &c., reporting taxes in June to the treasurer. All these officers were to give bond. The firing of guns, flying kites, leaving open cellar doors, racing horses, driving over foot-paths, leaving unhitched teams, letting hogs run at large, keeping stallions on Washington street, &c., was prohibited under penalties. Wood piles were not to remain on Washington street over twelve hours, or shavings in any place over two days. Shows and tippling houses were required to take out license. Offences against the ordinances were to be sued within twenty days, in the name of the trustees before a justice. Regular meetings were held the first Friday in each month, but meetings could be called at any time. The markets were held for two hours after daylight, Wednesdays and Saturdays, by a market master, who governed the markets, tested weights, &c. Huckstering was prohibited. The elections were held annually in September, and the town continued under this ordinance, or charter, until April, 1836. The officers so far as known with those elected at subsequent dates, are given in the table hereafter inserted.

On the 5th of February, 1836, the Assembly incorporated the town and legalized the acts of the first trustees. The wards were left as before, all east of Alabama being the first; thence to Pennsylvania, second; thence to Meridian, third; thence to Tennessee, fourth; thence west, fifth. One trustee to each ward was to be elected April 4th, and the board was to elect one of their number

president, and a clerk, marshal, lister, collector, trustees and other officers, whose election duties were prescribed. They could pass all necessary ordinances, levy taxes and improve the streets and sidewalks at the expense of property holders. Taxation was not to exceed one-half of one per cent, and was limited to the old plat, though the corporation covered the donation. The board elected under this act re-enacted, with but few changes, the ordinances formerly in force. The officers of the old board settled to the first of April, 1836. The treasurers' report showed $1,610 receipts for the year; $1,150 of this was paid for the Marion engine, five public wells, and other fire department expenses, and a balance of $124 was turned over to the new board.

On the 17th of February, 1838, the place was re-incorporated, the corporation covering the donation, but taxation being still limited to the plat, and not to exceed one-sixth of one per cent on real property. The town was divided into six wards, as follows: All east of Alabama, the first; thence west to Pennsylvania, second; thence to Meridian, third; thence to Illinois, fourth; thence to Mississippi, fifth; thence west, sixth. An election was to be held March 27th for a president, by the general vote, and one trustee for each ward, by the voters thereof, to hold office one year, and to constitute the "common council," four being a quorum. The president had justice's jurisdiction, and was to sign all ordinances, keep a dock-et, &c. The council met regularly once each month, but called meetings might be held. The trustees received twelve dollars each per year. They could pass all necessary ordinances for the improvement and government of the town, levy taxes, borrow money, regulate and license shows, groceries, saloons, fire companies, &c. They were to elect a clerk, marshal, collector, lister, treasurer, supervisor, clerk of markets, and other officers, and prescribe their duties. The marshal had a constable's authority, and was to enforce all ordinances. The officers were to give bond and receive such compensation as the council allowed. Tax sales on the municipal assessment were authorized and rules prescribed therefor.— Several sales were made under this authority, the first being held October 25th, 1839, at Washington Hall, but the records being all destroyed by fire in 1851, but few traces remain of them. North, South, East and West streets were declared public highways and ordered to be opened. The new board was elected in March under this act, and shortly after enacted ordinances regulating markets, prescribing the duties of the corporation officers, fire department, police,

street improvement, licensing tippling houses, groceries, shows, &c.

This charter, with some subsequent changes, continued in force till the city charter was granted in February, 1847. The changes were as follows: On the 15th of February, 1839, the Assembly ordered the council to expend the revenue collected in West Indianapolis in that part of the town, and to open the alleys in the donation. In February, 1840, the charter was amended so that councilmen were elected for two years, and received twenty-four dollars annually, as householders only being eligible. In February, 1841, the office of marshal was made elective by the people, and West Indianapolis was detached from the corporate limits; and on January 15th, 1844, all the officers were made elective by the people.

The first trustees made no effort to improve the streets, and no engineer was employed till 1836. The first street improvement was made that year in filling a pond near Wesley Chapel. No street grading was done, and few sidewalks existed, even on Washington street, till 1839-40. James Wood was employed March, 1841, to make a street profile, which was adopted in April, 1842, and thereafter followed in the street grades. The corporation officers and councilmen from 1832 to 1847 are given, as far as known, in the following table. The destruction of the records by fire in 1851 left no trace of them, and the table has been made from the contemporary journals and tradition:

TRUSTEES AND COUNCILMEN FROM EACH WARD, FROM 1832 TO 1846.

YEARS.	1st WARD.	2d WARD.	3d WARD.	4th WARD.	5th WARD.	6th WARD.
1832.	John Wilkens....	H. P. Coburn....	John G. Brown......	S. Henderson	Sam. Merrill	
1833.	John Wilkens....	H. P. Coburn....	S. Henderson.......	John Cain.....	Sam. Merrill	
1834.	Alex. Morrison...	L. Dunlap.........	Jos. Lefevre........	J V' Blaricum	Nat. Cox.... ·	
1835.	Jas. M. Smith....	Jos. Lefevre......	Charles Campbell..	H. Griffith....	N E Palmer	
1836.	Geo. Lockerbie.	John Foster......	S. Merrill.............	H. Griffith.....	J. L. Young	
1837.		Joshua Soule.....				
1838.					C. Scudder..	Nat. Cox.....
1839.	Geo. Lockerbie.	Wm. Sullivan....	John E. McClure..	P. W. Seibert.	G.Norwood	S.S. Rooker
1840.	Mathew Little...	S. Goldsberry...	Jacob Cox..........	P. W. Seibert.	G.Norwood	A.A.Louden
1841.	M. Little..........	S. Goldsberry...	Jacob Cox..........	A. A. Louden.	G.Norwood	C H Boatri't
1842.	Joshua Black.....	S. Goldsberry...	Jas. R. Nowland...	P. W. Seibert.	T. Rickards	A.A.Louden
1843.	Joshua Black ...	S. Goldsberry...	Jas. R. Nowland...	A. A. Louden..	T. Rickards	S.S. Rooker.
1844.	Wm. Montague.	S. Goldsberry...	Jas. R. Nowland...	A. A. Louden..	H. Griffith.	S.S.Rooker.
1845.	Wm. Montague.	S. Goldsberry...	Jas. R. Nowland...	A. A. Louden..	H. Griffith.	Wm. C. Van Blaricum.
1846.	Wm. Montague.	S. Goldsberry...	A. W. Harrison....	A. A. Louden..	C. W. Cady.	Wm. C. Van Blaricum.

NOTE. The first incorporation in September, 1832, was by vote of the people under the general law, the town being divided into five wards, and the councilmen chosen by general vote. The Assembly incorporated the place in 1836, making five wards, the trustees to be elected by general vote. On the 17th of February, 1838, the town was reincorporated and the trustees made councilmen, to be chosen by the voters of the several wards, with a president by the general vote. The wards were increased to six in number.

(3)

TOWN CORPORATION OFFICERS FROM 1832 TO 1847.

The following persons were the Corporation Officers, as far as can now be ascertained, from 1832 to 1847, when the City Government was organized. The records of the old Corporation up to 1839 were all destroyed by fire in the year 1851, and the list has been culled from the public prints and other sources.

Year.	Pres't of Council.	Clerk.	Marshal.	Collector.	Treasurer.	Assessor.	Engineer.	Clk. of Markets.	Supervisor of Sts.
1832.	Sam'l Henderson	I. P. Griffith	Samuel Jenison	Samuel Jenison		Gideon True			F. T. Luse
1833.	Sam'l Henderson	I. P. Griffith	Samuel Jenison	Samuel Jenison		Geo. Lockerbie			F. T. Luse (?)
1834.	Alex. F. Morrison	Jas. Morrison	John C. Busac	John C. Busac		Geo. Lockerbie			F. T. Luse (?)
1835.	N. B. Palmer	Joshua Soule	R'd D. Mattingly	R'd D. Mattingly	Thos. H. Sharpe	Geo. Lockerbie			F. T. Luse (?)
1836.	Geo. Lockerbie	Joshua Soule	Wm. Campbell	Wm. Campbell	Thos. H. Sharpe	John Elder	Wm. Sullivan		Wm. Ballenger
1837.	Joshua Soule	Hugh O'Neal	Wm. Campbell	Wm. Campbell	Thos. H. Sharpe		Wm. Sullivan	J. Wortzen....	Thos. Layton (?)
1838.	Jas. Morrison	J. Soule	Wm. Campbell(?)	W. Campbell(?)	Thos. H. Sharpe	A. G. Willard	Luke Munsell	W. Campbell	Thos. Layton.
1839.	N. B. Palmer	Hervey Brown	Jas. VanBlaricum	Jas. Van Blaricum	Chas. B. Davis	A. G. Willard	R. B. Hanna; Luke Munsell	J. Wortzen...	J. Van Blaricum
1840.	Henry P. Coburn	Hervey Brown	J. Van Blaricum	J. Van Blaricum	Humph. Griffith	Henry Bradley	Luke Munsell	J. Wortzen....	J. Van Blaricum
1841.	Wm. Sullivan}; D. V. Culley}	Hervey Brown	J. Van Blaricum	J. Van Blaricum	Chas. G. Davis	Thos. Donnellan	James Wood	J. Wortzen.....	J. Van Blaricum
1842.	David V. Culley;	Hervey Brown	Rob't C. Allison	Rob't C. Allison	C. B. Davis	Jas. H. Kennedy	James Wood	J. Wortzen.....	Rob't C. Allison
1843.	David V. Culley;	Wm. L. Wingate	Benjamin Bean	Benjamin Bean	C. B. Davis	Thos. Donnellan	Luke Munsell	J. Wortzen.....	Thos M. Weaver
1844.	Jaz. R. Wilson	Wm. L. Wingate	J. Van Blaricum	Henry ohr.	John L. Welshans	Thos. Donnellan	James Wood	J. Wortzen.....	J. Wortzen...
1845.	Joseph A. Levy	James G. Jordan	N. N. Norwood	Henry ohr.	John L. Welshans	Thos. Donnellan	James Wood	J. Wortzen.. n, E.}; Jacob Miller, W.}	Wm. Wilkinson
1846.	Joseph A. Levy	James G. Jordan	Jacob B. Fitler.	Henry ohr.	George Norwood.	John Cox	James Wood	Jacob B. Fitler, E. Jacob Miller, W.; Jacob Miller, W	

*Wm. Sullivan resigned November 12th, and D. V. Culley was elected by the Council.

NOTE.—In addition to the above-named officers, James Morrison was the Corporation Attorney in 1834 and 1837; Hugh O'Neal in 1838, and John L. Ketcham in 1846. John F. Ramsey was Weighmaster in 1836, and Adam Haugh from 1840 to 1846 inclusive. John Musgrove was Sexton in 1843, '45 and '46, and John O'Connor in 1841. David Cox was Messenger of the Marion Fire Company from 1843 to 1846 inclusive, and Jacob R. Fitler of the Good Intent in 1845-6. Thomas M. Smith was elected Chief Fire Engineer for 1846, the office being created that year.

1833. William Henry Harrison, the former Governor of the Territory, visited the town for the first time January 11th. He was received by the Assembly and tendered a public dinner at Washington Hall, January 17th, at which he made a Union speech. He visited the town again January 13th, 1835.

The first homicide here occurred on the 8th of May, Michael Van Blaricum drowning William McPherson by upsetting a boat in the river. The murder created great excitement at the time. He was tried and sent to the penitentiary in October, 1834. The first wholesale grocery was opened in June by Beard & Patterson.

The cholera had been prevailing elsewhere this year, and on the 18th of June one or two cases of supposed cholera—not fatal—occurred here. The churches assigned and kept the 26th as a special fast day. No other cases happened then, but in July it became very fatal at Salem, Indiana, and the trustees of the town called a meeting on the 17th at the court house. One thousand dollars were subscribed by the citizens, resolutions passed, a board of health consisting of five physicians and five citizens appointed, visiting committees were assigned to each ward, sanitary measures were adopted and medicines procured. The trustees were also requested to open a hospital. The Governor's Circle was accordingly secured for the purpose, and Dr. John E. McClure assigned as physician. There were no cases here however, and the building was not used.

The first circus, (combined with a menagerie, Brown & Bailey's,) exhibited at Henderson's tavern August 13th and 14th. A new graveyard was laid out cast of the old one, and lots sold in October by Isaac Coe. The great meteor shower on the 13th of November, from 2 A. M. to daylight, was witnessed with awe by the people, many of whom thought the end of the world was close at hand and they unprepared for the event.

1834. The State Bank of Indiana was chartered January 28th, 1834, for twenty-five years, with a capital of $1,000,000 in fifty dollar shares, one-half of the stock to be held by the State. Its charter was amended with its consent in several particulars at subsequent dates. Samuel Merrill was elected president by the Legislature, with Calvin Fletcher, Seton W. Norris, R. Morrison and T. H. Scott State directors. J. M. Ray was chosen cashier, a position he held till the charter expired. The bank was organized February 13th, with ten branches, (ultimately increased to sixteen,) and books opened for stock subscriptions for thirty days from the 7th of April. Samuel

Merrill served as president till 1840, James Morrison till 1850, Ebenezer Dumont till 1855, H. McCullough till 1859. Additional time was given to wind up the business. The bank was first located in the Governor's Circle in 1834, then on Washington street till 1840, when the banking house on Illinois street and Kentucky avenue being completed, it was removed to and remained there till 1859, being succeeded in its occupancy by the Bank of the State. The old State Bank was a safe and very lucrative enterprize for its stockholders, and made good and steady dividends. All the branches suspended specie payments under its direction May 18th, 1837, during the financial panic and bank run of that period, and did not resume payment till June 15th, 1842, when directed to do so by act of the General Assembly.

The Branch of the State Bank at this point was organized November 11th, 1834, with Harvey Bates, president, B. F. Morris, cashier. These officers served for two or three years, and were succeeded by Calvin Fletcher as president and Thos. H. Sharpe cashier, who served till the charter expired. The State and Branch Banks began business November 20th, 1834. The Branch banking house, on Pennsylvania street and Virginia avenue, was built in 1839, and occupied from 1840 to 1859, when it was sold for nearly $16,000 to the Sinking Fund, and by the Fund in 1867 for $30,000 to the Indianapolis Insurance Company, who now occupy it. For many years the rule of the bank was to loan but $200 to any one person, unless a greater sum was needed for stock or grain enterprizes, which were made special exceptions.

The old State Bank charter being about to expire, the General Assembly, on the 3d of March, 1855, chartered "The Bank of the State of Indiana," with seventeen branches, (three additional branches being afterward authorized,) and it was organized November 1st, 1855, Hugh McCullough being elected president, and J. M. Ray cashier, with seventeen directors—one from each Branch. It began business January 2d, 1857, with a capital of $1,836,000, and reported $132,216 profits over all expenses in the first six months. It continued an extremely lucrative business, rapidly extending its capital, until after the adoption of the National Bank system and the taxation of free and State bank paper. In January, 1865, the Assembly authorized it to reduce its capital, redeem its stock, distribute surplus funds, &c., to stockholders, and close up its branches and business, and at present it is about completed, the branches having nearly all been merged in National Banks. It was located in the building of the old

State Bank on Illinois street and Kentucky avenue, which was sold in May, 1868, to the Franklin Life Insurance Company, and now occupied by that corporation. Hugh McCullough, George W. Rathbone and J. M. Ray have been the presidents, J. M. Ray and Joseph A. Moore cashiers of the institution.

The Branch at this point of the Bank of the State was organized July 25th, 1855, with a capital of $100,000, afterward increased to over $290,000, W. H. Talbott being elected president. The stock was afterward sold at an advance to other parties, and the bank began business in January, 1857, at the north-west corner of Washington and Illinois streets, with George Tousey, president. C. S. Stevenson, cashier. Stevenson resigned to enter the pay department in June, 1861, and D. E. Snyder was cashier till November, 1866, being succeeded by D. M. Taylor, present cashier. Oliver Tousey was elected president in June, 1865, succeeding George Tousey, who had resigned to become president of the Indiana National Bank. The bank was removed in March, 1860, to the corner room of Yohn's block, where it remained till 1867, when it was removed to the back room in the same building and its affairs wound up.

A general bank law was adopted by the Assembly in May, 1852, and shortly afterward applications were filed by different parties for a number of banks at this point, some of which were afterward organized under other names, and others were never completed. Among these applications were the City Bank, nominal capital $500,000, in December, 1852, A. Defrees, proprietor; Bank of Indianapolis, J. Woolley & Co., proprietors, capital $100,000, January, 1853; State Bank of Indiana, $500,000, January, 1853; Agricultural Bank, $200,000, February, 1853; Traders' Bank, Woolley & Wilson proprietors, $300,000, May, 1853.

The banks actually organized here under the law were the Bank of the Capitol, J. Woolley & Co., proprietors, nominal capital $400,000, W. S. Pierce and J. H. Bradley successive presidents, J. Woolley, cashier. It began business in 1853 in a little frame house where Blackford's block now stands, then removed to Dunlop's building, then lately built on North Meridian street, and then to No. 6 East Washington street, which had just been finished. The concern carried more sail than ballast, and capsized September 15th, 1857, in the financial storm of that date, with liabilities to over $50,000, nominal assets $56,000.

The Farmers' and Mechanics' Bank, Allen May and G. Lee successive presidents, William F. May and O. Williams successive cashiers, began business February, 1854, in the basement of Masonic Hall. The avenue, which was sold in May, absconded in May, taking about $10,000 with him, crippling the bank so badly that it collapsed shortly afterward.

The Central Bank, Ozias Bowen and J. D. Defrees, successive presidents, Sidney Moore and W. H. McDonald, successive cashiers, with a nominal capital of $500,000, began business in July, 1855, at No. 23 West Washington street. The Traders' Bank, Woolley & Wilson, proprietors, began in 1851 at the office of Ellis & Spann on Illinois street; and the Metropolitan Bank, A. F. Morrison & Co., proprietors, J. D. Dunn, president, Jerry Skeen, cashier, in 1855 in Blake's Commercial Row, but neither of them did much business, and suspended payment soon after getting their notes in circulation, and were shortly after closed up by their owners or by the Auditor of State. The free bank system entailed great loss on the community from the depreciation of the circulation, the owners finding it much more profitable to buy in at a heavy discount than to redeem it or attempt to do a legitimate business.

The State and free bank systems have been superceded in the last five years by the National banking system. The First National Bank was organized August 1st, 1863, with $150,000 capital, under the National law. W. H. English was president, and W. R. Nofsinger, cashier. John C. New was chosen cashier January 11th, 1865. The bank was reorganized September 22d, 1864, and the capital increased to $500,000.— There are at present sixty stockholders. The bank was first located just north of Odd Fellows Hall, then in the north room of the hall, and removed thence October 1st, 1865, to the corner room of Blackford's block. It has been a government depository from its origin, and has done a very extended and lucrative business. Its circulation during the first quarter of 1868 was $450,000, deposits $790,000, discounts $900,000, surplus $75,000, profit and loss $125,000; exchange sales in 1867, $4,620,000.

The Indianapolis National Bank was organized December 15th, 1864, with $500,000 capital, Theodore P. Haughey being elected president, and Ingram Fletcher, cashier. He resigned in January, 1866, being succeeded by A. F. Williams, present cashier. The bank rented the corner room of Odd Fellows Hall, where it has since been located. It has been a government depository from its origin, and has done a large and lucrative business. The circulation during the first quarter of 1868 was $450,000, surplus fund $78,000, deposits $432,000, discounts $416,000; commercial exchange sales in 1867, $3,606,650.

The Indiana National Bank was organized, with $250,000 capital, March 14th, 1865. Oliver Tousey being elected president, David M. Taylor, cashier. The capital was increased June 6th, 1865, to $400,000, and on the 27th of July George Tousey was elected president, D. E. Snyder, cashier. D. M. Taylor was chosen cashier November 26th, 1866. The bank was opened at 19 North Meridian street in July, 1865, but the location being an unfavorable one, it was removed November 26th, 1866, to the corner room of Yohn's block, the Branch of the Bank of the State removing to the back room, and its business being transferred to the Indiana National Bank. The bank is a government depository, and since its removal to the present location has rapidly increased in business. The circulation during June, 1868, was $550,000, deposits $854,235, discounts $292,800; exchange sales in 1867, $2,787,370.

The Merchants' National Bank was organized January 17th, 1865, with $100,000 capital, Henry Schnull, president, V. T. Malott, cashier, and began business at 23 North Meridian street, but finding that location unfavorable it was removed in January, 1867, to 48 East Washington street, where it has since been located, and has done much more business. John S. Newman became president September 1st, 1866, The circulation for the first quarter of 1868 was $90,000, discounts $132,000, surplus funds $6,000, profit and loss $13,500; exchange sales for 1867-8, $950,000. The bank has nine stockholders.

The Citizens' National Bank was organized November 28th, 1864, with $200,000 capital, Isaiah Mansur, president, Asa G. Pettibone, cashier, and began business shortly after at No. 3 West Washington street. It was consolidated December 1st, 1865, with the Fourth National Bank. Isaiah Mansur being elected president, and Joseph R. Haugh, assistant cashier of the combined corporation, which retained the name of Citizens' National Bank, and the capital increased to $300,000. It was removed to No. 2 East Washington street November 20th, 1866. Joseph R. Haugh was elected cashier in January, 1866. Circulation June, 1868, $270,000, deposits $206,000, discounts $355,000, profit and loss $24,000, surplus fund $35,000; exchange sales in 1867, $1,067,000.

The Fourth National Bank was organized January 23d, 1865, with a capital of $100,000, Timothy R. Fletcher, president, Joseph R. Haugh, cashier, and began business at No. 11 North Meridian street. It was merged and consolidated in December, 1865, with the Citizens' National Bank, as above stated, losing its separate existence.

It is difficult to give with certainty the history of the different private banking enterprises of the city, some of which now vie with the public in business and importance, and organizations, so far as is known, the first private banking enterprise (though an incorporated company its banking privileges were at first taken advantage of only by the secretary, Mr. Gregg,) was the Indianapolis Insurance Company, chartered February 5th, 1836, with $200,000 capital, and with banking and favorable banking powers. It began operations in April, and for some years did considerable business in insurance and banking, but gradually declined, and suspended active operations about 1840. It was reorganized by Defrees, Morris and others in 1852 or 3, and continued till 1858, when it again suspended. In 1865 the stock was purchased, a new company organized, business resumed, and the capital increased to $500,000. The old Branch Bank building was bought in 1867. It now does an insurance and banking business. Its discounts in the bank department for the first quarter of 1868 were $99,220, deposits $159,617; exchange sales for fractional quarter in 1868, $67,884; average amount of discounted paper held during fractional quarter of 1868, $216,519.

John Wood, exchange broker and banker, began business in 1858 and continued till September, 1861, when he failed, causing considerable loss to the community from the shinplaster notes which he had issued, together with those of other equally responsible parties, that he had circulated. He soon after left this section.

E. S. Alvord & Co. did a banking business from January, 1839, to 1843, but nothing can now be stated as to its extent or character.

S. A. Fletcher, Sen., opened an exchange office in 1839 in a one-story frame shed next to Wolfram & Rommel's saddle shop, at the present No. 8 East Washington street, continuing there till 1850, when he moved to the room now occupied by Raschig's cigar store, and from thence in December, 1852, to the present bank, 30 East Washington street, then just built. Timothy R. Fletcher was a partner from 1839 to 1858, when he retired. On the 1st of June, 1864, S. A. Fletcher, Jr., and F. M. Churchman, became partners, S. A. Fletcher, Sen., retiring from the firm. On the 1st of January, 1868, S. A. Fletcher, Jr., and F. M. Churchman and S. A. Fletcher, Jr., dissolved. S. A. Fletcher, Jr., retiring from, and S. A. Fletcher, Sen., re-entering the firm. The bank has done a very lucrative business since its origin, increasing its capital from $3,000 in 1839 to $200,000 in 1868, and is now the leading private bank, doing the heaviest banking business in the

city. The deposits for the first quarter of 1868 were $635,000, discounts $500,000; exchange sales in 1867, $13,228,000.

Before the expiration of the old State Bank charter, Calvin Fletcher, Sen., and Thomas H. Sharpe, who had long been the president and cashier of the Branch at this point, started the Indianapolis Branch Banking Company on the 1st of January, 1857, now at the south-west corner of Washington and Pennsylvania streets, where the bank has ever since been located. As the capital of the old Branch was diminished and its business closed, the capital of the Banking Company was increased, and it has done a large and lucrative business, second only if after not equal to S. A. Fletcher & Co. Calvin Fletcher, Sen., died May 26th, 1866, and his interest in the bank descended to his sons, Ingram and Albert Fletcher. The capital of the bank is $200,000. The discounts for the first quarter of 1868 were $500,000, deposits $500,000; exchange sales in 1867, $3,147,2?0.

Alfred and John C. S. Harrison started an exchange office in May, 1854, in the second-story room of the Johnson building, remaining there till August, 1855, when the adjoining bank building was completed and the bank removed there, where it has since remained. No changes have occurred in its ownership since its origin. S. W. Watson is cashier. For the first quarter of 1868 the capital was $100,000, discounts $188,-000, deposits $227,347; exchange sales in 1867, $2,140,000.

The Indiana Banking Company, with seven partners, F. A. W. Davis, president, W. W. Woollen, cashier, was organized March 1st, 1865, with a capital of $100,000, and began business in Vance's building, corner Washington street and Virginia avenue, March 14th, 1865, where the bank remained till May 16th, 1867, when removed to 28 East Washington street. No changes in organization or amount of capital have since been made. The discounts for the first quarter of 1868 were $394,540, deposits $380,27?; exchange sales in 1867, $3,000,000.

J. B. Ritzinger opened a savings bank the 26th of March, 1868, at 38 East Washington street, J. B. Ritzinger, proprietor, A. W. Ritzinger, cashier; capital $50,000.

Dunlevy, Haire & Co., brokers, began business in Blake's Commercial Row in February, 1856, and continued here for a year or two. They were agents of the Cincinnati banks, and bankers, to run our State and free banks for gold, and within three months afterward had returned $2,000,000 currency for redemption. This action made their part made them and their principals at Cincinnati very unpopular, and produced the commercial convention of 1856.

But few failures of banks or bankers have occurred here, the following list comprising about all that have happened:

John Wood's bank, established in 1839, failed in 1841, as before stated.

In the spring of 1852 John Woolley & Co. began a private bank in a one-story frame, where No. 4 Blackford's block is now, remaining there till the establishment was merged in the Bank of the Capitol in May, 1853, and moved to Dunlop's building, and subsequently to No. 8 East Washington street. The failure of that bank has already been mentioned. It produced a run on the other banks, resulting two days in the failure of the savings bank.

William Robson, A. L. Voorhees and others started a savings bank in 1854 in the corner room of Odd Fellows Hall, Robson and Voorhees being successively the presidents, and Joseph K. Robinson cashier. Robinson became proprietor in 1857, and in the panic following the failure of the Bank of the Capitol was compelled to suspend payment September 17th, 1857, owing his depositors $15,000. The most if not all of this was paid by the receiver in April, 1858.

In the fall of 1862 Kilby Ferguson started ed the Merchants' Bank at No. 2 North Pennsylvania street, K. Ferguson, proprietor, G. B. Gosney, cashier, and continued business there till August, 1863, when by reason of unfortunate gold speculations he was compelled to suspend payment. The liabilities have lately been settled.

In the spring of 1856 G. S. Hamer started ed an exchange office in the basement of the American House, where shaving was closely done and shinplaster notes circulated, but the enterprising financier was arrested in November for passing counterfeit money, and shortly after disappeared.

No effort has hitherto been made to ascertain the extent of the dry goods and grocery trade here. The exchange sales by the banks in 1867, amounting to $34,614,180, may give an approximate measurement for that year, but a large additional sum should be added for currency transmitted by express. It may be safe to estimate this sum at $2,884,515, one-twelfth of the total, and by adding this we get $37,498,695 as the approximate importations of groceries and dry goods in 1867, and the trade has rapidly increased in 1868.

A number of railways were chartered and re-chartered in 1833-4-5, and efforts made to build them. Government surveyors ran the lines from Lawrenceburgh, Madison and Lafayette to this point, and from Columbus to Jeffersonville, in August, 1835. The first railroad meeting ever held here was on March 24th, 1834, to secure subscriptions on the Lawrenceburgh line, from

individuals and from the county commissioners.

The first meeting of the Whig party by that name, was held at the court house May 17th, Robert Brenton, president. John Hobart, Hiram Brown, Wm. Quarles, and John H. Scott were the speakers.

A meeting was held at the court house June 9th to devise means for the suppression of gambling. Resolutions were adopted, and prosecutions threatened unless the gamblers left. Meetings of a similar character were held in subsequent years, and an association formed to suppress the vice. Another raid was made in August, 1835, on the gamblers.

The Indianapolis Brewery, the first one in the place, was started this year near the canal, on Maryland street, by Young & Wernwag. A ropewalk was started on Market street, east of the market house.

The pension agency was removed here from Corydon in January.

1835. The State House being nearly completed, the Assembly, February 7th, directed the State treasurer to insure it, and to buy twenty fire-buckets, and ladders to reach the roof, and if the citizens subscribed the half the cost of an engine, to subscribe the balance for the State. A citizens' meeting was held on February 12th. The old fire-bucket company reorganized as the Marion Fire and Hose and Protection Company. The trustees were called on by resolution to subscribe the money for the engine, and levy a fire and public well tax. Caleb Scudder was chosen captain of the company. The trustees levied the tax, and subscriptions were also made by individuals; the State furnished her quota, and in the summer of 1835 the old Marion, a box, hand-brake engine, was bought in Philadelphia for about $1,800, and duly received here in September. A one-story frame house was first built for it by the State in 1836, but on the 6th of February, 1837, a two-story frame house was ordered to be built on the north side of the Circle, and was erected during the summer. It was occupied as an engine house and council chamber till the summer of 1851, when it was burned and the records of the town were destroyed with the house. On the 20th of February, 1838, the Marion Fire Company was incorporated. In the spring of 1840, the Good Intent, a box, hand-brake engine, was bought in Philadelphia, and used for a time by the Marion company with the old Marion, but in 1841 the company was divided, and the Independent Relief Company was formed and took the Good Intent. After the burning of the Marion house on the circle, a brick house was built in 1855-6, at the corner of Massachusetts avenue and New York

street, and the Marion was located there. The company disbanded in October, 1859, during the trouble preceding the introduction of the paid department, but re-entered the service in November, and was finally disbanded February, 1860. The old engine was used by the company till July, 1858, when a new, powerful side hand-brake engine was purchased by the council and given to the company. This machine was sold in April, 1860, to the town of Peru for $2,130.

The Independent Relief Fire and Hose Company was formed and incorporated with peculiar privileges in 1841, taking the Good Intent and using it till November, 1849, when it was given to the Western Liberties Company and a row-boat engine was bought by subscription and money realized from fairs, and used till August, 1858. The company became dissatisfied with it, and bought (aided by the city,) a powerful hand-brake engine at that time, which they used till they disbanded in November, 1859. Difficulty ensued between the company and the city authorities as to the ownership of the engines and other property, but in February, 1860, they surrendered everything to the city except the old row-boat engine, which was broken up and the materials sold in April, 1860, and the company finally dissolved. Their engine house during the greater portion of their existence was in Hubbard's block, on Meridian street.

The Western Liberties Company was formed in November, 1849, taking the old Good Intent, and occupying an old frame house at the fork of Washington street and the National road, near the race, using a large iron triangle for a bell, but they moved in 1857 to the house now used by the steam engine No. 1, west of the canal. In April, 1857, a new hand-brake engine, the Indiana, was bought for them, and used till November, 1859, when the company was disbanded, and the steam engine No. 1 afterward stationed in their house. The Indiana was afterward sold.

The Invincibles, a company mostly composed of Germans, was formed in May, 1852, in the first ward, and the Victory, a small hand-brake engine, procured shortly afterward, and used by them till March, 1857, when the Conqueror, a fine hand-brake engine, was bought and used by them till August, 1859, when the company disbanded and surrendered its property to the city. The house of this company, built in 1854-5, just north of Washington on New Jersey street, is now occupied by the hook and ladder company. The company was large, prompt and effective, and during its existence made several trips to other cities. After the new engine was bought the Vic-

tory was used by a company of boys. After the first paid department was organized, and its chief and assistant engine directors, the Invincible company was re-organized as pipemen, hosemen and brakemen for serving a part of it, and the Conqueror continued in ice. Use till the summer of 18-0, when the company was finally disbanded, and the engine sold shortly after to the town of Ft. Wayne.

The Union Company, No. 5, was organized in 1855, and a house built on South street for it in 1856, and in April of that year the "Spirit of 7 & 6," a Jeffers hand-brake engine was bought and used by the company till November, 1859, when the company was disbanded and surrendered its apparatus to the city. Some effort was afterward made to re-organize the company under the paid department, but without success. The engine was sold at $600 in October, 1860, as part pay for the steam engine No. 3, which was subsequently stationed in the Union house.

The Rover Fire Company was formed in the third and fourth wards in March, 1858. A house was secured for them, one of the old engines assigned to them, and steps taken to purchase an engine, but before anything was done the approaching change of system became evident, and the company was disbanded in June, 1859, and the house sold in 1860. Hose companies were simultaneously formed for each of the foregoing fire companies, and the necessary hose, reels and other apparatus furnished to them.

A hook and ladder company was formed in 1843, as a part of the old volunteer department, and the necessary wagon, ladders, ropes, hooks, axes and buckets procured. The company continued its organization till disbanded with the rest of the department November 14th, 1859, but was re-organized as a part of the paid department, and still continues in service, occupying the old Invincible house on North New Jersey street.

The Young America Hook and Ladder Company was formed in May, 1858, and got their wagon and apparatus in June, remaining in service till disbanded in November, 1859. In December, 1840, a number of boys formed the "O K Bucket Company," and procured a wagon and the old ladders and leather fire-buckets which belonged to the State and private citizens, and to the Indianapolis Fire Company in the earliest organization of the department. The council subsequently gave them a new wagon and buckets, and provided a house for them. They were effective—generally getting the first water on fires—until they disbanded in 1854. The company was revived in 1855, but disbanded finally in 1856, the boys taking the Victory formerly used by the Invincibles.

Under the volunteer system each company was independent, having its president, secretary and messenger for ordinary business, its chief and assistant engine directors, and brakemen for service. The corporate authorities exercised little control over the firemen until after the fire charter in 1847, and not much then till 1853, when the office of chief fire engineer was created and rules prescribed for the government of the department. Joseph Little was chosen first chief May 6th, 1853. His successors since that date have been Jabez B. Fitler, elected 1854; Chas. W. Purcell, 1855; Andrew Wallace, 1856; Joseph W. Davis, 1858; John E. Foudray, 1859; and under the paid department, Joseph W. Davis, 1859; Charles Richmann, 1866; Geo. W. Buchanan, 1867; Charles Richmann, May, 1868.

The volunteer system worked well till 1857. The rivalry between the companies produced good results; but the organization of the fire association in 1856, while rendering the department more efficient, also made it a political machine and increased the demands on the treasury. Conflicts and jealousies gradually arose between the companies, and on the choice of J. W. Davis as chief engineer in May, 1858, disputes arose as to the fairness of his election and management. The dissension impaired the efficiency of the organization, and the trouble was not entirely healed the next year under Foudray. It broke out afresh in August, 1859, on the proposition to substitute a paid department, which was earnestly advocated by Davis. The Invincibles disbanded in October, 1859, the Marions and Westerns in October, the Relief, Rover and Union in November, and the city was left for a short time without a fire organization. The Marions re-entered the service in November, but finally disbanded in February, 1860. The volunteer department in the spring of 1859 included six engine and six hose companies, with about four hundred and eighty men; two hook and ladder companies, with about one hundred men: one chief and two assistant engineers; seven houses, and about seven thousand feet of hose.

It was evident that a change would have to be made in consequence of the dissension arising over the election of engineer in May, 1858, and on account of the rapidly-increasing expense of the system. Fire alarms were very frequent, and the companies were charged with their origin. The council, in August, 1859, declared it inexpedient to re-organize the volunteer department. The fire committee reported, September 4th, in favor of a paid system, and the purchase of a third-class steam engine, and selling the old Relief and Good Intent engines. A Latta steam engine was exhibited here September 23d-4th at the county fair, and tried

at the Palmer House cistern before the build-
mittee. A Lee & Larned engine was also
brought here and tried October 13th and
22d, at the canal. It was determined to
buy one of the Lee & Larned machines, and
on the 30th of March, 1860, it was received
and stationed at the Western engine house.
On the 14th of November, 1859, the old
volunteer department was disbanded by ordinance, and a paid department, consisting
of one steam and two hand engines, and a
hook and ladder company, was authorized,
and J. W. Davis made chief engineer at a
salary of $800. C. Richmann and W. Sher-
wood were made captains of the two hand
engine companies. W. W. Darnell of the
hook and ladder company, and Frank Glazier engineer of the steamer. Some difficulty was experienced in forming the hand
companies on account of the general opposition to the chief engineer, but the force
was fully organized by January, 1860. The
engineer was ordered to sell the old and
surplus apparatus. The Marion engine was
sold in April, 1860, to Peru; the Union in
October to the Seneca Falls Company; the
Conqueror in February, 1861, and the remainder since that period, the last one being sold within the last year.

In August, 1860, a third-class Latta engine was bought, arriving here in October,
and was stationed at the old Marion house.
A Seneca Falls engine was exhibited at the
State fair, and tried October 22d before a
committee of the council in competition
with the other engines, the result being that
the council purchased it at $3,500, giving
the old Union at $600 in part pay, and sta-
tioned it at the Union house on South street.
Frank Glazier was appointed engineer of
the No. 1, Charles Curtis of the No. 2, and
Daniel Glazier of the No. 3. Hosemen and
pipemen were also appointed, and but few
changes have since been made in the force.
After seven years' trial of the three engines,
the council in 1867 purchased an additional
Seneca Falls machine, No. 4, which was received and put in service in December, and
the No. 3 sent back for repairs. These
were completed and the engine returned in
March, 1868, the whole cost of the new
engine and the repairs on the old one being
about $6,500. The Latta engine was then
relieved from service for repairs, and the
Lee & Larned will be repaired in its turn.
The department is now in an efficient state.
All the horses, hose, reels and other apparatus have been provided by the council.
For some years after the organization of the
paid department no central alarm existed,
but in the spring of 1863 an alarm tower
and bell was placed in the rear of Glenn's
block, and connected by wires and pulley-
with the watchmen's station on the tower of

the building. Two watchmen have since
been employed, giving the locality of the
fire by striking the number of the ward. In
February, 1868, a fire-alarm telegraph was
and the wires, boxes and fixtures
completed and put in operation by the end
of April, at a cost of about $6,000.

During the existence of the first bucket
fire company the dependence for water was
wholly on private wells. After the Marion
and Good Intent engines were bought a few
public wells were dug in the central
part of town. The first cisterns two in
number, holding three hundred barrels
each,) were built by the trustee government
in the spring of 1840, but it was not till October, 1852, when a cistern tax was ordered
by special election, that any number of cisterns were built. Sixteen were constructed
by the close of 1853, and since that date fifty
two, ranging from three hundred to eighteen
hundred barrels, have been built in various
quarters of the city, and though the supply
is still inadequate, the protection is ample
against all ordinary fires. In the spring of
1868 $300 were appropriated to bore an ar-
tesian well to test the project for supplying
cisterns from underneath the surface. At
present they are filled from wells, and the
creek and canal by the engines, or by a
steam pump, built for the purpose in 1864,
at a cost of about $1,000.

Though so largely built of wood, this
city has been remarkably fortunate in regard to fires. The streets are so wide, and
the department has been so prompt, that
fires rarely go beyond the houses in which
they originate. As the present buildings
are replaced by brick, stone or iron structures, with fire-proof walls and roofs, the
immunity from destructive conflagrations
will be still greater. The ordinary rates of
insurance are too high for this city, and our
people are now helping to insure property
in cities like Chicago, where more loss is
frequently suffered in a single fire than oc-
curs here in a year.

The State Board of Agriculture was chartered in February, 1835, Jas. Blake, Larkin
Simms, John Owen and M. M. Henkle, directors; James Blake, president, M. M.
Henkle, secretary. Premiums were offered
April 28th for essays on specified subjects,
and rules adopted for organizing county societies. The first State agricultural convention met December 14th, 1835, in Representatives' Hall, and several annual meetings
were afterwards held, but the enterprise
died in a few years. Meetings were held at
the court house June 6th and 27th, to form
a county agricultural society under the
State Board rules. N. B. Palmer was president, D. Maguire, secretary. Subscriptions
were made for premiums, and the Board of

(1)

Justices also appropriated fifty dollars. The first fair was held October 30-1 in the court-house yard. One hundred and eighty-four dollars were awarded in premiums. Much interest was manifested. Four hundred dollars were subscribed for the next fair. Annual fairs were held by the society for two or three years.

In the fall the papers said much improvement was going on. Property had doubled in value in two years, and business lots on Washington street were selling at fifty, sixty-two and seventy-five dollars per front foot.

The Benevolent Society was formed November, 1835, with a president, secretary, treasurer, depository and visitors, and has been active and efficient to the present date. Its system has always been the same, and prevents street begging. Funds and clothing are collected in specified districts in the fall by visitors, who deposit the same with the officers, and who also ascertain and report all cases needing aid. Written orders for money, clothes or provisions are given to applicants, and transient cases are cared for by a special committee. The society has been sustained by private contributions, the city and township authorities furnishing wood only when needed. Mr. James Blake has been the president for many years, and much of the good effected by the enterprize has been due to his zeal and energy.

The Young Men's Literary Society, designed for debate, composition and general mental improvement, was formed in 1835, and continued its meetings for twelve or fifteen years. It was incorporated in April, 1817, under the general law, collected a considerable library, and from 1843 to 1848 gave each winter a series of lectures by its members, and others from abroad. It was the successor here of the Indianapolis Athenæum, and the precursor of the lecture societies of the present day.

The winter of 1834-5 had been cold and protracted. The spring was backward. More rain fell in May and June than in any season before for ten years, and at Fort Wayne ten inches of water fell in two hours, the storm being limited to a small space. This statement was made by Jesse L. Williams, State engineer on the Wabash canal. There was a hard frost on the morning of July 1st, followed by a hot and dry season, closing on the night of August 18th in a tornado of wind and rain, unroofing houses, destroying fences, timber and crops, and killing horses, cattle and hogs. The following winter lasted till April.

1836. The want of natural channels for trade had prompted many improvement schemes in past years, and at an early day the Legislature had given $100,000 for opening roads, had often asked aid to improve the rivers, and had chartered many railways. From various causes these expenditures and efforts had effected little. With increasing resources the demand for greater facilities increased. The National road gave an impetus to other projects of more doubtful utility. A pressure from all sides was brought to bear on the Assembly, and on the 26th of January, 1836, the internal improvement bill was passed. The State not only undertook several great works, but extended aid to others under private companies. The act was erected with rejoicing. Bonfires and illuminations marked the spread of the news. Our citizens were especially elated, for several of the works terminated or crossed at this point, and more than one outlet would exist to the world. A general illumination took place here on the night of January 13th, when the passage of the bill had become a certainty. The bill at once improved the prospects of the town. Property rose in price rapidly, new houses were built, the settled limits extended westward, mechanics were busy, merchants sold large stocks, money was plenty, and every one prosperous. This continued nearly three years, when funds gave out, public works stopped, trade ceased, property declined, laborers went elsewhere, and ruin stared every one in the face. The hard times of 1839-42 were sorely felt. The leading business men were most involved, and for years their lives were struggles to save something from the wreck. The forbearance of creditors alone saved them from utter poverty. The bankrupt act of 1841 afforded relief to the whole country, easing the general distress, and enabling many to get another start. From this time till 1847 the town remained a dull country village, with so unfavorable an experience of internal improvements that our capitalists subsequently kept out of them or aided them but little.

Under the internal improvement system the central canal, from the Wabash to Evansville, together with several railroads from various points, had been intended to centre here. All were abandoned in 1839, after much work had been done. The Madison railroad had been completed nearly to Vernon and graded to Columbus. It was operated by the State till 1843, then surrendered to a company, and finally finished in October, 1847. Before competing lines reduced its traffic it made more money than any road in the country. The State was cheated out of her interest in the road, and the road itself, after losing business and importance, was finally bought and operated by the Jeffersonville line.

The canal was nearly done when abandoned; $1,000,000 had been expended. and a comparatively small sum would have completed it from Nobleville to Martinsville. It was begun in October, 1836, work being prosecuted simultaneously along its line by gangs of Irishmen, whose disputes with spade and shillelah gave animation to their encampments. A great debate of this kind occurred in 1838 near town, between the Corkonians and fardowners, several hundred disputants being engaged, and the discussion occupying the greater part of the day. The sections to Nobleville and Martinsville were nearly ready, and that to Broad Ripple was finished late in November, 1838. and opened for use June 27th, 1839, with an excursion by boats to Broad Ripple in July. Considerable preparations were made for traffic on it. Several freight and passenger boats were built, and flour, timber, grain, &c., were brought from Broad Ripple and above. The mill sites here were leased June 11th, 1838, and one woolen, one cotton, two paper, one oil, two grist and two saw mills built shortly afterward. The power proved less than was promised, the canal not having fall enough to cause a free flow of water, but the mills went to work, and with others since built have greatly benefited the place. The millers were always complaining of scant water and much moss; the people grumbled when the water was drawn off to clean the bed; and the Assembly, wearied by the incessant complaint, January 19th, 1850, ordered the canal to be sold. It was soon after sold to persons who were chartered as a company in February, 1851. In April the company sold to Gould & Jackson, who sold in October, 1851, to "The Central Canal, Hydraulic Waterworks and Manufacturing Company." This company sold to another company in 1859, who now rent out the power. For years after the first sale it was regarded as a nuisance, and propositions to fill it up were seriously considered in the council, both in 1855 and 1858, but having lately been kept in better order the opposition has measurably abated. It was dry for months in 1847, from the breaking of the banks and acqueduct, and in 1866-7 from the breaking of the feeder dam at Broad Ripple. It now furnishes mill power and transportation for wood and logs. The company owning it lately sued for the possession of a part of the military park, on the ground that it passed at the sale as an appurtenance of the canal.

The town having been specially incorporated in February by the Assembly, the new board of trustees was elected under the act in April, and the officers of the old board settled to April 1st, 1836. The treasurer's report showed $1,610 receipts for the year, and $1,150 of this sum had been expended for the Marion engine and in digging five public wells, and other fire department expenses. A balance of $121 was turned over to the new government. The new board passed ordinances regulating markets, ordering the streets to be opened, and prohibiting riots, drunkenness, horseracing and indecent language on the streets. The work on the National road in the last few years had attracted many men of bad character and habits to this point. These, banded together under a leader of great size and strength, were long known as "the chain gang," and kept the town in a half subjugated state. Assaults were often committed. citizens threatened and insulted, and petty outrages perpetrated, until at last a meeting was called March 9th at the court house to take the matter under advisement. Harrod Newland, a revolutionary soldier, was chosen president and made a radical speech against the gang. Resolutions were adopted to abate the nuisance. The citizens resolved to elect trustees and officers who would see the ordinances enforced, and pledged themselves to assist them. The determined stand taken somewhat awed the gang, and they became less bold in their demonstrations. At the camp-meeting in August on the military grounds, the leader made some disturbance and was knocked down and subjugated by Rev. James Havens, the preacher in charge, and shortly afterward was also soundly whipped by Samuel Merrill. These defeats broke his prestige, the gang was demoralized, and most of them left the town or ceased their lawless conduct.

The second homicide here occurred April 27th, Zachariah Collins being killed by Arnold Lashly. The county agricultural society held its second fair at the court house October 7th and 8th. C. Fletcher delivered an address, stating that 1,300,000 bushels of corn had been raised this year on the thirteen hundred farms in the county. Luke Munsell copyrighted a map of the town May 30th, and Wm. Sullivan published a map of the town in October. A great camp meeting was held on the military ground August 25-30, under James Havens and John C. Smith. One hundred and thirty experienced religion. Professor C. P. Bronson [died in New York, April, 1868,] gave the first lecture here on elocution, August 30th. Hiram Devinny began the manufacture of mattrasses, cushions and carpets here in October.

The new Washington Hall, a three-story brick hotel, built by a company in 1836-7, on the site of the old frame Washington Hall, at a cost of $30,000, was opened by E.

Browning November 10th, and kept by him till March 15th, 1851. It was then one of the largest and best western hotels, had a high reputation, and was the Whig head-quarters for its entire existence. It was damaged by fire $3,000 in February, 1843, and came near burning up. Several attempts were made to burn it in May and June, 1848. It was sold to F. Wright in March, 1851, was subsequently known as the Wright House, was successively kept by Henry Achey, Robert Browning, Burgess & Townley, W. J. Elliott, Louis Eppinger and others, and was bought in March and remodeled in the summer of 1859 by the Glenns, and is now known as Glenns block, the lower story being used as business rooms, and the upper by the council, city officers and police, with the fire tower and alarm on the roof. A very brief mention may be given here of the other leading hotels at various dates in the history of the town and city.

John McCormick was the first tavern and boarding-house keeper, beginning in the spring of 1820 on the river bank, in a little cabin with small pens around it as sleeping apartments for his guests. In 1821 Hawkins, Carter and Nowland each opened "taverns,"—Nowland in a cabin on Washington street west of the canal. He shortly after died, and his widow, Elizabeth Nowland, in 1823 opened a boarding-house where Browning's drug store is now, continuing there for many years. Carter's "Rosebush Tavern," a two-story ceiled frame, eighteen by twenty feet, built in 1821-2, at 40 West Washington street, was occupied by him till 1823. It was afterward moved near the canal, and then near the soldiers' home, where it yet stands. Carter in 1823 built a two-story frame tavern opposite the court house, which was burned in 1825. Hawkins' "Eagle Tavern," a double log house, was rebuilt in the fall of 1821, where the Sentinel office is now, the logs being cut from the lot and street. It stood there till 1826 or 7, when it was replaced with a small two-story brick. Bazel Brown took it in 1829, and was succeeded by John Hare, John Cain and others. It was torn down in 1849 and replaced by the Capital House, which was opened by John Cain July 14th, 1850, and subsequently succeeded by D. D. Sloan and others, till March, 1857, when it was occupied by the Sentinel as a printing office. It has since been used as a printing office and bindery, and for business rooms and offices. It was the first four-story house built here. The successive hotels on this site were the Democratic headquarters; and it was at the Capital House, as the most stylish in the city, that Kossuth was lodged during his visit here in February, 1852.

The Palmer House, a two-and-a-half-story brick, was built in 1840-1 by N. B. Palmer, the largest and best western hotels, had a on Washington and Illinois streets, and high reputation, and was the Whig head-opened by John C. Parker in the summer quarters for its entire existence. It was of 1841. It was enlarged and raised to four stories in 1856 by Dr. Barbour, the lessee. Parker, Barbour, J. D. Carmichael, D. Tuttle, C. W. Hall, B. Mason and others have been its lessees. It has always kept the same name, was for some time the leading house, and has had a fair share of patronage. Little's Hotel, first built in 1834 or 5, on New Jersey and Washington streets, by John Little, and known then as Little's Sun Tavern, (from the sign, a blazing sun,) was originally a small two-story frame house. A three-story ell was added by M. and I. Little in 1847, and in 1851 the old frame was moved to East and Washington streets, and a three-story brick front building put in its place. It also has frequently changed lessees but has retained its old name. The Duncan House, a three-story brick, subsequently the Barker and the Bay House, was built in 1847 on South and Delaware streets, by R. B. Duncan. It did a good business for some years, but has long been mostly devoted to boarders. D. J. Parker, M. M. Bay and others have been lessees. The Carlisle House, a three-story frame, built by Dan Carlisle in 1848, on Washington street, west of the canal, has so often changed names and lessees that they are unknown. From its position it never did as good a business as other houses, and is now used as a brewery. The Morris House, a two-and-a-half-story brick, subsequently much enlarged and raised to four stories, and known as the "American," "Mason," and "Sherman House," was built by Thos. A. Morris in 1852-3, north of the Union depot, and has done a good business. It has often changed its lessees. The Bates House, a four-story brick, which has retained its name though often changing lessees, was built on the corner of Washington and Illinois streets in 1852-3, by Harvey Bates, and has since been much enlarged, being the largest and leading hotel of the city, and doing perhaps the heaviest business. The Oriental, a four-story brick hotel, in 1856-7, and opened in June by Francis Costigan, has retained its name though often changing lessees, and has done a fair business. The Tremont, afterward the Spencer House, a four-story brick, was built on the corner of Louisiana and Illinois streets, near the Union depot, in 1857, and has done a good business under J. W. Canan and others, its lessees. The Farmers', now the Commercial Hotel, was built in 1856 by Henry Buchiz, as a three-story brick, and enlarged and raised to four stories by F. A. Reitz in 1864. It has often changed lessees.

The Macy House, a three-story brick, was built by David Macy, on Illinois and Market streets, in 1857, and has since been occupied mostly by boarders. A large number of other less important houses exist, mostly built in the last ten years, but want of space forbids further mention of them.

The Indianapolis Insurance Company was chartered for fifty years February 8th, 1836, with a capital of $200,000, in fifty dollar shares, and with very favorable banking privileges. It was organized March 16th with nine directors, D. Maguire being president and C. Scudder, secretary, and began operations in April. It did a limited business for many years, but finally suspended operations in 1859 or '60. In 1865 the old stock was purchased and a new company organized, with Wm. Henderson as president and A. C. Jameson, secretary. The charter was amended December 20th, 1865, increasing the capital to $500,000 by vote of the stockholders, and making the company perpetual. The old Branch Bank building was purchased for about $30,000 from the Sinking Fund, in April, 1867, and the office has since been located there. It is now doing a prosperous insurance and banking business, and ranks high among the home enterprises of the city.

The other insurance companies since started may be briefly mentioned here. The Indiana Mutual Fire Insurance Company was chartered January 30th, 1837, and amendments made to the act at several subsequent dates. It was organized in February with James Blake, president, Charles W. Cady, secretary, and began business in March in an office opposite the Washington Hall. It was prosperous and did a good business for two or three years, but from inherent defects in the plan, heavy losses and mismanagement, became involved, insolvent, and finally suspended operations about fifteen years ago.

The Indiana Fire Insurance Company was chartered in February, 1851, with a nominal capital of $300,000, and was organized May 1st, 1851, —————— being president, —————— secretary. It did a limited business, and suspended operations after a few years.

The German Mutual Fire Insurance Company was organized under the general law January 21st, 1854, and has successfully conducted its business to the present date. Its office was first located at 81 East Washington street, removed in 1859 to Judah's block, and in March, 1866, to 16 South Delaware street. Henry Busher, Julius Boetticher and A. Seidensticker have been the presidents, and A. Seidensticker, Valentine Butsch, Charles Volmar, Charles Balke, Adolph Miller and F. Ritzinger secretaries,

of the company. The risks assumed during the first year amounted to $136,000; its present risks to $3,146,000; cash and premium notes on hand in April, 1868, $284,487; losses in last year, $10,606; no unadjusted liabilities.

The Indiana Fire Insurance Company—a mutual company—was organized May 9th, 1862, under the general law of 1852, and the office has since been located in Odd Fellows Hall. Jonathan S. Harvey was chosen president, and W. T. Gibson, secretary, at the time of the organization, and have served till the present time. The amount of risks assumed by the company during the first fiscal year was about $600,000, and the amount now incurred is between eight and nine millions.

The Sinnissippi Mutual Insurance Company was organized November 18th, 1863, under the general law, with Elijah Goodwin president, John R. Berry, secretary, and continued its operations till 1865. It advertised extensively, did a large business, incurred risks (many of dangerous character) to the amount of millions of dollars, paid good salaries and commissions, and incurred heavy expenses and losses. Assessments were rapidly made on the premium notes, and the company broke in 1866, passing into a receiver's hands, and its affairs are now being closed up. The office of the company was at 35 East Market street.

The Equitable Fire Insurance Company was organized on the mutual plan in September, 1863, under the general law, W. A. Pellee, president, E. D. Olin, secretary, and its office opened in Odd Fellows Hall. The company was authorized by law in 1865 to change the character of its business substantially to the stock system, dispensing with premium notes and receiving premiums in cash. Its operations were limited mostly to the centre and north of the State, but its expenses and losses compelled its suspension in January or February, 1865, and its affairs are being adjusted by a receiver. The office was in Odd Fellows Hall.

The Home Mutual Insurance Company was organized in April, 1864, under the general law, with J. C. Geisendorff, president, J. B. Follett, secretary. Its business was conducted substantially on the same plan as that of the Equitable Company, but was mostly confined to risks in the city and vicinity. Not being very remunerative, and some losses having occurred, the company voluntarily suspended operations in June, 1868, and its business is being closed by a receiver appointed by the court. The office was most of the time at 64 East Washington street.

The Farmers' and Merchants' Insurance Company was organized on the same general plan and under the same law as the two foregoing companies, on the 1st of April, 1864, with Ryland T. Brown as president, and A. J. Davis, secretary, and the office located in Blackford's block. It continued its operations, doing a moderate business in the central portion of the State, till the summer of 1867, when it suspended, and its affairs are now in process of settlement.

The Union Insurance Company was organized on the stock plan under the general law, in the spring of 1865, with a capital of $200,000, James M. Ray being president, and D. W. Grubbs, secretary. The office was first opened in Talbott & New's building on Pennsylvania street, but removed in 1867 to Dunlop's building. E. B. Martindale was elected president, and George W. Dunn, secretary. The company continued its operations, doing a good business but meeting with considerable losses, till April, 1868, when it was determined to close its affairs and dissolve the company. Its risks were accordingly re-insured in the Home Fire Insurance Company of New York, and the Union Company discontinued.

The American Horse Insurance Company, (for security against loss by death, &c., of horses and other animals,) was organized under the general law in August, 1865, with a nominal capital of $100,000, Thomas B. McCarty being elected president, J. F. Payne, secretary, and has continued its business to the present date, at the office in Vinton's block on Pennsylvania street.

The Franklin Mutual Life Insurance Company was organized under the general law in July, 1866, James M. Ray being elected president, and D. W. Grubbs, secretary, (since succeeded by E. P. Howe,) and has been very successful, as all life companies are that are carefully managed. It has done a good business and met with few losses, standing well among such enterprises. The office was first opened at 19 North Meridian street, but in April, 1868, the company purchased the old State Bank building, at the corner of Illinois street and Kentucky avenue, and removed to that point.

Beside the foregoing home organizations, agencies, general and special, exist here for forty or fifty foreign life, accident and fire insurance companies. Most prominent among these is the Ætna, of Hartford, which, under William Henderson and A. Abromet as agents, has done a very lucrative business at this point, its net receipts here during the continuance of the agency, in excess of all expenses, amounting to nearly if not quite $200,000. The company

in 1858-9 erected a four-story brick building on North Pennsylvania street as an office and for business purposes.

1837. At a meeting held February 22d it was determined by the young men to form a military company, and at subsequent meetings a constitution, by-laws and uniform were adopted, members enrolled, and officers elected, Alexander W. Russell being captain, and serving till August, 1838, when Thomas A. Morris succeeded and commanded the company for years afterward. The uniform was gray with black velvet facings, and tall leather caps with pompons and brass mountings. The company was armed with muskets and drilled by Scott's tactics. It was the best organization in the State, attracted much admiration on parade, and existed till 1845. The "Graybacks" were the first independent company, and were specially incorporated February 14th, 1838. Their fine discipline and soldierly bearing aroused the long dormant military feeling, and other companies were shortly afterward formed in the town and vicinity. Prominent among these were the "Arabs," or Marion Riflemen, under Captain Tom McBaker, uniformed in tringed hunting shirts, and armed with breech-loading rifles. In August, 1842, the independent companies formed a battalion and elected Hervey Brown Lieutenant-Colonel, and George W. Drum, Major. Frequent parades and several encampments were held by the companies, and the military feeling was active till near the time of the Mexican war. Three companies of volunteers were raised here during that war, under Captains J. P. Drake, E. Lander and John McDougall. For two or three years after that war no organization existed. In 1852 the City Guards were formed under command of Governor Wallace, and in May, 1853, the Mechanic Rifles, but neither of these lived long.

The Saint Louis National Guards passed through here in February, 1856, and the effect produced was such that a similar organization was effected here on the 12th of March. The National Guards were uniformed in blue, with caps and white plumes, and were successively under the command of W. J. Elliott, Thomas A. Morris, George F. McGinnis, Irwin Harrison, J. M. Lord, and W. P. Noble. When the war occurred the company entered the eleventh regiment and closed its existence with the end of the war. An unsuccessful effort was afterward made to revive it. It was a well-drilled and officered organization, held frequent parades and a number of encampments, and supplied many competent officers to the army during the war. It revived the mili-

tary spirit here when it was at the lowest ebb, and aided in keeping it alive until the war demonstrated the absolute necessity of such organizations in time of peace. George F. McGinnis, W. W. Darnell, J. H. Livsey and others commanded the company through the war. Shortly after it was first formed the National Guards Band was organized, and under different names and with some changes, still exists, holding a high rank among the musical organizations of the State.

The City Greys and the City Greys Band were organized August 12th, 1857, and under the successive command of W. J. Elliott, E. Hartwell and others, attained a high state of discipline. It was uniformed in gray, wore bearskin shakos, and was armed like the Guards with muskets. It entered the eleventh regiment and closed its existence with the war, being commanded by R. S. Foster, S. W. Butler and Henry Kemper. The Greys Band, in March, 1859, during the Pike's Peak fever, started for that locality, but turned off toward Santa Fe, and thence down through Mexico to Matamoras, and through Texas to New Orleans and home, receiving a public welcome here June 7th, 1860, after their fifteen months of wandering and hardship. The band entered the service, though not as the old organization.

The City Greys Artillery was organized in 1859 as an adjunct to that organization, under J. A. Colestock as captain, but the commander lost his arm not long after by a premature explosion of the gun, and the company was suspended.

In July, 1858, the Marion Dragoons, Captain John Love, were organized, and for a year or two kept up their organization and occasional parades, but the difficulty of properly drilling and keeping up a cavalry company prevented their continued existence.

The Montgomery Guards visited the city on the 21st of February, 1860, and with our city companies paraded on the 22d. In the afternoon they gave a fancy drill by drumbeat, in Zouave dress, near the Bates House, in presence of an immense crowd, and excited great admiration. It was at once determined to form a Zouave company here, and on the 1st of March the Independent Zouaves, Captain F. A. Shoup, were organized, uniformed as Zouaves, armed with sabre-bayonet rifles, and persistently drilled. Shoup resigned in January, 1861, went south and joined the rebel army, in which he afterward became a brigadier general, and was noted as the first one on that side to propose using the negroes as soldiers in the rebel cause. The Independent Zouaves entered the eleventh regiment and terminated

their existence with the end of the war, being commanded by W. J. H. Robinson, F. Kneller and others. A military convention was held here June 27th, 1860, under the leadership of Captain Lewis Wallace, eleven companies being represented, and an encampment was determined on, to be held September 19th on the State military grounds. It was accordingly held September 19th–24th, the Greys, Guards, Zouaves, Montgomery Guards, Fort Harrison Guards, and Vigo Guards participating, General Love commanding, Captain Shoup Adjutant. The unfavorable weather prevented a large attendance.

The Zouave Cadets were organized in August, 1860, and the Zouave Guards, Captain John Fahnestock, in October. This company also entered the eleventh regiment and terminated its existence at the end of the war. The Cadets were in existence for a year or two after the war.

The news of the attack on Sumter was received April 12th, and the next day recruiting began. The Guards, Greys, Zouaves, and Zouave Guards at once filled up, and were all in camp by the 17th. Two reserve companies of National Guards were formed. Two companies of the Greys entered the service, leaving one reserve company at home. Two companies of the Independent Zouaves were in the eleventh regiment. The Zouave Guards left no reserve company. Besides these organizations an artillery company was formed, and Home Guard companies in every ward. Several thousands of men were raised here for the service during the war, without counting the gallant City Regiment, twelve hundred strong, with its artillery and cavalry wings, raised here during the Morgan raid, or the one thousand "hundred dayers" at a later date in the struggle. The military record of the city during the war was a proud one, and her quotas were always filled, although by the remissness of the authorities in securing the proper credits, a draft was ordered early in 1865, and a debt of several hundred thousand dollars incurred for bounties to volunteers to fill requisitions that should never have been made.

On the 4th of February, 1837, Calvin Fletcher and Thomas Johnson were appointed commissioners by the Assembly to receive subscriptions and drain the swamp to north-east of town, which discharged its waters by two bayous through the place. They proceeded to execute the work by cutting a ditch west to Fall creek, south of and

through the present fair grounds. During the flood of 1847 the banks of the drain broke and the water again came down the old channels, flooding the houses and alarming new comers. These bayou channels are now nearly obliterated by the street grades and filling of lots. On the 6th of February the Assembly authorized the Internal Improvement Board to use the half of square 50, which had been given to the town for market purposes in 1821, and in lieu thereof to set off the north half of square 48 to the town, the town and the State to exchange deeds on the transfer. On the 4th of February the first carpenters' association was incorporated, and it shortly after limited a day's work to ten hours.

The Episcopalians had met occasionally in 1835 for worship at the court house, as the services of a minister of that church could be secured, but in the winter of 1836 the meetings had been more frequent, and in March or April, 1837, a church was organized and Rev. James B. Britton chosen rector, preaching at the court house and seminary. Preparations were made for building in November, and on the 7th of May, 1838, the corner-stone of Christ Church was laid, a plain wooden Gothic structure, on the north-east corner of Circle and Meridian streets. The house was opened for services November 18th, 1838. This building was used till 1857, when it was sold to the African Methodist church and removed to West Georgia street. A new stone church (the first in the city) was begun in May, 1857, and completed in 1859. The spire yet remains unfinished. A peal of bells was placed in it in May, 1860, and taken out and replaced with a better one September, 1860. A tasteful brick parsonage was built near the church in 1857. Rev. J. B. Britton, S. R. Johnson, M. M. Hunter, N. W. Camp, J. C. Talbott, H. Stringfellow, T. P. Holcomb, J. T. P. Ingraham have been rectors of this church. In 1865 the church divided, a part of the members forming St. Paul's church, and in the spring of 1867 the corner-stone of a large brick edifice was laid at the corner of New York and Illinois streets, with appropriate services. Rev. H. Stringfellow has been the rector to this date. This church has recently been completed and dedicated as the cathedral church of the diocese. Grace church, on Pennsylvania and St. Joseph streets, was built in 1863-4, M. V. Averill rector. Several mission chapels of this denomination have since been built in different quarters of the city.

The Evangelical Lutheran church was formed in the spring of 1837, and the first communion held May 14th, Rev. A. Reck being pastor. It was at first proposed to build the church on the north-west corner of University Square, and a lease was obtained from the Assembly; but the house, a small, plain brick, was commenced in the south side of Ohio street, between Pennsylvania and Meridian, and was torn down in 1852 and a new church built in 1853-4 on the south-west corner of New York and Alabama streets. The German Lutheran church was built in 1860-1 on East and Georgia streets, Rev. Charles Freke, pastor.

The Indianapolis Female Institute was chartered at the session of 1836-7, and opened June 14th by Misses Mary J. and Harriet Axtell, in Sanders' building. It was subsequently removed to the upper rooms of the house opposite Washington Hall, and finally to a frame school-house on Pennsylvania street next the old Presbyterian church. The first examinations were held April 30th, 1838, and the school subsequently attained a high reputation, attracting scholars from abroad. Miss Axtell was a faithful and competent teacher, held in grateful remembrance by her pupils, but her health failing the school was discontinued in the fall of 1849, and she died at sea shortly after on her way to the West Indies. The Indianapolis High School, afterwards called the Franklin Institute, was opened on Washington street, opposite Washington Hall, October 25th, 1837, by G. Marston and Eliza Richmond. A frame school-house was built in the spring of 1838 on Circle street next the present high school building, and occupied by the school for four or five years. Marston left in 1839, being succeeded by Orlando Chester, who died in October, 1840, and was succeeded by John Wheeler, who taught until the school was discontinued. In December, 1837, it was proposed to establish a State Female Seminary as the counterpart of the Bloomington College for males, and use the Governor's Circle as the college building. The Indianapolis Academy, under Josephus Cicero Worral, had been in existence from 1836, and continued for several years after this date. Worral was a man of considerable education but peculiar idiosyncrasies, and his addresses to his scholars (often published) excited much amusement on account of the flights of fancy, classical allusions, and stilted style in which he indulged.

The first editorial convention in the State met May 29th in the town council chamber, twenty editors and publishers being present. John Douglass acted as president and John Dowling secretary. Fifty-two papers were then published in the State. An association was formed, constitution adopted, and advertising rates agreed on.

As the National Government was McAd-amizing the centre of Washington street, it was proposed in June that the trustees improve the sidewalks, and steps were accordingly taken to do so. The sidewalks as originally designed were fifteen feet wide on Washington and ten feet on other streets. At a subsequent date they were made twenty feet on Washington and twelve feet on other streets; and within the last ten years fifteen feet has been adopted as the standard width on the ninety-feet streets. The increased width of the pavement on Washington street was bitterly opposed by the property-holders on account of the increased expense entailed in their improvement. The first street improvements were begun in 1836-7.

A great hail storm occurred on the 6th of June, many of the stones weighing three and four ounces, and measuring three inches in length. Nearly all the windows in town were broken. The usual military and school celebration occurred on the Fourth of July, the exercises closing with a military reception, and ball at night in the Governor's Circle building. The Ladies' Missionary Society held the first fair here on the 31st of December, realizing $230 for the cause. Such fairs were afterward very frequently held by various societies and for various objects.

1838. The Assembly re-incorporated the town on the 17th of February, including the whole of the donation, but limiting taxation for municipal purposes to the old plat. The town was divided into six wards; all east of Alabama street constituting the first; thence west to Pennsylvania the second; thence to Meridian the third; thence to Illinois the fourth; thence to Mississippi the fifth; thence west the sixth. One trustee was to be elected by each ward, and a president by the whole town. They were to be freeholders, hold office one year, and constitute the common council, the president and four members being a quorum. The president had a justice's jurisdiction, was to enforce all ordinances, and keep a docket. The marshal had a constable's authority and was to keep the peace. The council met monthly, the members each receiving twelve dollars per annum. They had all necessary powers, to pass ordinances, levy taxes, (not over one-half per cent. on real property) improve streets, borrow money, tax shows, saloons and groceries, regulate markets, guard against fires, &c. The assessment was to be made annually by June 1st, and collected by September 1st. The council was to elect a secretary, treasurer, collector, marshal, supervisor, market master, lister and assessor. The election under this act was held the last Saturday in March, and resulted in the election of Jas. Morrison as president. In April and May the council passed ordinances governing the markets, regulating cases before the president, licensing groceries, and improving sidewalks and streets.

The summer and fall of 1838 was very sickly and many deaths took place. The first "steam foundry" in the town was started in January by Wood & Underhill, on Pennsylvania street, where the Second Presbyterian church now stands. The old steam mill was finally closed in February of this year and the machinery offered for sale, though not disposed of finally until a year or two afterward. Benjamin Orr opened the first ready-made clothing store here during this year.

1839. On the 13th of February the Assembly directed the State officers to buy a residence for the Governor, and early in the spring Dr. Sanders' two-story brick dwelling, erected in the summer of 1836 on the north-west corner of Market and Illinois streets, was purchased and used as the official residence till 1864. It was sold by order of the Assembly in 1865, and a row of business rooms built along the Illinois street front of the lot.

Three hundred and twenty-four votes were cast at the corporation election in March, N. B. Palmer being elected president. At the meeting in April the public wells were ordered to be repaired, by-laws adopted for the government of the town officers, and the streets which were still fenced up ordered to be opened. The corporation receipts for the year ending March 27th were $7,012, the expenditures $6,874; $550 of this sum was paid Elder, Colestock & Co., for building the west market house and adding to the east one; $413 were paid M. Shea, sexton, for clearing and fencing the old graveyard; $58 for printing, and $145 for street improvements and gravel.

The first revision of the town ordinances was made and published in July. In November $300 were appropriated to buy a new engine; a committee was appointed to see if it could be bought for $600, and donations solicited for the purpose.

An accurate survey of the donation this year showed a mistake in the original survey by which the title to eight acres, which had been laid off in lots and sold in 1831, was still in the general government. The Assembly memorialized Congress in February, 1840, stating the mistake and asking a donation of the eight acres. This was granted and the title quieted.

The first municipal tax sale took place October 25th at Washington Hall, by James Van Blaricum marshal and collector. A considerable number of sales were subse-

quently made, but the records have since been lost.

In November Mrs. Britton opened a female seminary near the foundry. This school—afterward known when under the care of Mrs. Johnson as the "St. Marys Seminary"—was subsequently removed to a building adjoining the Episcopal church, and for many years was quite prosperous.

The first Thanksgiving proclamation was issued on the 4th of November by Governor Wallace, the day fixed on being the 28th.

The Presbyterian church having divided in May, 1838, on the slavery and other questions, the church here was also divided, fifteen of the members forming the Second church November 19th, 1838, under Rev. J. H. Johnson. One or two calls were extended to pastors but declined, and in May, 1839, Rev. H. W. Beecher, then of Lawrenceburgh, was called, and began his ministrations July 31st. The congregation worshiped in the seminary. In 1839-40 a frame church (the present high school building,) was erected at the north-west corner of Market and Circle streets, and occupied by the congregation October 4th, 1840. Mr. Beecher remained till September 19th, 1847, and was succeeded by Rev. Clement E. Babb in July, 1848, who remained till January 1st, 1853. Rev. T. A. Mills was called as pastor January 1st, 1854, remaining till February 9th, 1857. Rev. G. P. Tindall became pastor in August, 1857, and Rev. H. A. Edson in November, 1863. In November, 1851, twenty-four of the members formed the Fourth Presbyterian Church, and erected a brick church in 1853-4 on Delaware and Market streets. In the spring of 1864 a new stone church, not yet fully completed, was begun on Vermont and Pennsylvania streets, and is now nearly completed at a cost of about $100,- 000. It is the finest church building in the place and city. The chapel was occupied December 22, 1867. The Fifth Presbyterian church is a colony from the Second, and their church was dedicated May 15th, 1864. The Olivet church is also a colony, dedicating their church October 20th, 1867. The old frame church was sold to the city for a high school building in the spring of 1867, and was last used as a church July 16th, 1867.

1840. Much political excitement occurred this year, and the Whigs carried the municipal election in March for the first time, electing the trustees and town officers. The corporation receipts for the year 1839 amounted to $5,975, the expenditures to treasurer $100, marshal $100, supervisor $4,753; $1,984 of this sum were spent on the market houses, $1,350 on streets and bridges, $197 on the fire department, $974 for salaries, and $244 for incidentals.

The first cisterns, two in number, of three hundred barrels each, were ordered to be constructed in the spring of this year.

The political excitement increased in intensity as the elections approached, both parties holding monster conventions. A very large convention was held at Tippecanoe about the last of May, many persons attending from this place. A great Whig convention was also held here on the 5th of October, and on the 14th of October the Democrats held a great meeting in the walnut grove north of the Blind Asylum to welcome Richard M. Johnson, Vice President and reputed slayer of Tecumseh. He was received with due honors and addressed the convention. Colonel Johnson visited the town once or twice afterward on private business. One thousand three hundred and eighty-seven votes were cast in the township at the November election, Harrison receiving eight hundred and seventy-two, Van Buren five hundred and fifteen.

The Indiana Horticultural Society was formed August 22d and continued active operations for several years, Henry Ward Beecher and James Blake being among its most prominent supporters.

The annual Methodist conference met here October 21st, Bishop Soule presiding.

1841. In March, James Wood, civil engineer, made a profile of the streets by direction of the council to establish a uniform system of grades, to be followed in their future improvement. The profile was filed with the authorities, adopted by the council April 8th, 1842, and has been followed in nearly all the subsequent improvements. The survey and profile cost $303.

On the 10th of April a meeting was held to make arrangements for funeral services for President Harrison. The exercises took place on the 17th, Governor Bigger and Henry Ward Beecher delivering addresses. Business was suspended during the day, and the funeral procession was imposing. The 14th of May was observed throughout the country as a fast day for the death of the President.

1842. By the treasurer's report in March the corporation receipts for the past year amounted to $3,197, expenditures $2,- 957; $1,138 had been expended for street improvements and $767 for salaries. The county receipts from March 1st, 1841, to June 1st, 1842, were $9,942, expenditures $3,194. The salaries of the town officers for 1842 were as follows: Secretary $200, collector $200, assessor $75, market messenger $140, messenger of fire company $100. An effort was made in the fall to repeal the act of incorporation on account of

the expenses attending the municipal government.

On the 25th of April at two o'clock A. M., the town was startled by a heavy explosion, and on examination it was found that the grocery of Frederick Smith, a one-story grocery, a frame house, where 96 East Washington street now is, had been blown up with powder, and further search revealed the body of Smith badly burned and wounded. He had attempted suicide during temporary insanity, sitting on the keg of powder and applying the match.

The first daguerreotype saloon here was opened by T. W. Whitridge in July or August. During the fall James Blake erected a mill and furnaces and attempted the manufacture of syrup and sugar from cornstalks.

This year was distinguished by the visits of two Presidential candidates, Van Buren and Clay. Mr. Van Buren arrived by stage on Saturday, the 11th of June, being received east of town by a procession composed of citizens, firemen, and four military companies, and was escorted with due honors to the Palmer House, where he made a speech in reply to the welcoming address. He visited Governor Bigger at the State house, and held a reception in the evening. On Sunday he attended the Methodist and Second Presbyterian churches, and left on Monday by stage for Terre Haute, being upset near Plainfield while *en route*. Henry Clay arrived October 5th, attending a Whig convention in response to an invitation of the party. The crowd on that occasion was generally estimated at thirty thousand, and considering the facilities for travel, then and since, it has never since been equaled. The procession included many bands, many military companies, representatives of all trades and professions, and was nearly two hours passing a given point. It proceeded to a grove north of Governor Noble's house, where a great barbecue was spread for the assembled thousands. Mr. Clay spoke for two hours after dinner, and was followed by Governor Crittenden, Governor Metcalf and other Whig leaders. The festivities lasted three days, and included a grand military parade, and review by the Governor, a fine exhibition of fireworks and an agricultural fair.

During this and several following years an excitement about mesmerism spread through the West. Lecturers went from point to point explaining the new science to the natives and giving experiments in illustration. Many amusing scenes occurred in the trials made on the "subjects" by committees appointed by the audiences.

1843. Physicians and philanthropists had repeatedly called the attention of the Legislature to the condition of the insane, blind, and deaf and dumb persons in the State, suggesting steps for their education and maintenance; and as early as January, 1839, the Assembly had memorialized Congress asking a grant for that object, and on the 13th of February, 1839, the assessors were directed to ascertain and report the number of deaf mutes in each county. The Governor was directed, January 31st, 1842, to correspond with the Governors of other States concerning the cost, construction and management of Insane Hospitals. Dr. John Evans delivered a lecture December 25th, 1842, before the Assembly on the treatment of insanity, and on the 13th of February, 1843, the Governor was directed to correspond with superintendents of hospitals and procure plans to be submitted with his suggestions at the next session. This was done, and a tax of one cent on the hundred dollars was levied January 15th, 1844, for hospital buildings. On the 13th of Jan., 1845, John Evans, Livingston Dunlap and James Blake were appointed commissioners to select a site of not more than two hundred acres. They chose the present site in the spring of 1845, and reported it, with a plan of the building, at the following session. On the 19th of January, 1846, they were ordered to begin the hospital according to the plan on the site, and sell hospital square, its proceeds, with $15,000 in addition, being appropriated to the building. The central portion of the hospital was begun in the summer of 1846 and finished in 1847, at a cost of about $75,000. The south wing was built in 1853-4, and the north wing several years afterward. Various additions, changes and repairs have also been made, and the house as finally completed has cost nearly if not quite $500,000, and is among the largest buildings in the West. It is situated on a quarter-section of land two miles west of the city, is from three to five stories in height, with a basement, and is about five hundred feet in length. It was first opened for the reception of patients in 1847, and has ever since been fully occupied. Dr. John Evans was its originator and first superintendent. He resigned July 1st, 1843. R. J. Patterson, J. S. Athon, J. H. Woodburn and W. J. Lockhart have since been the successive superintendents of the institution.

The first steps having been taken to provide for the insane, the Assembly, on the 13th of February, 1843, levied a two-mill tax to support the deaf mutes and build them an asylum. William Willard, a mute teacher from Ohio, arrived here in the spring of 1843 and opened a private school for mutes on the 1st of October, having sixteen pupils during the first year. This

school was adopted by the State on the 15th of January, 1844, and the Governor, Treasurer and Secretary of State, with Henry Ward Beecher, Phineas D. Gurley, P. H. Jamison, L. Dunlap, James Morrison and Matthew Simpson appointed trustees, with instructions to rent a room and employ teachers. They rented the house on the south-west corner of Illinois and Maryland streets, and opened the school there October 1st, 1844. The Governor was also to receive proposals for site, &c. The Governor was authorized on the 15th of January, 1845, to appoint five trustees in place of the former board. He did so, and in the fall of 1846 the new board rented the Kinder building on East Washington street and removed the school there, where it remained until the completion of the Asylum in October, 1850. The institution was permanently located here January 9th, 1846, the trustees being directed to buy thirty acres near the city, $3,000 being appropriated therefor. They were subsequently directed to buy one hundred acres in addition to instruct the pupils in agriculture. The site was bought east of the city in the summer of 1846 and the building began in 1849 and finished by October, 1850, at a cost of about $80,000. It was rough-casted and completed in 1853. On its completion the school was removed there and has been prosperously managed ever since. Many mutes have received their entire education there and been fitted for active business pursuits. Prior to 1848 pupils who were able were required to pay tuition and board, but since then the education and maintenance of all have been free. William Willard was the originator and first teacher of the school. James S. Brown was the first superintendent from 1845 to October, 1852, and since that date Dr. Thomas McIntyre has been in charge of the institution.

The insane and the deaf mutes being thus provided for, the blind were still neglected; but during the session of 1844-5 pupils from the Kentucky Institution gave an exhibition before the Assembly with such success that a two-mill tax was at once ordered for the support and education of the blind. James M. Ray, George W. Mears, and the Secretary, Treasurer and Auditor of State were appointed commissioners at the next session to expend the fund thus created in starting a school or maintaining pupils at the Ohio or Kentucky institutions. They appointed William H. Churchman as lecturer to present the case to the people and to ascertain the number of blind in the State. On the 27th of January, 1847, G. W. Mears, J. M. Ray and Calvin Fletcher, were appointed commissioners to erect asylum buildings and arrange for a school.

$5,000 being appropriated for a site, furniture, &c. Mr. Fletcher declining to serve, W. Norris was appointed trustee. Two blocks on North street were purchased for a site, a plan selected and the building commenced. The school was opened October 1st, 1847, in the building on the south-west corner of Illinois and Maryland by Mr. W. H. Churchman, who had been appointed superintendent. Nine pupils were in attendance on the 4th, and thirty during the session. In September, 1848, the school was removed to a three-story brick building erected on the grounds and afterward used as a workshop. The asylum was commenced the same year and finished, with some changes of plan and details, in 1851, at a cost of $60,000, and the pupils and school at once removed to it. The surrounding grounds have since been tastefully laid out and planted with trees and shrubbery. W. H. Churchman, G. W. Ames, W. C. Larrabee and James McWorkman have been superintendents of the institution. The asylums are creditable to the city and State. not only for extent, management and arrangement, but also that they were built when the State was heavily in debt and the people unprepared for the extra taxation necessary for their support.

In February, 1843, a fire damaged the Washington Hall to the extent of $3,000, and seriously threatened its entire destruction. The weather was excessively cold, the water freezing as it fell, and the house was saved after several hours' hard work by the engine companies, aided by hundreds of citizens in passing buckets.

The Millerite delusion, which had some of the citizens among its adherents, created some excitement during the winter and spring. The belief in the approaching end of all things was strengthened by an earthquake on the 4th of January between eight and nine o'clock, lasting nearly a minute and sensibly shaking the buildings. It was also encouraged by the great comet which nightly flamed in the south-west during February and March, its train reaching across the sky like a destroying sword. The weather however was adverse, being cold and stormy during March and April, with deep and drifting snows, followed in May by heavy rains, filling the streams, sweeping off bridges, breaking the canals, and raising White river over the bottoms. The 22d of February and the 4th of July were celebrated by the military, four companies participating, and the last anniversary by the schools in the usual style. In the month of June R. Parmlee began making pianos here, and continued the business two or three years. In November "The New York Company of Comedians" gave

a series of concerts in Gaston's carriage shop on Washington west of Illinois street, each concert being succeeded by a theatrical representation. John and Mary Powell, Sam. Lathrop, Mr. Wallace, Tom. Townley and others were the actors. The company had considerable merit and attracted good audiences. During the season, which lasted for ten weeks, the noted tragedian, Augustus A. Adams, Mrs. Alexander Drake and Mr. Morris were the stars. This company was the third which performed here, Lindsay's company having performed several years before, and Mr. and Mrs. Smith in 1823-4.

The Indianapolis Female Collegiate Institute, Miss Lesuer, principal, began in September in the Franklin Institute on Circle street, and continued two or three years.

The Roberts Chapel Methodist church was built during this and the following year at a cost of eight or ten thousand dollars, on the corner of Market and Pennsylvania streets, under J. S. Bayless, the first pastor. The congregation worshiped in the court house until the completion of the church. The present lot and building were sold in June, 1868, and steps are being taken to erect a larger and finer edifice at a cost of about $80,000, on the north-west corner of Vermont and Delaware streets.

1844. The Union Cemetery was laid out in April adjoining the old burying ground. In 1852 Messrs. Ray, Peck and Blake, laid out the ground north and east of this cemetery for burial purposes, and in 1860 the Greenlawn Cemetery, west of the last-named ground and next the river and Terre Haute railroad, was added.

A meeting was held on the 5th of August to make arrangements for the contemplated visit of Lewis Cass. He came on the 25th and was received with due honors and conducted to the State military grounds, where a welcoming address was made by Governor Whitcomb, and a long speech made by General Cass in response. He was followed by Senator Hannegan and others. The procession and audience was large and enthusiastic. A reception was held for several hours at the Palmer House, and he left at six in the evening for Dayton.

1845. The Thespian Society, composed of young men of the town, gave a series of dramatic performances during July, August and September. They also performed during September and October of the following year. Several of the performers evinced decided talent for the stage, and their efforts attracted good audiences.

The usual celebrations occurred on the Fourth of July, but the day was signalized by a riot, resulting in the murder of John Tucker, a negro, on Illinois street opposite

the present site of the Bates House. Balon Washington west of Illinois street, each lenger, the principal in the affray, made his escape. Nick Woods was sent to the penitentiary, and the others were acquitted. Washington street was graded and graveled in July. In August and September Seton W. Norris built the present Hubbard block, then the best business house in the place.

On the 16th of August John H. Ohr, apprentices in the Journal office, issued the first number of the Locomotive, and continued its publication weekly for three months. It was revived by them April 3d, 1847, and again issued for three months. Its size was seven by ten inches, and each three months' issue formed a volume. Douglass & Elder revived it January 1st, 1848, and issued it weekly from an office on South Meridian street in Hubbard's block, till July, 1861, when its publication was suspended and its subscription list transferred to the Sentinel. Its size when first issued by them was eight by thirteen inches, and after several enlargements it was finally published on a sheet twenty-three by thirty-one inches. Elder & Harkness became proprietors March 30th, 1850, and continued such till its suspension. For a number of years it had the greatest circulation in the county, and published the letter-list. It was neutral in politics, and devoted to literary and news matters.

The old Methodist church, erected in 1825-9 on Meridian and Circle streets, having become unsafe from the cracking of the walls, was torn down and Wesley Chapel erected in this and the following year on its site. It has since been in constant use by Wesley Chapel charge, but will probably be sold this year and a finer and larger edifice will be built on the south-west corner of Meridian and New York streets.

1846. The corporation receipts for the year ending March 31, amounted to $2,636. This had all been expended and a debt of $870 contracted. This debt caused some uneasiness to the citizens.

The Mexican war began early in April, and the news was received here early in May. The Governor's proclamation calling for volunteers appeared May 23d. Recruiting at once began and a company was formed in June under captain J. P. Drake, and lieutenants John A. McDougall and Lewis Wallace, and marched to the rendezvous at New Albany. This company was attached to the first Indiana regiment under colonel Drake, and spent the year of its enlistment guarding stores in Matamoras. Two additional companies, under captains Edward Lander and John A. McDougall, were raised in May and September, 1847,

and attached to the fourth and fifth regiments. A number of recruits were also secured here for the regular army. But little excitement existed here in regard to this war, and it was generally viewed from a party stand point.

The Madison railroad depot was located this summer on the high ground south of Pogue's run, nearly half a mile from the settled portion of the town. The location caused much dissatisfaction, and the company was strongly urged to build its depot on Maryland street; but, the location having been finally determined on, the council ordered the improvement of Pennsylvania and Delaware streets across the low valley of the run, and the creek bed was straightened from Virginia avenue to Meridian street by the property holders.

The citizens became provoked during the summer at the bold operations of the gamblers. Meetings were held, a committee of fifteen appointed, resolutions to abate the nuisance adopted, and Hiram Brown, the oldest member of the bar, retained to prosecute the offenders. Vigorous measures were taken, and repeated in December, 1847, and the gamblers compelled to leave the town. Much feeling was aroused by these measures and the fifteen were denounced as a vigilance committee, but the desired object was attained and the town rid of the presence of many bad characters.

1847. Heavy and continued rains, amounting to twelve inches in forty-eight hours, had fallen over the State during the last days of December, 1846, producing by the first of January the greatest flood in White river and its tributaries since 1824. The whole valley was flooded, washing off soil, cattle, hogs, fences, hay, and causing in various ways so much damage that the Assembly authorized a deduction of taxes for the year to parties residing on the streams. The swamp north-east of town becoming full, the banks of the drain broke flooding the two bayous, and causing loss and inconvenience to parties who had built along them. West Indianapolis was covered, and the National road and canal badly injured. The aqueduct by which the canal crossed Fall creek was broken, and not repaired till late in the fall, the mills meanwhile lying idle. This flood was almost equalled by another in November.

The 22d of February was celebrated by the mechanics with a procession, speeches, dinner, &c. A meeting was held on the 26th of February to take measures for the relief of the starving poor in Ireland. An organization was effected, committees appointed, subscriptions of money and grain procured and forwarded, and for several

weeks the work was actively and effectively prosecuted.

The Assembly on the 15th of February, 1847, granted the town a city charter, its acceptance or rejection to be decided by a vote of the citizens on the 27th of March, and in case of its acceptance the Governor was to proclaim the fact and that it had become a law. The donation east of the river was included in the corporation, and was divided in seven wards. Washington street was the boundary between the north and south wards. All east of Alabama and north of Washington was the first; thence west to Meridian the second; thence to Mississippi the third; thence west, fourth; all west of Illinois and south of Washington, fifth; thence east to Delaware, sixth; thence all east the seventh. The first city election was to take place April 24th. The Mayor was to serve two years, had a justice's jurisdiction and the veto power. One councilman was to be elected from each ward at $24 annual salary and serve one year. The council was to elect one of their number president, hold monthly meetings, two-thirds being a quorum. They had full power to pass ordinances, levy taxes, establish district schools and levy taxes therefor, grade streets, suppress nuisances, &c., and were to elect a secretary, treasurer, assessor, marshal, (who was to have a constable's authority,) street commissioner, attorney, and such other officers as might be needed. Taxation for general purposes was limited to fifteen cents on the $100, but could be increased if specially authorized by vote of the people. At the election for city officers in April a vote was also to be taken on the question of tax for free schools.

Joseph A. Levy, the last president of the old town council, issued a proclamation directing an election to be held in the six wards of the town on the 27th of March, to determine the acceptance or rejection of the new charter. The election resulted in 449 votes for to 19 against it. This vote was certified to Governor Whitcomb on the 29th, and on the 30th he proclaimed the adoption of the charter and that it had become a law. Joseph A. Levy, president of the old council, then issued a proclamation directing an election, on the 24th of April, in the seven wards of the city, for mayor and councilmen, and also to decide whether a tax should be levied for free schools. The election was held and the tax almost unanimously authorized, Samuel Henderson was elected the first mayor, and the following persons from the several wards the first city councilmen: Uriah Gates from the first, Henry Tutewiler from the second, Cornelius King the third, Samuel S. Rock-er the fourth, Charles W. Cady the

LIST OF PRINCIPAL CITY OFFICERS FROM 1847 TO 1868.

Year.	Mayor.	Prest. of Council.	Clerk.	Treasurer.	Marshal.	Engineer.	Attorney.	Assessor.
1817.	S. Henderson	S. S. Hooker	James G. Jordan	N. Lister	Wm. Campbell	James Wood	A. M. Conaham	Joshua Black
1848.	S Henderson	C. W. Cady	James G Jordan	H. Ohr	John Bishop	James Wood	N. B. Taylor	Chas J Hand
1849.	H C Newcomb	Geo A Chapman	James G Jordan	James Greer	S A Colley	James Wood	Wm B Greer	H Ohr
1850.	H C Newcomb	Wm Eckert	Jos T Roberts	J H. Kennedy			Ed Coburn	
1851.	C Scudder	A A Louden	Jos T Roberts	John S Spann	B Pillican	James Wood	Wm Wallace	S P Daniel
1852.	C Scudder	D V Colley	D B Colley	A F Shortridge	S A Colley	James Wood	A G Porter	D Vanbushench'n
1853.	C Scudder	D V Colley	D B Colley	A F Shortridge	E McNeely	James Wood	A G Porter	Jacob S Allen
1854.	Jas McCready	D V Colley	D B Colley	A F Shortridge	B Pillican	James Wood	N B Taylor	M Luth
1855.	Henry F West		Jas N Sweetser	A F Shortridge	B Pillican	James Wood	N B Taylor	John G Waters
1856.	Wm J Wallace		Alf Stevens	H Vandegrift	G W Pitts	A B Condit	N B Taylor	J H Kennedy
			Fred Stein	Francis King	Jeff Springsteen	D B Hosbrook	John T Morrison	John B Stough
1857.	Wm J Wallace		Geo H. West	Francis King	Jeff Springsteen	D B Hosbrook	B Harrison	John B Stough
1858.	Sam D Maxwell		John G Waters	J M Jamison	A D Rose	James Wood	S V Morris	S V Morris
1859-9	Sam D Maxwell		John G Waters	J M Jamison	Jeff Springsteen	James Wood	B K Elliott	R W Robinson
1861-2	Sam D Maxwell		John G Waters	Jos K English	D W Loucks	James Wood	J N Sweetser	John B Stough
					John Unversaw	James Wood, Jr		
1863-4	John Caven		C S Butterfield	Jos K English	John Unversaw	James Wood, Jr	R J Ryan	R J Ryan
1865-6	John Caven		C S Butterfield	W H Craft	John Unversaw	James Wood, Jr	B K Elliott	Wm Hadley
1867-8	Dan McCauley		Daniel Ransdell	Robert S Foster	John Unversaw	Joshua Staples	B K Elliott	Wm Hadley
						R M Patterson		Wm Hadley

LIST OF PRINCIPAL CITY OFFICERS FROM 1847 TO 1868—CONTINUED.

Year.	Street Com'r.	Market Master.	Weighmaster.	Sexton.	Ch'f Fire Eng'r.	Sealer Wei'ts & Meas.	Printers.	Chief Police.
1847,	Jacob B Fitler.....	Sampson Barber.	John Patton........	B F Lobaugh......				
1848,	John Bishop.......	Jacob Miller......	A Haugh........	J I Strecker.......			State-man and Locomotive...	Jeff Springsteen.
1849,	George W Pitts....	Jacob Miller......	A Haugh........	J I Strecker........			Sentinel and Locomotive...	Jeff Springsteen.
1850,	Geo Youngerman	Jacob Miller......	A Haugh........	Phil Stocks......			Locomotive......	Jeff Springsteen.
1851,	Jos Batsch........	Jacob Miller......	A Haugh........				Locomotive.......	J M Van Blaricum
1852,	Hugh Staten	Jacob Miller......	A Haugh........	Phil Stocks.......			Locomotive......	Chas G Warner...
1853,	Wm Hughey	H Ohr............	A Haugh........	Phil Stocks.........	Joseph Little....	J W Davis......	Elder & Harkness	A D Rose........
1854,	Wm Hughey	Jacob Miller......	A Haugh........	Geo Bishing...	Jacob B Fitler...	J T Williams....	Chas G Berry......	Samuel Lefevre...
1855,	J B Fitler..........	Richard Weeks...	A Haugh........	John Meditt....	Chas W Purcell..	J T Williams....	Larrabee & Cottan	A D Rose.......
1856,	J B Fitler..........	Geo W Harlan....		A Linguetcher...	Samuel Keeley....	H J Kelley......		
1857,	H Colestock...	B Weeks......	Now.......	John Meditt.....	Andrew Wallace..	J M Jamison....	Ind'p's Journal Co	A D Rose.......
1858,	H Colestock.......	Chas John.......		John Meditt....	Jos W Davis......	J G Henning....	Ind'p's Journal Co	Thos A Bonney..
1859-60	H Colestock.......	Chas John.......		G W Alfred.....	John E Fequthay.	C S Butterfield...	Ind'p's Journal Co	Thos O Ames....
1861-2	Jno A Colestock,	Thos J Foss.....		G W Alfred.......	Jos W Davis.....	Jas Loucks.....	Ind'p's Journal Co	Point Powell....
1863-4	John M Kemper,	J I Wenner.......		G W Alfred.......	Jos W Davis......	Jas Loucks......	Ellis Barnes.......	J Van Blaricum
1865-6	August Richter...	Chas John.....		G W Alfred.......	Chas Richmann...	Jos Loucks...... Joseph Bishop...	James G Douglass	
1867-8	August Richter...	Sampson Barber		G W Alfred........	Geo W Buchanan Chas Richmann...	Aug Bremer....	James G Douglass	Thos S Wilson ...

NOTE.—The city was incorporated by the Assembly February 13th, 1847, the act being accepted by the people at a general election held March 27th. A mayor was to be elected in April for two years, one councilman from each of the seven wards for one year, and the council were to elect the city officers, who also served one year. This government continued till March 7th, 1852, when the council accepted the general law of June 18th, 1852, as the city charter. By this act the mayor became president of the council, and all the officers and councilmen were to be elected by the people and serve one year. Two councilmen were to be elected from each ward by the voters thereof. This charter was amended in 1857, extending the term of mayor and councilmen to two years, and on the 1st of March, 1852, it was amended so that the city officers elected by the people were to hold office two years and the councilmen four years. This act was superseded by the act of December 20th, 1865, under which the officers and councilmen were elected for two years, the auditor, assessor, attorney and engineer being elected by the council. This act was superseded by the act of March 14th, 1867, under which the city is now governed. This act provides for a police judge, John N. Scott being elected the first incumbent May, 1867. The mayor, clerk, assessor, judge, marshal, treasurer and councilmen are elected by the people, and hold their offices for two years; the other officers are elected by the council, and hold office for one year.

fifth, Abram W. Harrison the sixth, William L. Wingate the seventh. The new council was organized May 1st, and elected Samuel S. Rooker president, and James G. Jordan sec'ry, at a salary of $100; Nathan Lister, treasurer, at $50; James Wood, engineer, at $300; William Campbell, collector, with per cent. compensation; William Campbell, marshall, at $150 and fees; A. M. Carnahan, attorney, with fees; Jacob B. Fitler, street commissioner, at $100; David Cox and Jacob B. Fitler, messengers of the fire companies, at $25 each; Sampson Barbee and Jacob Miller, clerks of the markets, at $50; Joshua Black, assessor and Benjamin F. Lobaugh, sexton. [The city officers, from 1847 to the present time, are named on pages 47 and 48.] The tax duplicate for 1846-7 amounted to $4,226, and $865 of this sum were delinquencies from former years. Though there was little money in the treasury the council at once began to improve the streets, and it was waggishly suggested that they employ a squad to tramp down the dog-fennel and thus give the place a business appearance.

Little had been done by the old trustees and councilmen in the way of street improvements, beyond filling mud holes, cutting drains or grubbing stumps, and though James Wood had been employed to make a street profile in March, 1841, which had been adopted in April, 1842, and followed in the subsequent improvements, and considerable sums expended, no permanent results had been achieved. The street profile was re-adopted by the new city council June 21, 1847, and a new system commenced, beginning at the centre of the city and extending gradually outward. Property holders were required to bear the expense of grading and gravelling in front of their lots, and the city finished the crossings. The first bouldering was done in May, 1850, by Looker and Lefevre, on Washington between Illinois and Meridian streets, and by the summer of 1860 it was completed from Mississippi to Alabama streets, and from thence it has been extended east and west and north and south. Nearly all the present street improvements, culverts and bridges, have been completed in the last twelve years.

The free school tax having been authorized by a large majority, at the election held April 24, 1847, the council levied it and made arrangements for the schools. Each ward was made a district under the supervision of a trustee. Houses were rented and teachers employed, the schools being free only for one quarter each year under the State law. Donations little and money were asked, and the thanks of the council extended, in December, 1847, to Thomas

D. Gregg, for a gift of $100. Lots were purchased at from $300 to $500 in the seven wards in 1848-9, and in 1851-2 plain, cheap, one story brick structures, so planned that additional stories could afterward be added, were built in five of the wards. Those in the second, fourth and sixth wards, had two rooms each, and in the others but one room each. A second story was added to the first, second and fifth ward houses in 1854-6, and all except the old seventh ward house enlarged or raised. A good two story house was built in the eastern part of the seventh (now in the eighth,) ward in 1857, and it was raised an additional story in 1865. Lots were bought in the fourth and present ninth wards in 1857, and in 1865-6 large, well finished, three story buildings, with basements, were erected on them at a cost of about $32,000 each. Other lots have been purchased for sites, and in view of the future extension of the city beyond the donation it would be good policy to secure sites for future houses on or beyond the present boundaries of the city. In 1867-8 a large, four story building, with basement, was erected in the south part of the sixth ward and will cost, when fully completed, about $43,000. It is at present the largest and finest school building in the city. The houses recently built are well designed, well finished, and have far more architectural pretensions than the earlier ones. Additional buildings are still needed as the schools from the start have been much cramped for room.

The first tax levy, in 1847, produced $1,981; that of 1848, $2,885; that of 1849, $2,851. In 1850 the fund amounted to $6,160, $5,938 of which sum was spent that year and the beginning of the next for lots and buildings. The tax produced a larger sum each year with the increased growth of the city, and in 1857 yielded $20,320. At first the entire amount was expended for buildings, the teachers being paid by tuition fees, but after the first houses were finished the annual return was mostly expended in salaries, the schools being kept open longer, more teachers employed and better salaries paid.

In 1847 the several wards were constituted independent districts, each under the supervision of a trustee, and schools were opened in the fall of that year or spring of 1848, in rented houses. This continued till January, 1853, when the council elected Henry P. Coburn, Calvin Fletcher and Henry F. West, a board of trustees under the new law, giving them the sole control and management of the city schools. A code of rules was drawn up by Calvin Fletcher, arrangements made, and on the 25th of April the free schools were opened

for the first time, two male and twelve female teachers being employed. Until that date the number of pupils had averaged only 340, but by the first of May the attendance rose to 700, and over 1,000 out of the 2,600 children in the city were enrolled. Until the election of this board of trustees the schools had been conducted independently, without a common system, text books or course of study. At the request of the trustees the principals of the leading private schools prepared a list of text books and a course of instruction which was adopted and subsequently followed. In August the graded system was adopted, and the high school, for more advanced pupils, was opened September 1st, by E. P. Cole, with one assistant, in the old county seminary, which had been repaired and refitted for the purpose. From this date to February, 1855, the system was under the sole supervision of the trustees, who served without compensation and almost without thanks, to the detriment of their private interests, but they persevered in the work, overcame all obstacles, and at last interested the people in the enterprise. The work, however, proved too great, and at their request the council in February, 1855, elected Silas T. Bowen superintendent, at a salary of $400 per annum, (which he earned twice over,) requiring him to give a large share of his time to the duties of the office. He effected a marked improvement, but it was soon evident that the duties required more labor and time than he could bestow, and the council, in March, 1856, appointed George B. Stone (who had succeeded E. P. Cole as principal of the high school,) superintendent at a salary of $1,000 a year, requiring him to give all his time to the schools. He at once perfected the system, adopted improved methods of teaching, held meetings of the teachers and examined and drilled them for their work, inspired them with his own zeal and energy, and made the system so thorough and popular that the prejudice which had existed against it died out. The school tax was willingly paid, and the private schools sank into the back ground or languished for want of their former support. With the increasing revenue better salaries (ranging from $300 to $600,) were paid, the terms were lengthened, more teachers engaged, 35, mostly females, employed in 1857. The average attendance of pupils had risen from 340 in April, 1853, to 1,400 in 1856, and 1,800 in 1857. The total number enrolled at that date was about 2,800. Ten houses were occupied, seating comfortably only 1,200, but crowded with 1,800 pupils. Forty-four per cent. of the children in the city were enrolled, and 73 per cent. of those enrolled were in average daily attendance. The schools were graded as primary, secondary, intermediate, grammar and high schools. The system was working prosperously and a bright career seemed certainly before it when the supreme court decision on the tax question in January, 1858, struck a fatal blow at the whole fabric. The city council was immediately called to consider the question. It called meetings of citizens in the several wards to devise measures by which the schools could be continued. The meetings were held January 20th, and 1,100 scholarships were subscribed amounting to $3,000, and it was resolved to sustain the free system for the current quarter, and as a pay system afterward. The schools were closed, however, at the end of the quarter, the superintendent and teachers left for other points, and the houses remained vacant or used occasionally for private schools for a year or two afterward.

No free schools were opened in 1859. A small tax was levied for the repairs of houses and furniture, and from the State fund free terms of eighteen weeks each were held in 1860 and 1861. The system was reorganized under the law of 1862, and a term of twenty-two weeks held that year and since that date it has been gradually regaining the ground occupied in 1858. Prof. George W. Hoss acted as superintendent in 1862-3, having 29 teachers employed and 2,374 pupils enrolled. In September, 1863, the system was again reorganized, A. C. Shortridge being elected superintendent. and since that date full terms of thirty-nine weeks have been held each year. The schools are graded as primary, intermediate and high, with four subordinate grades (A. B. C. and D.) in each. Common text books are used in the similar grades, and all the children in any given subordinate grade of all the schools are simultaneously pursuing the same course of study, graduating from the lower to the higher subordinate grades, and from the primary to the intermediate and thence to the high school, the whole course requiring twelve years, (ten months in each year,) and giving the pupils a thorough English education. Daily registers are kept showing the conduct, attendance and scholarship of each pupil, and a average must be attained before promotion to a higher grade is granted. The registers thus kept show a great improvement in attendance and scholarship in the last three years.

The school buildings and the whole system are controlled by three trustees elected by the city council, but accountable for their acts and expenditures to the county commissioners and the superintendent of public instruction. They have charge of the ex-

penditures for buildings, tuition, employ-ment of teachers, &c; the expenditures be-ing made from two separate funds, one being for buildings and repairs, the other for tuition, and derived partly from the State school fund and partly from a special city tax. The immediate management of the schools devolves on a superintendent, who devotes his whole time to them and receives a salary of $2000. The teachers (sixty-two of whom are now employed, three male and fifty-nine female,) receive salaries ranging from $400 to $700, and are only employed after a thorough examination of their qual-ifications for the position. Improved methods of instruction have been promptly adopted, object teaching, gymnastics, music, penmanship and other branches, are taught by special instructors, who visit the schools in turn for that purpose.

The following table shows the number of houses, teachers, children enrolled in the schools, average number enrolled, daily average attendance and per cent. of atten-dance from 1863 to the present time. No reliable returns exist as to the total number of children of school age (6 to 21,) in the city for the several years, and no records exist as to above items for the years 1853-8. When the new sixth ward building is open-ed, 4,200 children can be accommodated with seats, and 75 or 80 teachers can be employed.

Years.	School Houses.	Teachers	Children Enrolled.	Average No Pupils	Per Cent. Attended
1863-4		30	2,374	1,260	86
1864-5		28	2,533	1,428	92
1865-6	9	34	3,212	1,900	91.1
1866-7	11	58	4,369	2,505	94.2
1867-8	12	62	4,940	3,137	95.3

In September, 1853, when the graded system was adopted, the schools were rated as primary, intermediate, grammar and high school, the last being opened in the old seminary building, on the first of Sep-tember, by E. P. Cole, with one assistant. It was held there till the downfall of the schools in 1858. It was re-established in 1864, and held at the first ward house, and from the spring of 1867 in the old Second Presbyterian Church on Circle street, which was then purchased for $13,500. This building is now undergoing alterations and being better fitted for school uses at an ex-pense of about $4,500. The principals of this school from 1853 to 1858 were E. P. Cole, George B. Stone and W. B. Henkle. Since 1864 W. A. Bell, Pleasant Bond, W. J. Squier and W. A. Bell. The present salary is $1,600.

From 1847 to January, 1853, the schools were conducted independently in the seven wards, under the supervision of seven trus-tees, one to each district or ward. A board of three trustees was then elected by the council to take charge of the entire system, and retained the control of it till April 12, 1861, when (under the new law) an ordi-nance was passed making the wards districts, and requiring the voters of each of the seven wards to elect a school trustee for their ward. They were elected in May of that year for two years. This system continued till April, 1865, when, under the law of that year, the council elected three trustees, W. H. L. Noble, T. B. Elliott and C. Vonne-gut, who have since been continued in office and had the entire management of our city school system. The city is greatly indebted to the early trustees (prominent among whom were Henry F. West, Henry P. Co-burn, Calvin Fletcher, sr., Silas T. Bowen, David V. Culley, David S. Beatty and Jno. B. Dillon,) for their zeal, energy and perse-verance under very discouraging circum-stances, and to the present board, Messrs. Noble, Elliott and Vonnegut, for reviving and carrying forward the system. Silas T. Bowen, George B. Stone, George W. Hoss and A. C. Shortridge, have been the super-intendents. To Mr. Stone belongs the cred-it for perfecting the system and demonstrat-ing its usefulness, and to Mr. Shortridge its revival and present efficiency. The city may well be proud of the system, and of the thoroughly drilled corps of instructors now employed, and with continued careful man-agement the free schools will be among the first of her future glories.

In May, 1847, the Grand Masonic Lodge bought a lot at the south-east corner of Washington and Tennessee streets and formed a stock company to build a hall. A plan drawn by J. Willis, architect, having been accepted, the corner-stone was laid with appropriate ceremonies October 25th, 1848, and the hall built in 1849-50 at a cost of about $20,000. It was opened in the spring, but not finished till the fall of 1850, and was finally dedicated by the Grand Lodge May 27th, 1851. The concert room in the second story was the first large hall opened here for public meetings, and was in almost constant use from the time of its opening till the erection of Morrison's Opera Hall on Meridian street in 1865, since which time it has been comparatively little used. The constitutional convention of 1850 was held in Masonic Hall, and nearly all the conventions, concerts, lectures, panoramas, and exhibitions, dramatic and otherwise, for fifteen years, were given in it. Almost all the leading speakers, lecturers and singers of the country have appeared on its stage. The stock in the building was long since purchased by the Grand Lodge, and it is

now proposed to change and improve the building.

A meeting was held in May to make arrangements for a formal welcome to the First Indiana Regiment of Volunteers expected soon to return from Mexico. The welcome proved a failure, as the volunteers returned in small squads in wagons and stages at different periods, and it was impossible to divide the "enthusiasm" accordingly.

The first instalment of female teachers sent by Governor Slade from New England arrived here in June and were sent to various parts of the country. They were soon married, and others were afterward sent in their stead. In July, the remains of Captain T. B. Kinder, brought from Buena Vista by his company, were buried with military honors in the old cemetery.

The near completion of the Madison railroad awakened the interest of the community in such enterprises, and frequent meetings were held during the summer and fall to advocate roads to different points and organize companies. A new impetus was given to business, street improvements were begun, new buildings and work-shops erected, and new residents were met daily on the streets.

Arrangements were made September 25th at a citizens' meeting to celebrate the completion of the railroad on the 1st of October. The last rail was laid at about nine o'clock that morning, just as two crowded excursion trains arrived from below, greeted by a great crowd of rejoicing natives, many of whom then first saw a locomotive and train, and who joyously filled an excursion train to Franklin and back. The great even was celebrated by the firing of cannon, and by a procession which included Spalding' entire circus outfit, Ned Kendall's band and a country cavalry company. An address was also delivered by Governor Whitcomb from the top of a car at the depot, and an illumination and fireworks exhibition closed the festivities at night. The excursionists were hauled across the low and muddy valley of Pogue's run in carriages and wood wagons, and the few hotels were crowded with hungry guests. The depot had been located on the high ground south of the creek, a quarter of a mile from the town, during the preceding summer, its location there being opposed by many persons who urged that it should front on Maryland street, which was then the southern settled limit. A cluster of warehouses was built around it, and for several years it formed a separate settlement until the expansion of the city included it in the body of the place. The depot was built in 1846-7, the engine house and shops in 1850, and the road had,

a flat bar track till 1850-2, when it was taken up and T rail substituted.

The Madison road had been begun in 1838 by the State, the cost being estimated at $2,240,000, of which sum the inclined plane was to cost $272,000. Twenty-eight miles were finished in 1841 at a cost of $1,500,000. Branham & Co. leased the road receipts, the State keeping up repairs and supplying motive power. The work was surrendered to a company in 1842, and completed October 1st, 1847. N. B. Palmer, S. Merrill, John Brough, E. W. H. Ellis, F. O. J. Smith and others were presidents till the line was sold. In January, 1854, it was consolidated with and operated together with the Peru road, but the arrangement was severed after a few months. It was sold by the United States Marshal March 27th, 1862, for $325,000, and a new company organized, and was bought a year or two afterward by the Jeffersonville Company, and has since been operated by that organization. For some time after its completion this road paid better than any other in the country. In 1852 its stock sold at $1.60, and in January, 1856, had fallen to two and one-half cents on the dollar. The State held stock in the road valued at $1,200,000, but was ultimately cheated out of it, receiving scarcely anything for it.

The isolation of the town ended with the completion of this road. An outlet for travel and surplus products at last existed, and the town became a centre of traffic for a considerable region around it. Wheat, which had been selling at forty cents per bushel, rose in a few weeks to ninety cents. Other farm products advanced in proportion, and goods and groceries declined. Trade improved, building increased, work-shops were started, property advanced in price, and city airs were timidly assumed.

The Madison road exacted such high rates for fares and freights, and for several years made such heavy profits that opposition was aroused; other routes were demanded, and roads to Bellefoutaine, Terre Haute, Peru, Lafayete, Lawrenceburg and Jeffersonville, were advocated. The old companies were resuscitated, or new charters obtained; the projects were energetically pushed in 1848-9, meetings were held, stock subscribed, surveys made and contracts let. In 1849-50 a railroad ever prevailed in the community, and did not subside until eight lines were completed, and the city became widely known as "the railroad city" of the west. From under estimates as to cost and over estimates as to immediate business, the lines failed to realize the hopes of stockholders, but while not at once remunerative to them,

the gain to the State and city was very great. The construction, in a few years, of many depots, shops and warehouses, disbursed much money, attracted many workmen, and stimulated manufacturing enterprises. The population of 4,000 in 1847, increased to 8,100 in 1850, 10,800 in 1852, 15,000, in 1857, and 18,000 in 1860.

For sometime each road used its own depot; passengers and freights being transferred from one to the other by hacks and drays, but a connection by rail was soon proposed, and an agreement having been made in August, 1849, between the companies, and the right of way having been granted December 20, 1818 by the council, the Union Railroad Co., was organized, the Union track located and laid in 1850, (relaid in 1853,) the ground bought and a Union passenger depot, 120 by 420 feet, built in 1852-3, on Meridian, Illinois and Louisiana streets. It was opened September 28, 1853, William N. Jackson being appointed general ticket agent, a post ever since held by him. It has since been used by eight separate lines, and was enlarged, improved and an eating house added in 1866. In December, 1867, the Junction Railroad Co., and the Crawfordsville and Vincennes lines unsuccessfully applied for admission to the depot, and it is possible that a Union passenger station will yet be erected in the western part of the city. Such a depot will ultimately be erected, for the present one can not accommodate all the business of the future.

A brief statement of the history of the several roads projected and built since the Madison road, may be given here. Prominent among these was the Bellefontaine road to Union City on the State line, which was energetically pushed by the first President, Oliver H. Smith, its construction being largely due to his efforts. It was chartered in 1848, meetings held. stock subscribed and right-of-way secured in 1848-9; contracts were let in the fall of 1849, track-laying began April, 1850, cars ran to Pendleton, twenty-eight miles, December. 1850, and the road was finished, eighty-four miles, to the State line. December 1852, at a cost of $21,550 per mile. The brick depot and shops were built in 1851, in the north-east part of the city and used till the Union depot and track were finished, when a frame freight depot and brick engine house and shops were built in November, 1853, at the corner of Virginia avenue and Pogue's run. These were used till 1864 when the large frame freight depot and brick shops and engine house were completed and occupied in the eastern part of the city. The engine house and shops on Virginia avenue were then torn away,

but the frame depot is still used for way freights. The first depot and shops, with 1,100 feet of track and five acres of ground were sold in July, 1853, for $17,500 to Mr. Farnsworth, and were used by Farnsworth & Barnard as a car factory from November 1853 till 1859. It then remained vacant till after the war began and was occupied as a Government stable from 1862 to 1865, when it was burned down. The Bellefontaine road was consolidated in 1855 with the connecting Ohio line to Galion. The stock was "watered" and the name changed to the Indianapolis, Pittsburg & Cleveland Railroad. In the spring of 1868 a further consolidation was effected with the Cleveland, Columbus & Cincinnati road, and the new road is known as the Cleveland, Columbus, Cincinnati & Indianapolis Railroad. O. H. Smith, Alfred Harrison, Calvin Fletcher, John Brough, S. Witt, and others, have been Presidents of this corporation since its charter. It has been one of the best freight and passenger roads leading to this point.

The Lawrenceburg and upper Mississippi road was originally begun in sections, or several short roads, in 1850, a through road being bitterly and successfully opposed by the Madison Co., but was finally chartered in 1851 and finished to Lawrenceburg, 90 miles, in October 1853, under Geo. H. Dunn, the first president. The name was changed December 1853 to the Indianapolis and Cincinnati road. The Ohio and Mississippi road having been finished from Cincinnati to Lawrenceburg in April 1854, a third rail was laid and the cars run to that city, 110 miles, under a lease. In 1854-5 the old White-water canal was bought, and a separate track laid in its bed, and a fine passenger and freight depot built. The shops of the company were built south-east of the city in 1853, but were burned in 1855, and soon afterward rebuilt. They were removed to Cincinnati in 1865 and are now located there. The brick freight depot was built on Louisiana and Delaware streets in 1853, and is now used by the consolidated roads. In 1866, after an effort to build a rival line via Crawfordsville to Lafayette, a consolidation was effected with the Lafayette road and the name adopted for the united corporation is Indianapolis, Cincinnati and Lafayette road. Branch roads have been built up the Whitewater valley on the canal bank, and from Fairland to Martinsville, and in March 1868 a consolidation was effected with the Vincennes road.— Much opposition was aroused by this last movement, but Mr. Lord, in a speech to our business men, in April 1868, greatly allayed the feeling, and promised that his

policy should not prove detrimental to the interests of this city. Geo. II. Dunn, Thos. A. Morris and Henry C. Lord have been presidents of this corporation.

The Jeffersonville road was begun in 1848 and finished to Edinburgh, 78 miles, in 1852, at a cost of $1,185.000. It had been designed to extend to this point, but in August 1853 a lease was obtained from the Madison road, by which the use of that road with its shops, depots and houses was perpetually secure l, and in 1853 the Jeffersonville company bought the entire road and equipment and now operate both lines. A branch road was built in 1852 from Edinburgh to Shelbyville and Rushville, 26 miles, at a cost of $525.000, but was afterward abandoned. The war traffic and travel was immense over the Jeffersonville road, it being the only direct southern line leading to the seat of war. John Zulauf, Dillard Ricketts and others, have been its presidents.

The Terre Haute and Richmond road was projected in 1846, surveyed December 1847, contracts let in 1848-9, commenced in 1850, and finished to Terre Haute, 73 miles, in May 1852, at a cost of $1,415,000, under Chauncy Rose, its first president. The eastern section was abandoned and its construction undertaken by the Indiana Central Railway Co. in 1851. The brick freight depot (remodeled in 1857,) was built on Louisiana and Tennessee streets in 1850-1. Its roof was partly blown off in 1865 by the explosion of the pony engine of the Central company, inside the building. The engine house and the frame bridge over White river were built in 1851-2, and the bridge was replaced by a handsome iron structure in 1866, without interrupting traffic on the line. The road has been prosperous, well managed, has met with few accidents, and is the main line for western trade and travel. It is also the only coal road yet built. The company have no shops here, the repairs being made at Terre Haute. Chauncy Rose, S. Crawford, E. J. Peck and others, have been its Presidents.

The Peru and Indianapolis road was chartered at the session of 1845-6, the company organized July 1847, road surveyed October 1847, located July 1848, commenced 1849, cars were run to Noblesville, 21 miles, March 1851, and the road completed to Peru, 73 miles, April 3, 1854, at a cost of about $760,000. It was consolidated June 1, 1854, with, and operated for several months by the Madison road. The road traversed a new country, encountered many obstacles, and has not been as successful as other lines. It has been the main source of supply for lumber and tim-

ber, and since its northern connections were finished has had a fair share of the north-western trade and travel. It passed into a receiver's hands in 1857, and has since been operated for the bondholders.— Its shops are at Peru, and its buildings here have never been of much value. It was originally laid with flat bar, taken up from the Madison road, but T rail was substituted in 1855-6. The first frame depot was commenced in August, 1856, on New Jersey street and Pogue's run, but was blown down during a storm. September 17, burying about a dozen men in the ruins, and badly injuring several of them. Another was built in November following.— W. J. Holman, Jno. Burk, E. W. H. Ellis, J. D. Defrees and David Macy, have been presidents.

The Lafayette and Indianapolis road was begun in 1849 and finished to Lafayette, 65 miles, in December 1852, at a cost of about $1,000,000, under Albert S. White, the first president. The stock subscription was small, the road being mostly built by loans which were subsequently paid off from the earnings of the road, making its stock very valuable. Until the completion of the northern connections of the Peru road it was the main route to the north-west, and did a very lucrative business during the war. In 1866 Henry C. Lord having failed to buy the road or effect a consolidation with it, began the construction of a rival route to Danville and the north-west via Crawfordsville, and after doing considerable work achieved his object, and obtained a perpetual lease of the line, and it is now controlled and operated by the Cincinnati company. The Lafayette freight depot was built in 1852-3, on North street and the canal, but was burned in 1861, and rebuilt in 1865. Since the consolidation it has been but little used, the business of both roads being done at the Delaware street depot. The company never had any shops at this point, the construction and repairs being done at Lafayette. A. S. White and Wm. F. Reynolds, were the presidents of the company.

The Indiana Central Railway Company was organized in the spring, surveys made in the summer, and contracts let in the fall of 1851. Track-laying began November, 1852, and the road, was completed to the State line, seventy-two miles, December 8, 1853, at a cost of $1,223,000, under John S. Newman, the first President. It divides eastern trade and travel with the Bellefontaine road, and was consolidated with the Ohio connecting road in 1863, and afterwards known as the Indianapolis & Columbus road. A further consolidation was effected in 1867, with-

the Chicago and Great Eastern road, and the offices and shops are to be removed elsewhere. The brick freight depot was built on Delaware street and Pogue's run in 1852, and its shops just east of the city, in the same year.

At and since the date of completion of the foregoing roads, several others were projected, or in course of construction; among them was the Junction road, ninety-eight miles long, from Hamilton, Ohio, via Rushville and Connersville, to this city. It was begun in separate sections, in 1850, by the Ohio and Indianapolis, and the Junction Companies, which were consolidated. April, 1853, with $1,800,000 stock subscriptions. Several hundred thousand dollars were expended on the line, the depot grounds here were purchased, and the road half finished, when the hard times of 1855-6 caused its suspension and the sale of its lands at a nominal price. The company was re-organized in 1866, work was resumed, a subsidy of $45,000 voted to it by our city, depot grounds bought, and the road finished to this point in May, 1868. The freight depot will be built on Virginia avenue, south of Pogue's run, and the shops and offices are to be located here by contract with the city. Caleb B. Smith, Jno. Ridenour and others have been Presidents of the Company.

The Vincennes road was first projected in 1851, and a company organized in 1853, with John H. Bradley, President; but only a preliminary survey was made, and the enterprise was abandoned during the subsequent monetary revulsion. A new company was organized under General Burnside, in 1865, the contracts let, and a subsidy of $60,000 granted by the city in 1866, and right of way secured; work is now being rapidly prosecuted along the line, and the road will be finished from Gosport to this city during the present year. The shops and offices, by agreement with the city, are to be located here. The road traverses the best iron, coal, stone, timber and grain region of the State, and will be second to none in importance, and it is all important that its management should not be adverse to our interests. On the 31 of April, 1858, it was consolidated with the Cincinnati road.

A direct road to Evansville, one hundred and fifty miles long, had been projected in 1849, but nothing was done till April, 1853, when Oliver H. Smith and Willard Carpenter organized a company under the general law, and held meetings, subscribed stock, surveyed the line, let contracts, and pushed the work rapidly forward till 1856, when the monetary pressure stopped the enterprise, and caused the loss of nearly

everything invested in it. It is still dormant, but its importance, and the rich agricultural and mineral region it traversed, the amount expended on it, and the heavy south-western trade, certainly demand a renewal of the enterprise, and its favorable consideration by our people, especially since the management of the Vincennes road will probably be adverse to our interests.

The Cincinnati & Indianapolis Short-line Railroad Company, from this point via Rushville, Laurel and Brookville to Cincinnati, was organized in January, 1853; subscriptions were obtained, surveys made, contracts let, and other steps taken, but the enterprise was suspended by hard times in 1854-5, before any tangible results were obtained, and has not since been revived.

The Toledo & Indianapolis Railroad Company, via Muncie to Toledo, one hundred and eighty-five miles, was organized February, 1854, under the general law. Seventy-five miles of road, only, were to be built to make connections with existing roads, and secure a short and direct route for grain to the lake. Surveys were made, and efforts to obtain subscriptions, but the financial pressure of 1855 put an end temporarily to the scheme.

The Indiana & Illinois Central Railroad, one hundred and sixty miles long on an air line, to Decatur, Illinois, was proposed in December, 1852, and organized February 15, 1853. Surveys were made, subscriptions obtained, and contracts let in July, 1853, for the whole line, at $22,000 per mile, to be done in 1855, and $500,000 of work was done. The hard times intervened, the work stopped, and the company lands were sold to pay the contractors. The line is almost straight, traverses a beautiful and rich country, opens up coal and iron regions, and gives a direct western line to the Pacific road. Its importance merits renewed effort, and the company—which was re-organized in 1866—should attempt its construction.

In 1866, before the Cincinnati road had succeeded in forcing the sale of the Lafayette line, H. C. Lord, as the final effort, determined to build a rival line via Crawfordsville. The city voted a subsidy of $45,000, right of way secured, surveys made, contracts let, and considerable work done at this end of the line, when the Lafayette road consented to sell, and the new line was at once abandoned. This summary disposal of the matter displeased the residents along the line; the company was soon re-organized, contracts relet, and the work is now in progress. It is to be hoped that a new outlet to the north-

west will be speedily found through the rich region traversed by this line.

In 1857 an effort was made by the eastern roads to force a sale or consolidation of the Terre Haute road, which having failed, it was announced that a straight-line road to St. Louis would be built from this point. Surveys were made, right of way secured, subscriptions voted, and the contracts, it is said, will be let this year. The road should be built, as it will give an additional and competing route to the coal and iron beds of the western part of the State, and the city can well afford to aid the enterprise, first providing that no consolidation shall be made with competing roads. The Terre Haute company is also engaged in building a straight line from that city to St. Louis, as a continuation of their own route.

It will be seen from the foregoing brief statement of facts connected with the several roads, that only one of the completed lines, (the Bellefontaine,) ever located its principal shops at this point, and even that road, since its consolidation, has its main shops in Ohio. The excuse advanced for this general action has been that work could be done cheaper elsewhere; but this, even if true in one or two cases, can scarcely be true of every little town in this or other States, and the solution of the problem is to be found partly in the jealousy of other cities toward this, and mostly in the want of enterprise on the part of our own people. They have not deemed it necessary, either for their own interests or those of the city, to hold a controlling interest in the highways leading here, and the consequence has been that as little as possible has been done by the railways toward building up our manufacturing interests. In many respects this city is better situated for manufacturing than any other in this or the adjoining States, and its advantages increase with the opening of every additional line; and, if it fails to achieve a high rank in this respect, the fault will lie solely with our own capitalists, and the blame should lie where it belongs. It has been too much the fashion here to wait for others to increase the value of property which is held by the few, and the money on hand, instead of creating wealth by producing manufactured articles from comparatively valueless raw material, is doled out sparingly at one and two per cent. per month, taxing the life out of those who do attempt to create such articles. It seems singular that, while the railway companies combined and successfully operated a union track and depot, that they never entered into a union company for the manufacture of

locomotives, cars, and all other articles needed in the equipment of their roads. One great establishment, under competent management, could combine the iron and brass foundries, rolling mills, machine shops, saw and planing mills, forges, upholstery, paint and other shops, needed in the fabrication of every item used by them. Such an establishment, with the capital it could employ, the thorough subdivision and supervision of labor, the extent and variety of articles manufactured, the steady demand therefor by the stockholding roads and outside lines, located here where the influx and efflux of materials and articles would be so ready and certain, and skilled laborers, so readily brought, could defy private competition, furnish all articles to its stockholders at cost, and pay all expenses and a profit from outside work.

But few mills or manufactories existed here till after the completion of the Madison road, for the local demand was very limited, and shipments to other points almost impossible. Underhill's foundry, on Pennsylvania street, started by Grover in 1835, was the only one here. The grist mills of West and of Carlisle, West's cotton and woolen mill, Hannaman's woolen and oil mill, and Sheet's paper mill, were on the canal, and had been built since 1838. Patterson's grist mill was on Fall creek, and the old steam (grist, woolen and saw) mills, on the river, had been repaired by Geisendorff's in 1817, and used as a woolen mill till 1852, when they built a mill (subsequently enlarged,) on the west branch of the canal. Of mills and manufactories, built since 1847, the more prominent may be briefly mentioned here. The principal grist mills were Carlisle's, (his old mill was burnt January 18, '56,) now Sohl & Gibson, on the canal, built 1863; Underhill's, south of the city, 1851; Skillen's, 1863; Capital mills, 1856; Morris' mills, south Pennsylvania street, 1848, burnt 1851; Bates' mills, Pogue's run, 1859. Of saw mills, Kortpeter's, south Pennsylvania street, 1849; Fletcher & Wells, Massachusetts avenue, 1857; Gay & Stevens, Madison depot, 1857; Hill's, East street, 1858, burned and rebuilt October, 1859; Off & Wishmire's, Railroad street, 1858; Helwig & Blake's, canal, 1858; Marsee's, New Jersey street, 1859; McKernan & Pierce, Kentucky avenue, 1855. Of planing mills, Shellaberger's, east Market, 1852; Blake & Gentle's, (the first one here,) Vermont street, 1849; Kreglo & Blake, canal, 1855, burned and rebuilt in Aug., 1840; Byrket's, Tennessee street, 1857; McCord & Wheatley's, Alabama street, 1855; Tate's, New Jersey street, 1864; Hill & Wingate's, East street, 1858,

burned in October and rebuilt November, 1859; Builders & Manufacturers' Association, Delaware street, 1866; Carpenters' Association, South and Meridian streets, 1866; Emerson's, near the canal, 1863; Beam's, west Washington street, 1865; Behymer's, east Market street, 1854.

Shingle mills, Evarts', south Pennsylvania, 1857; Smock's, east Washington, 1858.

Of furniture and chair factories, John Ott, west Washington, 1855; Sloan & Ingersoll, 1850; Espy & Sloan, 1848; John Vetter, Madison depot, 1857, burned 1866; Philip Dohn, south Meridian, 1865, burned and rebuilt, 1857; Spiegel and Thoms, east Washington, 1855, and East street, 1863, enlarged to double size, 1866, and the first five-story house built in the city; Helwig & Roberts, canal, 1857, burned and rebuilt 1860; M. S. Huey, west Washington, 1855; Field & Day, Vermont street, 1850; Wilkens & Hall, west Washington, 1854; C. J. Meyer, east Washington, 1860; Cabinet-makers' Union, east Market, 1859.

Of coopering establishments, there have been Detrees, on the canal, Murphey's and May's on East street; Careys and Brennon's, near Soldiers' Home; McNeeleys, near Lafayette depot; Kingans and others.

Of peg and last factories, Crawford & Osgood, south Pennsylvania street, 1818, and burned 1851; Osgood & Smith, south Illinois, 1852, burned and rebuilt once or twice afterward; Yandes & Kemper, south Illinois, 1857.

Of wagon or carriage manufactories, Hiram Gaston, Kentucky avenue, 1853; Lowes, east Market, 1853; Drews, east Market, 1852; Shaws, Georgia street, 1866.

Of spokes and felloes, Osgood Smith & Co., south Illinois, 1852.

Of woolen mills, Geisendorffs, on the canal, 1852; Merritt & Coughlen, in Hannaman's old mill, on the river, 1849 or '50, were burned out in January, 1851, and rebuilt in May, 1851; West's, 1830; Younts, 1849, on the canal.

Of paper mills, Sheets, on canal, 1839; Gay & Bradens, canal, 1862; McLean & Co., river, 1861.

Of cotton mills, West, canal, 1839, and the Cotton Mill Co., on the river, 1867.

Of agricultural and farm implements and machinery, W. M. Gause, 1855; Beard & Sinex, and Beard & Forsha, Tennessee street, 1857; Hasselman & Vinton, south Meridian, 1852; Chandler & Taylor, west Washington, 1859, burned and rebuilt 1863(?); Binkley & Co., south Tennessee, 1860; Beard & Starr, north Tennessee, 1860; Agricultural Works Co., south Tennessee, 1864.

Of oil mills, J. P. Evans & Co., south Delaware, 1862.

Iron manufactures have taken the lead-ing rank at this point, and promise still more rapid growth in future. The interest has risen in the last fifteen years from a very small beginning. The first steam engine ever built here, a small affair of three or four horse power, was completed in June, 1848, by Mr. Sergeant, at Bardwell's shop, in the basement of Crawford & Osgood's factory, on south Pennsylvania street. The first foundry in the place was started in July, 1832, by R. A. McPherson & Co., near the bridge, west of the river. Joshua Glover had been doing some iron work on a small scale in 1831. Underhill & Co. started a foundry in July, 1835, on north Pennsylvania street, and in 1838, Underhill applied steam power in it, being the first to use it in a foundry here. He manufactured plow points, skillets, and other small castings, remaining there till 1852, when he built a large foundry on south Pennsylvania street, and failing in business the building was applied to other purposes, and burned up in November, 1858. Taylor, Watson & Co., in 1848 built a small foundry in the low ground south of Pogue's run, and first began to make steam engines here in 1849. This establishment subsequently passed into Hasselman & Vinton's hands, who built the present foundry, boiler and machine shops in 1852. The firm suffered heavy losses in May, and also in July, 1858, from fires. In 1865 the establishment passed into the control of the Eagle Machine Works Co., who now carry on a heavy business in the manufacture of castings, boilers and agricultural implements, their trade extending over a large territory, and employing a heavy capital. In March, 1851, Wright, Barnes & Co., afterward Ira Davis & Co., built a foundry on Delaware street and Pogue's run, which burned down in 1857. Curtis & Dumont began the manufacture of boilers on south Pennsylvania street in 1852, next north of Underhill's foundry, and Kelshaw & Sinker began the same business at about the same time, just south of the same foundry. Their shop was burned in December, 1852, and rebuilt in 1854. Dumont & Sinker became partners, continuing the business, and adding a foundry. In 1863, Dumont left, and the establishment, now greatly enlarged, is carried on as a foundry, machine shop and boiler factory, on the site of Underhill's old City Foundry, by Sinker, Allen & Yandes. In 1851, Deloss Root & Co., built a small frame stove foundry, south of the Gas Works on Pennsylvania street. It was burned up in January, 1860, but soon rebuilt of brick on a much more extended scale, and stoves, heavy castings and boilers, are now largely manufactured by the

establishment. Wiggins & Chandler, in June, 1859, built a small foundry and machine shop on the Canal and west Washington street. It was burned in 1863, (?) but soon after rebuilt on a more extended scale by Chandler & Taylor, and has since done a large business. In 1858, Redstone, Bros. & Co., started a foundry and machine shop on Delaware street south of the Union track, making small castings and sawing machines. Spotts & Thompson started a foundry near the same place in 1859, but both establisments were shortly afterward burned. The Hoosier Stove Foundry was built in 1861, by Cox, Lord & Peck, on Delaware street and Pogue's run, and was operated by them for two or three years and then discontinued. It passed into the hands of A. D. Wood in 1867, and is now carried on by him. Ruschaupt & Co. built a large foundry and machine shop on South Meridian street in 1855, but as they soon afterward became interested in the Eagle Machine Works, the establishment was vacated, and is now used by the Carpenter's Association. Frink & Moore started the Novelty Works in 1860, for the manufacture of small castings, and have done a good business. A foundry was started in 1863, on East Market street, by some one, (unknown to the writer,) and has since mainly been doing railroad work. B. F. Hetherington & Co. started a foundry and machine shop on south Delaware street in 1866 or '67 and are still located there.

Jos. W. Davis & Co, started a brass foundry in 1855, on south Delaware street, and has since added steam and gas-fitting, building up a good business. Garrett & Co., in 1858, started a brass and bell foundry, on the railroad between Meridian and Pennsylvania streets, but failed a year or two afterward.

In 1856, Williamson & Haugh began the manufacture of iron railings, and jail work, on Delaware street opposite the Court House, and at a subsequent date B. F. Haugh & Co. removed to south Pennsylvania street, erecting new buildings and continuing the business on an enlarged scale.

In 1857, E. C. Atkins began the manufacture of mill and other saws, in the old City Foundry building on south Pennsylvania street, but being burned out in 1858, he built a small shop near by, which was also burned in June, 1859. A new shop was then built on south Illinois street, a company formed in 1863 or '64, and the business and buildings have since been greatly enlarged, and a heavy trade carried on. In 1867 Farley & Sinker built a shop and began the manufacture of saws on south

Pennsylvania street, and are doing a good business.

Cottrell & Knight, in 1855 or '56, began the copper-smithing business on south Delaware street, and have since built up a large trade.

In addition to the foregoing, other establishments exist or have existed, and the different railroads have nearly all had repair shops of greater or less extent at this point.

The Indianapolis Rolling Mill was built by R. A. Douglass & Co., and a railroad track down Tennessee street constructed to it, in the summer of 1857, and work began October 29. The owners became involved in the spring of 1858, and for some time it was doubtful whether the works would be continued, but the mill was purchased shortly after by a new company, with John M. Lord as president, and has since been much enlarged and profitably operated. The company have purchased coal and iron mines in Clay county, have erected a furnace to supply their mill with iron, and have also supplied coal for the use of the citizens. The success of the company stimulated other parties, and during the summer of 1867, the White River Iron Company was formed, and a rolling mill was erected on White river, at the foot of Kentucky avenue, and put in operation in April of the present year, for the manufacture of bar iron, about $100,000 of capital being invested in the enterprise.

Several pork and beef packing establishments have been built since 1847.— Blythe & Hedderly began the first one, on Fall creek race in the fall of 1847. It was afterward carried on by Blythe & McNeely. Mansur & Ferguson built one west of White river in 1850. It was burned and rebuilt in 1858. Their packing establishment was located at the Madison depot.— Macy & McTaggart built one near Terre Haute railroad bridge in 1852. Gulick & Tweeds was built just north of it in 1854-5. Allen May's was built north-west of the city in 1855, and burned in 1858. Kingen & Co., built in 1864, on the river bank, the largest and best packing establishment in the country. It was of brick, five stories high, slate roofed, and finished in the best style. They were putting mill machinery in it in the spring of 1865, intending to use it as a mill in summer and packing house in winter. It was filled at the time with lard and pork, on storage, when it was fired by an incendiary and utterly destroyed, involving a loss of $250,000 to the insurance companies, and being by far the largest and most destructive fire that ever occurred here. It was rebuilt in 1866, but not so large or expensively as before. Want

of space prevents further mention of the different manufactories of the city. They are almost wholly the growth of the past fifteen years, and with proper encouragement and enterprize could be easily doubled in the next ten years.

The first wholesale dry goods house in the place was started in 1847 by J. Little & Co., at 28 west Washington street. It was burned May 14, 1848, when owned by Little, Drum & Andersons.

1848. It was announced about the middle of December, 1847, that Andrew Kennedy, an ex-member of Congress from Indiana, was ill of small-pox at the Palmer House, and he died in January, 1848. Many members of the legislature having visited him before the disease was known, a panic ensued and the assembly adjourned. This act excited much ridicule at the time, b t as a number of other cases occurred in January and February, the mirth soon ceased, and panic seized the citizens. The council ordered a general vaccination, established a board of health, and authorized the construction of a hospital. A lot was accordingly bought, material collected and a contract made with Seth Bardwell for a frame house, but before its erection the disease and panic subsided, and a citizens' meeting protested against further taxes for hospital purposes. The council in April gave the contractor $225 with the material, to give up the contract; the lots were sold, and Bardwell built the Indiana House, on west Market street out of the material. A citizens' meeting in the summer of 1847, had recommended the building of a hospital, and parties had then offered to advance the necessary funds. In July, 1849, another case of small-pox ocurred, and as the cholera was prevailing severely on the river, another first class panic ensued. A citizens' meeting recommended the cutting of the dog fennel in the streets, and appointed a committee to quarantine the cars, several miles south of town, and remove the cholera and small-pox patients who might be on board. The plan was very brilliant, but failed for the want of a sufficiently self-sacrificing committee. The board of health also recommended dog fennel mowing, general sanitary precautions, and the erection of a hospital. The mowing was accordingly done, but the dog fennel was found to be worse when cut than when standing. This recommendation having failed, no hospital was erected, and but few sanitary measures taken. Many German emigrants were arriving at that time, and the first fatal case of cholera happened among them, July 18, 1849, and several of them subsequently died. The President appointed the first Friday of August,

1849, as a fast day, on account of the cholera. It was generally observed as such throughout the country.

On the 14th of February, 1848, the assembly passed an act chartering telegraph companies, and on the 26th, Henry O'Reilly advertised for subscriptions to build a line from here to Dayton. It was constructed immediately afterward, and the first dispatches sent to Richmond, May 12th. The first published dispatches appeared in the *Sentinel* May twenty-fourth. The office in the second story of Norris', now Hubbard's block, was crowded by excited natives, who doubted the genuineness of the invention; and the first operator, Isaac H. Kiersted, was greatly worried in explaining it. In 1850, Wade & Co built a second line, which was consolidated with the first in April, 1853, and since that date other lines have been built by companies and railways, till twenty-nine wires now centre at the office in the third story of Blackford's block, all under one corporation, with Jno. F. Wallack as superintendent. Isaac H. Kiersted, J. W. Chapin, Anton Schneider, Sidney B. Morris, J. F. Wilson and J. F. Wallack, have been chief operators and superintendents at this point.

A merchants' exchange was formed in June, for the reception of dispatches and the transaction of business. C. W. Cady being secretary, K. Homburgh, treasurer. It failed in a few weeks for lack of money. A citizens' meeting was called at College Hall in August, 1853, to revive it, and after discussion it was resolved to form a board of trade. N. McCarty, J. D. Defrees, Ignatius Brown, R. J. Gatling, A. H. Brown and J. T. Cox, were appointed to prepare a constitution, circular and map, and solicit funds. D. Maguire was elected president, J. L. Ketcham, secretary K. B. Duncan, treasurer. Funds were subscribed and a circular and map, prepared by Mr. Brown, were published and sent over the country, calling attention to the advantages held by the city for manufacturing and wholesaling. Active efforts continued for about two years, and did much good, but the interest died out, and the effort was suspended. The board was again revived in 1856, and for two years actively disseminated information concerning the city.— The establishment of the rolling mill here was owing to its efforts. It again suspended for want of funds. In 1864, the chamber of commerce was formed. T. B. Elliott, (succeeded in 1865 by W. S. Pierce,) president, Jehiel Barnard, secretary, and has since continued operations at its office in Vinton's block, though not supported as it should be. The merchants and manufacturers' association was formed in the

spring of 1858,' with objects substantially similar to the old board of trade, and opened an office at 10 south Meridian street.

A new engine was demanded by the Relief Company, and subscriptions being scanty, the Council ordered an election in June, for a special tax to buy one. The decision was against it, as also at another election in July, ordered for the same object. The first foreign paper published here, the Indiana *Volksblatt*, a democratic weekly journal, edited and published by Julius Boetticher, appeared from an office at Temperance Hall, in September, and has since been regularly issued under the control of Mr. Boetticher. It is now published at 166 east Washington street.

The companies commanded by Captains Lander and McDougall having returned from Mexico, a procession and barbecue in their honor took place, October 4th, in the woods where the Soldiers' Home was afterwards located. Senator Hannegan, Thomas J. Henley and others, were the speakers.

The Central Plank Road Company was formed in November, contracts let May, 1849, and the road finished from Plainfield to Greenfield, in April, 1851, on the old National road, which, with its bridges, was taken by the company. Gates were located at the east and west ends of Washington street, and tolls charged on the bridge. Citizens' meetings were held, denouncing this action on the part of the Company, and the Council finally procured the removal of the eastern gate, by releasing the Company from all liability for improving Washington street.

The railroads being desirous to connect their several depots by rail, the Council, on the 20th of December, prescribed by ordinance the conditions on which they might lay the present Union track, and in the following August the Companies formed the Union Railroad Company, and laid the track in 1850.

1849. The street improvement ordered in 1847-8, had caused a debt of about $6,000, and William Eckert, President of the Council, ordered an election June 9th, to authorize a special tax of ten cents to pay it. Two hundred and fifty-eight votes were cast, and the tax carried by eleven majority. The people grumbled greatly that the tax was now forty-five cents on the one hundred dollars. H. C. Newcomb was elected Mayor at the April election, succeeding Samuel Henderson, the first incumbent of that office. The population this year was found to be 6,500.

Much improvement was taking place, three hundred houses were supposed to have been built, shops and factories were

started, and steam engines were at last made here.

The Central Medical College, a department of the Indiana Asbury University, was organized during the summer, with J. S. Bobbs, Richard Curran, J. S. Harrison, George W. Mears, C. G. Downey, L. Dunlap, A. H. Baker and D. Funkhouser as Professors, and began its first session, November 1st, (lasting four months,) in Matthew Little's two-story brick dwelling, south-east corner East and Washington streets, which had been fitted up as the College Buildings. Twenty or thirty students were in attendance the first session, and several were graduated in March, 1850, President Simpson delivering the diplomas. Annual sessions were held for two or three years, when the institution was discontinued. The Assembly, January 21, 1850, authorized the sale of one acre of University Square, at its appraised price, to Asbury University, for the buildings of the Central Medical College, but the selected acre being appraised in April at $8,500, the price was thought to be too high, and opposition arising to the sale, it was abandoned.

The Court of Common Pleas of Marion county was organized, and began its first session, on the second Monday of July, 1849, under a special act of the preceding session, Abram A. Hammond being first judge and ex-officio clerk. He was afterwards succeeded by Edward Lander, who served till the Court was abolished, in 1851-2. About fifty cases were on the docket at the first term. The present Court of Common Pleas was established by the revised laws of 1852, Levi L. Todd being elected by the people first Judge, in August, 1852. His successors since have been Sam'l Corey, David Wallace, Jno. Coburn, Charles A. Ray and Solomon Blair.

The Widows and Orphans Society was organized early in December, 1849. The receipts for the first year were $113.16, expenses $98.30. It has been mainly sustained by private contributions, and by fairs and exhibitions held for its benefit, and has steadily grown in usefulness and importance. Two lots in Drake's addition were donated to the Society by Allen May, and a third bought in 1852. A neat brick building was erected on the property in 1855, at a cost of about $3,000, and the affairs of the society have been successfully administered to the present date. The thanks of the community are due to the noble women who struggled against every disadvantage in the inception of this great charity, and direct and sufficient aid should be annually given them by the city government. For the last

two or three years small appropriations have been annually voted to the Society by the City Council.

1850. An earthquake, which was felt all through the west and south, occurred at 8 o'clock A. M. on the 4th of April, shaking the buildings.

The City Treasury receipts for the year ending April 25th, were $9,327, expenditures $7,554. The total taxables for 1850 amounted to $2,326,185. The school fund was slowly accumulating, amounting to $3,205, the receipts for the year being $2,385. Polls, 1,243, an increase of 400 over last year. The population, as shown by the census in October, was 8,097, an increase of 1,530 over 1849. The wealth had increased about $800,000. There were twenty-five physicians, thirty lawyers, and one hundred and twenty industrial establishments.

Governor Crittenden and suite arrived May 28th, on invitation of Gov. Wright, and a Union meeting was held in the State House yard on the 29th, when resolutions were passed, and speeches made by the Governors and others.

A union funeral service was held July 27th, by all denominations and parties, for President Taylor, Rev. E. R. Ames delivering an able eulogy on the deceased President.

Many German emigrants were arriving this year, and brought the cholera with them, nine or ten of them dying during the summer. There was no panic, however, and the disease did not spread.

The Christian Church was built during this and the next year, on the south-west corner of Delaware and Ohio streets.

The Indiana Statesman, a weekly, democratic paper, was first issued September 4th, by Ellis & Spann, from the old Sentinel office, on Illinois street. It was merged with the Sentinel in September, 1852.

The Indiana Female College was organized, and the house and lot on the south-east corner of Ohio and Meridian streets purchased during the summer, and the school opened there in the fall by Rev. T. A. Lynch. His successors in the Presidency of the institution have been Rev. Charles Adams, G. W. Hoss, B. H. Hoyt, O. M. Spencer and W. H. Demotte. The college was suspended in 1859, but in 1865 the old lot and buildings were sold, and the lot and buildings of the former McLean Female Seminary bought and used from that date by the institution. The school was well conducted and prosperous, but was closed with the June term, 1868, and in that month the house and lot was purchased by the trustees of Wesley

Chapel, for about $16,000, and a church will shortly be erected there by that congregation, at a cost of seventy-five or eighty thousand dollars.

1851. The Toledo Theatrical Company, under Mr. Shires as manager, with H. A. Perry, Robert Buxton, Mrs. Coleman Pope and other good actors, gave a series of dramatic performances, January 7–26, in Masonic Hall, and though sadly embarrassed by lack of scenery and stage room, did themselves credit, and drew large and enthusiastic audiences.

The Indianapolis Gas Light and Coke Co., (originated by John J. Lockwood,) was incorporated by the assembly in February 1851, for thirty years, with $20,000 capital. Stock books were opened March 6th, and on the 20th the Company organized with D. V. Culley, President; W. W. Wright, Secretary and H. V. Barringer, Superintendent. The City Council, by ordinance, March 3d, gave the Company the exclusive right, for fifteen years, of supplying the city and its inhabitants with gas, prescribing the conditions on which pipes might be laid in the streets, and stipulating that gas should be furnished for the street lamps at the price then prevailing in Cincinnati. In July the Company bought a lot on Pennsylvania street, south of Pogue's run, and built a retort house and gas-holder during the fall. Mains were also laid on Pennsylvania and Washington streets. The works were finished in December, and gas was first furnished for consumption on the 10th of January, 1852. In the following April 7,700 feet of pipe had been laid. Thirty bushels of coal were daily consumed, 675 burners employed and 116 consumers using gas. Before the construction of the gas works, the only building in the city lighted by gas was the Masonic Hall, which was furnished with a gas-making apparatus, and the first street lamps in the city were the two in front of the hall, supplied from its apparatus. For two or three years the Company was unsuccessful, the machinery and works being defective in construction and the Superintendent inexperienced in the business. An additional sum was then expended in modifying the works. Christopher Brown was appointed Superintendent, an increased pressure was put on the mains, more gas was consumed, and the Company began to prosper. The mains were extended on additional streets, and further improvements were made in the works. But little gas was used by the city until within the last ten years. The first lamps were put up on Washington street, between Meridian and Pennsylvania streets, in the fall

of 1853, and were supplied with gas at the expense of the property-holders on that square, the tax for gas lighting having been defeated at the elections in 1851-2. The first contract for supplying street lamps was made by the Council and Company in December, 1854, and portions of Washington and some of the adjacent streets were lit in 1855. In 1858-9, a large increase was made in the length of streets lighted and number of lamps, and the increase has been steady since that date. In May, 1860, there were eight and one-half miles of street lit, two hundred and sixty-five lamps were used and eighty-five more were being erected. At present twenty-one miles of streets are lit and nearly nine hundred lamps have been erected, only seven hundred and fifty of which are used, the Council having recently decided to light only those at the street corners. The lamp posts and lamps are put up at the expense of the property-holders and kept in repair by the city. Twenty-three miles of mains and nearly seventy-five miles of service pipe are now in use. There are one thousand five hundred and fifty consumers. Extensive changes, additions and repairs have been made to the works, and they have also been largely extended. In 1863, the Company built, on Delaware street, a new receiving reservoir, or gas-holder, of about 300,000 cubic feet capacity, at a cost of about $120,000. The retort house, which originally held six retorts, now has fifty-five. The average daily production of gas at present is about 175,000 feet.

No rule was at first adopted as to the number and position of street lamps on each square, and some trouble and irregularity resulted from it, but on the 12th of February, 1859, the Council fixed the number at four to each square, placed at equal diagonal distances, and so arranged that the opposite street corners should be lit.

As the charter granted, March 3, 1851, for fifteen years, by the city, would expire March 4, 1866, the Council, in May, 1865, ordered the clerk to advertise for proposals to light the city for twenty years with gas. It was done, and on the 4th of September the Gas Company submitted the only proposition that was received. They had been charging private consumers $4.50 per 1,000 feet, and this for $20.00 per lamp, with $8.44 per annum for lighting and cleaning. They now offered to supply the city and citizens, for the ensuing twenty years, at $3.48 per thousand feet, light and clean the lamps at $5.40 each per annum, all payments to be in currency at par, free of Government tax,

which was to be paid by consumers. They also claimed the exclusive right, under Legislative charter, to supply the citizens for five years longer with gas. The committee on gas made long reports in July and October on the subject, setting forth that eighteen miles of mains had been laid, five hundred and thirty three lamp posts erected and one hundred more being erected: that the gas used by private parties in 1864 amounted to about 17,000,000 feet, and by the city to 4,500,000: that one thousand two hundred meters were in use, and 90,000 bushels of coal consumed. They considered the question of cost and price here and elsewhere, and submitted a proposition that the Company be given the contract for fifteen years at $3.00 per one thousand feet, and the lamps at $28.80 per year, consumers to pay tax, and the city to light and clean the lamps—a gas inspector was recommended. They also denied the Company's asserted right to continue for five years longer than the period fixed by the original contract with the city. It was afterward proposed to capitalize the property of the Company at $850,000, the city to divide profits above 15 per cent., and on the 22d of January, 1866, a gas ordinance was passed granting the company the right for twenty years on a capital of $856,000. The Company, on the 31st of January, declined to accept it, and said they would continue to furnish gas to all consumers at $3.75 per thousand by actual measurement, consumers to pay tax. Matters remained in this state till the 5th of March, when R. B. Catherwood & Co., offered to take the charter for thirty years, with the exclusive privilege, and furnish gas at $3.00 per thousand feet, the city to contest the claim of the old Company. In response to this offer the Gas Committee, on the 12th of March, reported an ordinance giving Catherwood & Co., or "the Citizens' Gas Light and Coke Co.," the exclusive right for twenty years, reserving the right of the city to buy the works after ten years, and all profits over 15 per cent. on the capital were to be divided equally between the Company and city. The new Company was to test the claim of the old Company by suit. The capital was to be appraised every five years, and the Company was to fix the rate on the first of March annually for gas, at not over $3.00 per thousand feet.

They were to extend mains whenever fifteen burners were promised to the square, and lay them and repair streets at their own cost. The company were to insure the works against fire, and forfeit their charter if the conditions were not fulfilled. While this ordinance was pending, the old

company got alarmed, and came forward with another proposition, offering to furnish gas for twenty years at $3 per 1,000 feet, to make no charge for meters, to charge only actual cost of pipe connections, to extend mains whenever fifteen burners to the square were promised, &c. This offer was accepted, and on the 19th of March the council passed an ordinance rechartering the old company for twenty years from March 4, 1866. Good gas was to be furnished at $3 per 1,000 feet, with no charge for meters, the company to lay mains when fifteen burners to the square were promised, and make all pipe connections at actual cost. The price of gas was to be reduced if improvements in its manufacture were adopted; all streets to be repaired when torn up to lay pipes, and damages paid by the company in case of injury to any party. The city was to light and clean the lamps, and have the quantity and quality of the gas tested. The company accepted this charter on the 21st of March, and has since been acting under it.

It was found, shortly after the new contract was made, that the city gas bills were rapidly increasing under the meter-measurment system; and on investigation, in the spring and summer of 1867, it was discovered that the city had been paying for sixteen or twenty lamps beyond the actual number, and for all of them whether lighted or not, and that by defective burners and too heavy pressure, more gas was consumed than was necessary — nearly 6,000,000 feet having been burned in eleven months in 1866-7. The committee recommended the election of a gas inspector, and George H. Fleming was chosen to that office in the spring of 1868, and furnished with a set of instruments at a cost of $800. Rules were adopted for testing quantity, quality and pressure of the gas, and the number of hours the lamps were to be lighted. It was also resolved to light the lamps only on the street corners, and to shut off the gas at midnight. By this action the cost to the city has been reduced from nearly $40,000 to little over $20,000 annually.

The original capital of the gas company was $20,000; but the works and mains, as first built, cost $27,000. They were rebuilt in 1856, at an additional expense of $30,-000—making the total outlay, before the works proved profitable, about $57,000. From that time the enterprise has been successful. Few or no dividends have been declared, the profits all being devoted to the additions, repairs and extensions of the property; the works being again entirely rebuilt in 1860, and an additional gas-holder of 75,000 feet capacity built. Three reservoirs, one of 20,000, one of 75,-000 and one of 300,000 cubic feet capacity are now in use; 700 bushels of coal are daily used in making gas, the average product being 175,000 feet. In the spring of 1868 the company built a three-story brick office on the north-east corner of Pennsylvania and Maryland streets, at a cost of about $12,000. The present value of the property and franchise of the company is over $500,000. D. V. Culley, D. S. Beatty, E. J. Peck and S. A. Fletcher, Jr., have been the presidents, and H. V. Barringer, Christopher Brown, E. Bailey and H. E. Stacey superintendents.

The State Board of Agriculture was chartered by the Assembly, February 14th, 1851, and was organized May 27 with a board of directors, Gov. Wright being chosen president, John B. Dillon, secretary, and R. Mayhew, treasurer. The first fair was held here on the military grounds October 19-25, 1852—1,365 entries were made, a large crowd of visitors attended, many of whom experienced difficulty in procuring food and lodging, but the railways enabled most of them to come and return the same day. The citizens were then first astonished with the numberless side-shows, since so common, at such gatherings. The fair of 1853 was held October 11-13, at Lafayette; that of 1854 in October, at Madison. Those of 1855, '6, '7 and '8 at Indianapolis. Receipts, respectively, $11,-000, $13,000, $14,000 and $11,000; that of 1859 at New Albany, receipts $8,000. Those of 1860, '2, '3 and '4, were held at Indianapolis, receipts $11,000, $4,200, $8,-000, $10,000. That of 1865 at Ft. Wayne, receipts $10,500. That of 1866 at Indianapolis, and of 1867 at Terre Haute. No fair was held in 1861. It will be seen that the most successful fairs have been held at this point, and the fact would be still more marked by the comparison of the entries made at each. The most successful fair was that of 1857, both in receipts and in number of entries. The fairs here until 1860, and during the war, were held on the military grounds, which were fitted up by the Board and citizens for the purpose. Those held elsewhere were on grounds furnished and fitted up by the citizens of the respective cities. In 1859 the Board determined to locate the fair permanently at this point and procure larger grounds. Proposals were invited, and during the winter and following spring much competition arose between the partizans of different sites adjoining the city, and some ill feeling was caused. The Otis grove, north of the city, was bought by the board and railway companies in 1860, and ex-

pensively fitted up during the summer, and the first fair held there in October. It was not very successful pecuniarily; many of the premiums were left unpaid, and for a number of years the board was much embarrassed financially, being relieved at last by State appropriations and damages received from the general government. The fair of 1861 was announced, but the war intervening, it was abandoned.

With the first rush of troops to this point, the fair ground was occupied, called Camp Morton, and used at intervals afterward until the capture of Fort Donalson, when it was selected as a prison camp, and used as such till after the close of the war—having, often, 5,000 inmates. Its use as a camp and prison injured the grounds exceedingly and destroyed nearly all the trees. It is now being improved, the city having voted $3,000 for that object; and when the improvements are completed will again be used by the board. The State fairs have all been alike in their essential features, and are now what they were at the beginning. Gov. Wright, Jos. Orr, A. C. Stevenson, G. D. Wagner, D. P. Holloway, J. D. Williams, Stearns Fisher and A. D. Hamrick have been the presidents of the society; and J. B. Dillon, W. T. Dennis, Ignatius Brown, W. H. Loomis and A J. Holmes the secretaries.

Nine hundred and fifty-five votes were cast at the city election, April 26th. H. C. Newcomb was elected mayor, but resigned November 7th, and the council elected Caleb Scudder for the balance of the term. A tax of five cents was authorized at the April election for the fire department and purchase of engines.

John B. Gough made his first visit to this city in May, and gave a series of temperance lectures in Masonic Hall. He has lectured here many times since before different societies, but never equalled the impression he then made, when he was in his prime, and before his English trip injured his voice and manner.

A violent storm of wind and rain occurred on the 16th of May, blowing down fences and trees, and prostrating the M. & I. R. R. car house, and on the 22d a heavy hail-storm broke thousands of panes of glass. On the 28th of May Gov. Reuben Wood, of Ohio, visited the city and was suitably received by the authorities.

The papers in May stated that there were then two foundries, three machine shops, and a boiler factory in operation; fifty steam engines had been built, and the manufacture of threshers had been commenced at the Washington foundry. Charles Mayer was also building a three-story business house with an iron front, the first one in the city. An "old resident," in a communication, asserts that "nobody is crazy enough to think the city will have 30,000 inhabitants during this century." The receipts of the city treasury for the year ending May 1st, 1851, were $10,515; expenditures the same; debt $5,407; school fund from last year $3,308, amount collected $2,851, expended $5,935 on building; balance $221. The number of children in the city was stated to be 2,126.

W. McK. Scott started the first commercial college here in March, 1851, continuing it for several years, and in October 1851, he originated a library and reading room association. Rev. N. W. Camp, president, A. M. Hunt, secretary, and W. McK. Scott, treasurer and librarian; but the enterprise lived only about a year. He also started the first real estate agency that had existed here for many years. Commercial colleges have been founded since that date by Bryant, Hayden, Gregory, Purdy, and others, graduating many young men for active business pursuits.

It being proposed to light Washington street with gas, and to buy a town clock, a vote was taken September 13, to authorize a gas tax of eight cents, and clock tax of one cent. The first was heavily defeated, and the last authorized. It was levied, and a sufficient fund having accumulated, Jno. Moffatt was employed in April, 1853, to build the clock for $1,200, and after much dissension as to where it should be placed, it was located in Roberts' Chapel steeple in 1854, and remained there till July 1868, when it was removed and put in charge of the chief fire engineer.

The first express office here was opened September 15, by the Adams Express Co., the line being over the Madison road, Blythe & Holland, agents, till December, when Charles Woodward was appointed. He was succeeded a year or two after by John H. Ohr, who held the office till it was discontinued in March, 1858. Offices of Wells, Fargo & Co.'s Express, of the United States Express, of the American and Merchants' Union have been established here at different dates. Since the consolidation of the companies in March, 1868, the Merchants' Union and American have been the only offices open here.

The county agricultural society was formed in August, and held its first fair in October. Fairs have been held nearly every year since with moderate success, doing well when the State fairs were held elsewhere.

On the 23d of September, twenty-two members of the First Presbyterian

church formed the third church. Rev. David Stevexson was called to the pastorate Nov. 17. He has been succeeded by Rev. Geo. Heckman, and Rev. Robt. Sloss. The church building on the corner of Illinois and Ohio street, was begun in 1852, and partly completed in May, 1859, at a cost of about $25,000 for house and lot. The towers have not yet been built. The congregation occupied College and Temperance Halls till January, 1854, when they went into the basement of the church, using it till 1859. The United Brethren Church was built during 1851-2, on the corner of Ohio and New Jersey streets.

Washington street had formerly been planted along portions of its sidewalks with trees, but they had gradually been cut away, and on the first of October the old locust trees in front of the present Dunlop corner, the last ones in the center of the city, were cut down.

Madame Anna Bishop and Bochsa, the first noted musicians who visited the place, gave a concert at Masonic Hall, on the 24th of November.

In November the experiment was tried of having markets at noon instead of at daylight, but it was abandoned after a short period. The weather in December and January was excessively cold.

1853. On the 10th of January a fire broke out in the old frame and brick houses extending east of the Capital House to the alley, utterly consuming them, and burning up nearly all the records in the City Treasurer's office. The present buildings were erected there during the summer and occupied in the fall.

P. J. Ash opened a theatre with a small company at Masonic Hall, in February, but failed and discontinued shortly afterwards.

The Assembly, on the 20th December, 1851, had invited Kossuth to visit the city, and at a subsequent public meeting, fifty citizens had been appointed a committee of reception. They met him February 26th, at Cincinnati, and on Friday, the 27th, he arrived here via Madison, and was escorted by a procession across the muddy valley of Pogue's run to the State House, where he was welcomed as the guest of the State by Governor Wright, and replied in an address of some length, to the vast crowd assembled in the yard. The party was quartered at the Capital House, (now the *Sentinel* office,) then the best and largest hotel in the city. A reception was held at the Governor's residence at night. On Saturday he was received by the two houses of Assembly, and received delegations, and contributions for Hungary. Sunday he attended

Roberts Chapel and the Sunday schools. On Monday he received delegations and contributions, and at night delivered a long and elaborate address, at Masonic Hall, before the society of "The Friends of Hungary." On Tuesday he left for Louisville, after collecting about $1,000.

Dr C. G. McLean built, during this summer, a three-story brick building, on the corner of New York and Meridian streets, and opened the first session of the McLean Female Seminary at that place in September; one hundred and fifty pupils were in attendance during the first year, and the school soon took high rank. Dr. McLean died in 1860, and the school was continued until 1865, under Professor C. N. Todd, Professor Sturdevant, and others. It was then discontinued, and the property bought by the Indiana Female College, which was located there till June, 1868, when it was discontinued, and the property sold to the Wesley Chapel congregation for about $16,000, as the site for their new Church.

The North Western Christian University was chartered by the Assembly, Feb., 1852. A meeting of the commissioners was held June 22, and stock subscriptions reported, amounting to $75,000. Twenty-one directors, with Ovid Butler as President, were elected July 14th. A site of twenty acres of fine woodland was donated to the institution by Ovid Butler. Plans by Wm. Tinsley, architect, were adopted, and the contracts were let in July, 1853, for the west wing of the building. It was erected in 1854-5, at a cost of $27,000, and dedicated November 1st, 1855, by Horace Mann, who delivered an able address on the occasion. John Young, J. R. Challen and A. R. Benton were the first Professors. John Young, S. K. Hoshour and A. R. Benton have been the Presidents. The institution has been prosperous under an able corps of instructors. Three societies, Pythonean, Mathesian and Threskomathian, are sustained by the students. Pupils of both sexes are in attendance at the institution. The College buildings are still incomplete.

The City Assessor returned the population of the city in July, at 13,812. The fourth of July was celebrated with more display than usual. The Sabbath School procession, embracing about two thousand children and teachers, marched to the State House square. The firemen and military, comprising the City Guards, the Marion, Western, Independent Relief and Invincible fire companies, and the O. K. bucket company, headed by Downie's band, (which had been formed in August, 1850,) also paraded the streets, with the

fire engines and hose reels fancifully decorated.

The first balloon ascension here, was made at 4 o'clock p. m., July 29th, at the State House square, (which had been enclosed for the purpose,) by Wm. Paullin. The balloon rose to a great height, remaining above the clouds for an hour, and lighting in the evening near Greenfield. At night, Diehl of Cincinnati, gave a fine exhibition of fire-works inside the enclosure. The show was gotten up by Jas. H. McKernan, and the ascension was witnessed by over 15,000 persons, nearly all of whom held curb-stone tickets. Since that time balloon ascensions have been made here by Pusey, Bannister, Bellman, and a number of others.

Much improvement was made in the place this year, and many buildings erected or begun; among these were the Bates House, Morris (now the Sherman) House, McLean's Seminary, three brick school houses, Lafayette and Union depots, Terre Haute shops, Washington foundry, Sinker's boiler factory, Osgood & Smith's peg and last factory, Geisendorff's woollen factory, Drew's carriage factory, Shellabarger's planing mill, Macy's pork-house, Blake's Commercial Row, Blackford's building on Meridian street, and others. The railroads were being actively constructed, streets improved, and cisterns built for the fire department, as voted for in October by a small majority. The first State and county fairs were held by the present societies, drawing large crowds; great conventions were also held during the summer, by the political parties.

1 8 5 3 . Among the side shows in attendance at the State fair, in October, 1852, had been Yankee Robinson's atheneum, or tent theater, placed where Gallup's building now is, east of the State House. He returned here during the winter, and on the 21st of January opened in the Washington Hall, (which had been fitted with stage and raised seats,) with the Alphonso troupe of vocalists, the concert being a blind for the theatrical performance which followed. After ten days or two weeks, he announced himself as manager, and continued the performances till March 7th, drawing very good houses, and employing a good company; among them were Henry W. Waugh, J. F. Lytton, D. W. Waugh, Robinson and his wife, Mr. and Mrs. Sidney Wilkens, and others. After Robinson left, H. W. Brown opened the hall as a theater, with Sidney Wilkens and wife, Meehen, and others, forming a good stock company. The season lasted from July 1st to the 26th, and Uncle Tom's Cabin was first represented here to crowded houses. Sidney Wilkens

again opened it as manager, on the 10th of August, and continued for a short time with nearly the same company. Wilkens was an actor of considerable merit.

The first old settlers' meeting was held at the State house, January 31st. Speeches were made, anecdotes of the early settlement related, and an organization effected with arrangements for annual meetings. These were subsequently held till 1860, at Calvin Fletcher's and James Blake's, and at the fair grounds, but were abandoned during the war, and have not since been revived.

The Odd Fellows had determined to build a grand lodge hall here, and during the winter had organized a stock company.— Subscriptions to about $45,000 were taken by the grand and subordinate lodges and encampments, and by individuals, and in February the lot at the corner of Pennsylvania and Washington was bought for $17,000. A plan was adopted, afterward modified by F. Costigan, architect, and during 1854-5 the present building was erected on the site of the two-story brick and frame houses which had formerly occupied the lot. It cost about $30,000, and was occupied in the summer of 1855, the city council room and city offices being on the second floor, where they remained till the present offices were occupied in Glenns' block, in May, 1862. The style of the hall is peculiar, probably unlike any other on earth. The lower floor is occupied as business rooms, the second as offices, and on the third are two large halls and anterooms, used by the lodges and encampments, who occupy them each secular night of the week. The house is stuccoed inside and out, and is surmounted by a dome, designed by D. A. Bohlen architect. The hall was dedicated, with appropriate ceremonies, May 21, 1856.

The dates of organization of the several lodges and encampments, and the names of their first officers are as follows:

Lodges—Centre No. 18, December 25, 1844, Wm. Sullivan, N. G., E. B. Hoyt, secretary, J. B. McChesney, treasurer; Philoxenian, No. 44, July 8, 1847, Hervey Brown, N. G., W. W. Wright, secretary, John J. Owsley, treasurer; Capital No. 124, January 20, 1853, John Dunn, N. G., Wm. Wallace secretary, Geo. F. McGinnis, treasurer; Germania No. 129, January 24, 1853, Chas. Coulon, N. G., Julius Boetticher, secretary, B. H. Mueller, treasurer; Encampments—Metropolitan No. 5, July 20, 1846, J. P. Chapman, C. P., Edwin Hedderly, H. P., B. B. Taylor, secretary, A. C. Chrisfield, treasurer; Marion No. 35, March 24, 1853, Obed Foote, C. P., J. K. English, H. P., A. Dereis, secretary, Geo. G. Holman,

treasurer; Teutonia No. 57, August 13, 1855, Geo. F. Meyer, C. P., Chas. Coulon, H. P., F. H. Tapking, secretary, Alex. Metzger, treasurer.

A State convention of brass bands was held at Masonic Hall, February 22, under George B. Downie, as leader. Twelve or thirteen bands were present, and engaged in a contest for a prize banner, which was taken by the New Albany band. A similar convention, eight or nine bands being in attendance, was held at the same place, November 29, 1853, under C. W. Cottam, as leader.

The taxing power of the council being restricted under the charter of 1847, it was proposed in December, 1852, to adopt the general incorporation act of 1852, but much opposition arising, the project was not pressed at that time. In March, 1853, however, the council adopted the general act, and the city was governed under it till March, 1857. The elections were changed from April to May, and all the officers and councilmen were elected annually. 1450 votes were cast at the election, May 3d, under the new law. Caleb Scudder being chosen mayor, Daniel B. Culley, clerk, A. F. Shortridge, treasurer, Matthew Little, assessor, Benj. Pilbean, marshal, N. B. Taylor, attorney, Wm. Hughey, street commissioner, and James Wood, engineer. The new officers and council assumed their duties May 6th, and Joseph Little was elected first chief fire engineer. The receipts of the city for the year ending May 1, 1853, were $10,905, expenditures $7,030. The fire tax amounted to $2,033, expenses, $2,018; clock tax, $1,005, expenses, $18; school fund, $6,745, expenses, $6,458, in building houses, etc. $895 had been expended for cisterns, five of which were finished, five in progress, and six others located. The council chamber was removed in June, from Hubbard's b'ock to Dunlop's building, then lately finished, and in 1855, to Odd Fellows' Hall, then completed. The new city assessment in July, gave of personal property, $1,239,507; real, $3,891,875; total, $5,131,682, and 1,460 polls. 35 persons paid tax on over $20,000 of property, and 59 on from 10 to $20,000. Until July, the marshal was the only police officer in the city, but in that month he was authorized to appoint a deputy. The council fixed the salaries of the officers in September; that of the mayor being $600; clerk, $600; marshal, $500; engineer, $800; street commissioner, $400; clerk of markets, $350; sexton, $80; deputy marshal, $400; councilman, each meeting, $2.

The fourth Presbyterian church on Delaware and Market streets, was contracted for in May, and built during this and next year, though not finally finished till within a few years past. The third Presbyterian church, on Illinois and Ohio streets, was also begun this year, but not completed for several years after. The towers are now being built. The tower of the fourth Presbyterian church, about one hundred and forty feet in height, is entirely of brick, the only one so built, and is the tallest brick structure in the city. The outside of the church is stuccoed. These were the finest and most expensive church edifices in the city when erected, but have since been surpassed by the first and second churches.

John Freeman, an old and respectable colored citizen, was arrested, May 21st, as the fugitive slave of Pleasant Ellington, and taken before William Sullivan, U. S. Commissioner. The case caused great excitement. Crowds thronged the court room, writs of habeas corpus were issued, and successful efforts made to delay the case to get evidence. Freeman, in the mean time, had to lay three months in the jail, guarded by special marshals, while his attorney went south to get witnesses. Several planters came on from Georgia, proved his freedom, and on the 27th of August he was released. This case had no small influence on political matters afterward, and made many earnest opponents of slavery among those who had been formerly indifferent on the subject.

The fourth of July was celebrated in the forenoon in the usual manner, by sixteen Sabbath schools, at the State House; by four fire and hose companies, with the Franklin band, in the afternoon, and by the Turners in the evening, south of the city.

A temperance excitement arose during the summer, and out-door meetings were held on the corners, and in front of the saloons, during July, August and September. A committee was appointed in the last month, to wait on the sellers, and reported forty-four then engaged in the business, most of whom had agreed to quit it. The meetings were kept up at intervals for a year or two.

All the omnibuses in the city having been bought by Garner & Plant, an omnibus company was formed on the 1st of August, and lines established from the depot, and along Washington street, but the enterprise was abandoned as unremunerative, after two or three months trial.

A great fire, on the evening of the 10th of August, consumed the extensive stables on Maryland and Pearl streets, back of the Wright House, and surrounding buildings were repeatedly on fire, but by great exertions on the part of citizens and fire-

men, the fire was confined to the stables alone.

The Indianapolis Coal Co. was formed in the spring, working mines in Clay county, and the first loads of coal were sent to our market during the summer and fall. Hitherto wood had been the only fuel used here, being cheap and plentiful. The first horse-power wood-sawing machine was used on street during the fall, creating much excitement among the boys.

The first number of the *Frie Press*, a German independent weekly paper, appeared September 3d, and has been regularly issued to the present time. It is owned by a stock company, and has generally supported the republican party. The company is also publishing the *Daily Telegraph*, the only German daily paper in the city.

An auction stock exchange was started by William Y. Wiley, in October, weekly sales and meetings being held, but the city was too small to support such an enterprise, and it was abandoned after several weeks trial. No subsequent effort has been made to revive it.

The famous dissenting Priest Gavazzi delivered two eloquent lectures on the papacy, at Masonic Hall, October 28-9, to crowded houses. Lucy Stone, at the same place, on the 24th, 25th and 26th of November, and 3d of December, delivered addresses on woman's rights and wrongs. Ole Bull gave his first concert here, in the same hall, on the 6th of December, in company with Maurice Strakosch and the now world-renowned Adalini Patti, then a child of twelve or thirteen years of age. Ole Bull, since that time, has given several concerts here, the last being in February, 1868. During Christmas week, W. H. Howard gave several theatrical performances, which he terminated by running off and leaving his company unpaid.

Much improvement had taken place in the city during the summer and fall, and it was supposed that $500,000 had been expended in the erection of houses.

1854. The Young Men's Christian Association was organized on the 21st of March, and has since steadily and successfully pressed forward in a useful work. It made efforts to collect a library, and from 1855 to the present time, has given, each winter, a series of lectures by distinguished persons. Rooms have been rented, an agency office opened, a city missionary appointed, and sabbath schools organized under its direction.

2012 votes were cast at the city election on the 1st of May. The officers elected will be found in the table heretofore published. A great storm occurred May 13, blowing down trees, fences and Robinson's atheneum tent, injuring several persons in the audience. Robinson, during the summer and fall, fitted up the third story of Elliott's building, on the corner of Maryland and Meridian streets, and commenced the theatrical season in the fall, ending April 14, 1855. The company was unusually good, comprising R. J. Miller, Yankee Beirce, Yankee Robinson, F. A. Tannyhill, McWilliams, J. F. Lytton, H. W. and D. W. Waugh, Mrs. Robinson, Mrs. Beirce, Miss Mary McWilliams, and others. He introduced Miss Susan Denin to an Indianapolis audience. She had two engagements during the season, and aroused great interest among the drama-loving part of the community. She was succeeded by Maggie Mitchell and J. P. Addams.

The marshal was the only police officer until July, 1853, when he was authorized to appoint a deputy, but on the 14th of September of this year, the council established a police force of fourteen men, with a captain; Jefferson Springsteen being chosen the first chief. This force was continued till December 17, 1855, when the ordinance was repealed, and the whole squad and the deputy marshal discharged; the marshal again being left the only police officer in the city. The repeal arose from the general discontent at the expense attending the maintenance of the force, and at the conduct of the police in enforcing the liquor law. Conflicts had occurred immediately after the law took effect, between the Germans and the police, and on the 1st of August, an attempt to make an arrest on east Washington street resulted in a riot, in which several of the Germans were shot. A citizens' meeting, held immediately afterward, at the court house, sustained the police, proffered the aid of one hundred special policemen in each ward, and determined on the enforcement of the law, and preservation of the peace. The council also commended the act of the police. The ill feeling gradually subsided, but the general discontent over the matter resulted at last in the discharge of the force. For a month or two afterward, the streets were much disturbed by noisy rioters, among whom (as it was charged at the time,) were a number of ex-policemen, who thus evinced their desire for re-employment, and demonstrated its necessity. The papers soon asked for another force, and the council, on the 21st of January, 1856, created one of ten men, one to each ward and three at large, with a captain; Jesse M. VanBlaricum being chosen chief. This force continued till

after the May election, when the new democratic council discharged it, and by ordinance allowed the city marshal to appoint one policeman to each ward, with a captain; Charles G. Warner being selected for the post. The republicans repealed this ordinance, May 18, 1857, and passed another, by which the council elected seven policemen and a captain; A. D. Rose being chosen. Two additional policemen at large were appointed in 1858, and Samuel Lefever elected captain. A. D. Rose succeeded in 1859. The force was increased May 11, 1861, to two men from each ward, and on the 2d of July, 1861, was fixed by new ordinance at fourteen men and a captain; A. D. Rose retaining the post. He held it till October, and then entered the army, being succeeded by Thos. A. Ramsey. The two day policemen were discharged in November. John R. Cotton was chosen chief in May, 1862. Two day patrolmen were again added, and the men first uniformed at the expense of the city. Thos. D. Amos was chosen chief, May 19, 1863, and the force increased to one lieutenant, seven day and eighteen night patrolmen. D. M. Powell succeeded as chief, May 25, 1863. During the fall much trouble was experienced in preserving the peace, in consequence of the great number of rowdies in the city, and on the 4th of December a new ordinance was passed reorganizing the force. On the 4th the mayor was authorized to appoint detectives, and on the 21st the military authorities were asked to detail guards to assist the police. The request was granted, and until after the war a strong guard materially aided in preserving order in and around the city; the guard headquarters being at the police office. A new ordinance fixing police districts, was passed March 21, 1864, and amended May 9th, and Samuel A. Cramer elected chief. On the third of October, twenty-six special policemen were added, during the State fair. Complaints being made of the insufficiency of the force, the council, on the 5thof December, 1864, authorized an addition of sixteen men until the second Tuesday in May, 1865, and raised the chief's salary to $1,500. The pay of the men was also increased once or twice during 1863 and 1864, being finally fixed at $2.50 and $3.00 per day. Jesse VanBlaricum was chosen chief in the spring of 1865, with two lieutenants, nine day and eighteen night patrolmen, two detectives, and sixteen special men under his command. He served till April, 1866, when Thos. S. Wilson was elected chief, and still holds the office. The force has been maintained for the last three or four years at an annual cost of $25,000 or $30,000, and now consists of about thirty men.

In September, 1865, Mr. A. Coquillard organized a merchants' police force for the patrol of the business squares along Washington street, and on the 16th of October the council recognized the force, granting it police powers. A. D. Rose took the control of it in September, 1866, and is now at its head. It is composed of twelve men, paid by the parties whose property it guards. In addition to the regular and merchants' police, there is a force of three or four men at the Union Depot, appointed by the company, and confirmed by the council, and invested with police powers.

1855. A financial panic had occurred in the West during the fall of 1854. The Free state-stock banks had very generally stopped payment, and their notes, which formed the great bulk of the circulation, were passing at a heavy discount. Railway and other pending enterprises, were greatly embarrassed, and nearly all those in progress suspended operations. Traders and manufacturers were much cramped, and general distrust prevailed among business men. A bankers' convention was held here on the 7th of January to classify the notes of the suspended banks and fix discount rates according to the value of their securities. The rates were accordingly fixed, but not adhered to even by those who made them, and the discounts were raised or lowered at the caprice of brokers, entailing great losses on the community, and making large sums for the operators in the business.

The mayors of the several cities of the State met in convention at this point on the 22d of January, for consultation and mutual improvement, but without any visible result.

A colored lithographic engraving of the city, as seen from the top of the Blind Asylum, was published in January by J. T. Palmatary.

A deep and lasting snow fell in February, affording fine sleighing.

A number of cases of small pox occurred in January, and as the disease began to spread during February, the council, on the 10th of March, ordered the erection of a hospital. Several lots were bought in the north-west corner of the plat, plans adopted, and the house begun; but the disease and panic soon subsided, funds ran low, and the house was suspended or prosecuted at intervals for years, and was not finished till the spring of 1859, requiring a new roof and other repairs in the meantime. Its erection was due to Dr. Livingston Dunlap, councilman from the Sixth

ward, who persevered against all obstacles till his object was achieved. It cost about $30,000, and remained unused, except as a rendesvous for bad characters, till April, 1851. It was proposed in February, 1860, to sell it, but the council committee reported in favor of renting it. During the summer it was proposed to use it as a city prison or a house of refuge, or a home for friendless women; but each of these projects was successively defeated. The Sisters of Chartiy, on the 21st of June, asked its use, under their control, as a hospital, but other christian denominations opposed the plan, and the application was withdrawn. The council finally, on the 21st of July, granted it to a society of ladies as a home for friendless women. It was not occupied, however, for that purpose, and was given rent free to a keeper, who was to take care of it. After the war began and the sudden concentration of men at this point, the sick were taken there, and the council, on the 18th of May, granted its use to the government for a hospital, and it was occupied as such till July, 1865, and as a soldiers' home till November, 1865, when, with the additions and improvements, it was surrendered again to the city. These improvements consisted of two large three-story ells, several outbuildings, fences, trees, gardens, &c. They had been offered for sale by the government authorities, but were finally surrendered to the city with the building in lieu of rent. After the government vacated it, Rev. August Bessonies, January 2d, 1866, submitted a proposition to the council to give the house to the Sisters of the Good Shepherd, as a city prison for females, and also asked that the unfinished house of refuge be deeded to them, to be finished and used as a reformatory school for abandoned females. These propositions were opposed by the citizens, and a subscription of $5,000 made to finish the house of refuge, and Mr. Bessonies' proposition was defeated. The house remained vacant till the spring of 1856, when about $2,000 were spent in buying hospital furniture and supplies at the government sales at Jeffersonville. A board of directors was elected, Dr. G. V. Woollen chosen superintendent, a corps of consulting physicians and surgeons appointed, and the hospital opened for patients July 1st, 1866. It has since been conducted at an expense of six or seven thousand dollars per year.

Two thousand, six hundred and ninety votes were cast at the May election. The revenue for general purposes, for 1854 amounted to $20,500; school fund $10,300. The general expenditures exhausted the receipts and left a debt of $537—the balance left in the school fund was $6,880. The street improvements requiring considerable labor in the engineer department, the council, in July, first authorized the office of assistant engineer, at $300 salary. A wood-measurer was also appointed for the newly-established wood markets. A market house was built this year on South street, between Delaware and Alabama streets. But few markets were held there, and the house was torn down in 1858.

The first city directory was issued this year by Grooms & Smith. Directories have since been issued by A. C. Howard, Henry E. McEvoy, J. T. Talbott, Sutherland & McEvoy, J. C. Sutherland, H. H. Dodd & Co., Richard Edwards, A. L. Logan and others.

The liquor law took effect June 12th, and the county agency was started. The law was generally observed for a few weeks, and unusual order and quiet reigned on the streets, but on the 2d of July R. Beebee was arrested for selling liquor, fined and imprisoned; the case went to the Supreme Court, and the impression gaining ground that the law would be declared unconstitutional, it was soon generally disregarded and the traffic reopened.

Blake's, Drake's, Fletcher's, Drake & Mayhew's, Blackford's and other additions to the city were made in 1854-5, and the lots mostly disposed of and their improvement begun. Between sixty and eighty additions and sub-divisions have been made to the city since the first one was made by John Wood, in June, 1836.

The fourth of July was celebrated by the Sabbath Schools at the State House yard, in the usual manner. Nineteen schools, comprising 2,100 children, participated. The firemen paraded in the afternoon, making a fine display. The Hope company, of Louisville, then visiting here, was in the line.

The Indianapolis Building, Loan Fund and Savings Association was organized in October, and continued its existence for several years, its object being to make loans to its members at ostensibly low rates of interest, to aid in building houses. The Marion Loan Fund and Savings Association, a similar organization, was started in March, 1856. These organizations when wound up, failed to realize the hopes of their projectors. The Indianapolis Fuel Association was formed on the 31st October, and supplied its members during the winter, with wood and coal at but little over one-half the rates charged in the open markets.

A women's rights convention was held at Masonic Hall, October 22d and 23d, Mrs. Rebecca Swank, President. Mrs.

Lucretia Mott, Ernestine L. Rose, Frances D. Gage, Adaline Swift, Harriet L. Cutler, and Joseph Barker, of Pittsburg, and other speakers addressed the convention. But few persons attended, and the movement excited no remark.

The city was well supplied with amusements this year. The Black Swan, with the African Mario, sang at Masonic Hall on the 2d of May, (she again visited the place in the spring of 1858.) Du Bufe's paintings of Adam and Eve were shown May 22–6, at Washington Hall. Powers's Greek Slave, October 19–25, at College Hall; Parodi, with Maurice and Madam Strakosch and others, sang, Dec. 10th, at Masonic Hall. Brown and Commons opened the Atheneum, May 14, ending the season June 25, with C. J. Fyffe, manager, and J. F. Lytton, Beaver, and others, in the company; Harry Chapman and his wife, Mrs. A. Drake, William Powers and James E. Murdoch were the stars. Murdoch left in disgust before the close of his engagement. Commons re-opened the Atheneum, September 15th, ending the season December 8th, with Thos Duff, manager, and about the same company; Eliza Logan, Joseph Proctor, Susan and Kate Denin, Peter and Caroline Richings, and Mr. and Mrs. Florence were the stars. Yankee Robinson had returned during the fall, and wintered here with his circus company. An amphitheatre was fitted up in Delzell's stable, on east Pearl street, and horse opera given during the winter.

The first effort at numbering the houses on Washington street, was made during the fall, but no settled system was adopted and the numbering was partial and faulty. The Council, in July, 1858, authorized A. C. Howard to number all the streets of the city, and the work was completed during the fall, but the system was defective in numbering only the houses then built, and the work was badly done, resulting in confusion as new buildings were erected. The Council, in June, 1864, adopted a system authorizing fifty numbers to the square. The work of renumbering was done by A. C. Howard, and the plan has since been followed in the numbering of new buildings.

The Young Men's Christian Association gave their first course of lectures during the fall and winter, Park Benjamin, Rev. Mr. Butler, David Paul Brown, Edwin P. Whipple, Henry B. Staunton, H. W. Ellsworth, Bishop Simpson, and Edward P. Thompson being the lecturers.

1856. The General Conference of the Methodist Episcopal Church met on the 1st of May, in the hall of the house of representatives, and continued in session for about a month, attended by the full board of Bishops, and the leading men of that denomination. The delegates were the guests of citizens of all the churches, and the pulpits of the churches were filled each Sabbath by preachers in attendance at the conference. The session was important and interesting, and drew the attention of the whole country to this city. It was the first national body meeting here.

The city election took place May 6th, 2,776 votes being cast, the democrats electing the whole city ticket, with ten out of fourteen councilmen.

The assessment for this year amounted to $7,146,670, $1,892,152 being personal property. The receipts in the general fund for the past year were $27,880, expenditures $46,105. The debt on the 1st of May, 1854, was $567; May 1st, 1855, $11,090; May 1st, 1856, $15,295. It was proposed to fund the debt by a loan, and Jeremiah D. Skeen was chosen in August, by the Council, as financial agent, to sell city bonds in the New York market. He accordingly went there, and not succeeding in negotiating a loan for the city, hypothecated the bonds for $5,000, which he applied to his own use. The defalcation was discovered in the spring of 1857, and unsuccessful efforts made to recover the bonds. The money was finally paid by the city to the parties who had advanced the money to Skeen. Suit was brought against Skeen and his sureties, and judgment finally recovered in January, 1858, for the principal and interest of the defalcation.

Alfred Stevens, the City Clerk, died October 26th, and George H. West was appointed Clerk pro tempore, to fill the vacancy. Henry F. West, Mayor of the City, died November 8th, and was followed to the grave by an immense concourse of citizens. He was the only incumbent of that office who has died during the term. He had been an earnest and active promoter of the public schools, and their success had been largely due to his efforts as trustee. The Council ordered a special election to be held, November 22d, to supply vacancies in the offices of Clerk and Mayor. It was held, and for the first time in several years the democrats were beaten. Two thousand nine hundred and thirty-one votes were cast; William J. Wallace was chosen Mayor, and Fredrick Stein, city Clerk. The republicans indulged in wild demonstrations of delight when the result became known.

Early in February, Dunlevy, Haire & Co. began business as brokers and run-

ners of the State and free banks, in the interest of Cincinnati bankers. In two months $2,000,000 of the circulation was returned for redemption, causing such financial stringency that a State commercial convention was held here, in April, to protest against the course of the Cincinnati and Indianapolis brokers in crippling the trade and resources of the State, by contracting the circulating medium. Delegates from Cleveland, St. Louis, Toledo and Louisville, were in attendance. Bitter resolutions were adopted in regard to the conduct of Cincinnati business men and bankers, and efforts were made to divert the trade of Indianapolis to other points. The meeting had the effect to seriously diminish the war on Indiana banks, and open other markets to our people.

Clinton Watson opened an exchange and reading room in August, in the room over Harrison's bank, but the enterprise failed in a few weeks from want of patrons.

Professor Pusey made a balloon ascension on the 28th June, and attempted another on the 4th of July, but failed for want of sufficient gas. The usual celebration of schools and firemen occurred, and in the afternoon the first fantastic parade attracted great crowds.

The political canvass this year was unusually animated and bitter, both parties putting forth their full strength, and holding frequent great conventions. The largest republican demonstration was held on the 15th of July, attended by many thousands of persons from all parts of the State. A great procession took place, and an almost equally great torchlight procession at night, closing with fireworks and balloon ascensions. During the afternoon, a border ruffian demonstration and dramatic representation of the designs of the slave interest, and life in Kansas, was given by a club of young men in fantastic dress, and with proper accessories. It created great amusement at the expense of the opposite party, and was repeated with effect by the club at several other points during the canvass. The largest democratic convention followed on the 17th, closing also with a torchlight procession at night, and in numbers and enthusiasm vied with that of their opponents.

A great storm of wind and rain took place November 21st, doing considerable damage, not only here, but all over the western States.

The Indianapolis Art Society was formed during this or the next year, and held annual drawings for several years, under the direction of a committee, at Herman Lei-

ber's print and picture store, where the pictures (mostly by Indianapolis or Indiana artists) were placed on exhibition.— Messrs. Jacob Cox, P. Fishe Reed, Jas. F. Gookins and others, being contributors.— The paintings were purchased by an association, at their value, each member contributing a stipulated sum, and the pictures were divided by lot. Many good paintings were thus distributed at small cost among the citizens.

The Young Mens' Literary, and the Young Mens Christian Associations each gave a course of lectures during the winter. Charles Sumner, J. B. Gough. T. A. Mills, S. S. Cox, Elihu Burritt and others, appearing before our people. Judson, John and Asa Hutchinson sang. January 22, at Masonic Hall. Ole Bull appeared February 27, Signor Blitz, (the elder,) in April, Tom Thumb in July, Miss Richings October 10th, and 30th: Strakosch, Parodi, Tiberini, Morini, and Paul Julien, November 24th; and a State musical convention under George F. Root, was held there November 20-1. W. L. Woods opened the atheneum in March, for one month; W. Davidge being the only noted star. It was reopened by Vance & Lytton, May 16. closing June 3; Eliza Logan, Miss Richings, and Mrs. Coleman Pope, being the stars.— It was opened by Maddocks & Wilson several times in June and July, for a day or two at a time. Wilson, Pratt & Co. appeared there during the State fair; Yankee Bierce and the Maddern sisters early in December, and on the 19th of December it was opened by Lytton & Co. for the season, closing March 9, 1857. The company included Mr. and Mrs. R. J. Miller, Mr. and Mrs. Lacey, Tannyhill, Lytton. and others. Sue Denin, Dora Shaw, John Drew, Charlotte Crampton, Mrs. Drake and Miss Duval, appeared as stars. It was reopened for a few days, afterward, for benefits, and in March 1857, for a week or two, under C. J. Smith, as manager.

1857. The Germans, during the fall of 1856, had requested that a portion of the city free school fund should be set apart for the support of German schools, and the council in December had requested the trustees to report whether the project was feasible and proper. They reported against it in January, 1857, stating that the fund and school accommodations were insufficient for the schools then in operation. There were nine houses (two of them rented,) and the old seminary, in use. properly accommodating twelve hundred pupils, while eighteen hundred were in attendance. The fund for 1856 had amounted to $27,050, the expenses to $19,428; balance $7,616. There were thirty-five teach-

ers employed in June, and 2,730 children enrolled, being about forty-four per cent. of the children in the city, and but seventy-three per cent. of those enrolled were in daily attendance. The first ward house had been raised to two stories, in 1854, and the fifth ward house in 1856. The eighth ward house was built this year. D. V. Culley, John Love and N. B. Taylor, were elected trustees in January. In August there were twenty-nine sabbath schools, with two thousand nine hundred and fifty scholars.

The city council on the 10th of March adopted the new incorporation law as the city charter, under which the city officers and councilmen were elected for two years. Three thousand three hundred votes were cast at the May election, each party electing part of its ticket. The council organized and drew for short and long terms, and elected Andrew Wallace chief fire engineer. The receipts in the general fund for the past year were $82,667; expenditures $31,003; balance $1,232; debt $23,-740; school fund $20,620; expenses $15,-354; balance $4,915. The assessment was $9,874,700, and a tax levy for general purposes of sixty cents on each $100. The salaries of the city officers were fixed as follows: Mayor $800, clerk $600, marshal $500, deputy $400, attorney $400, street commissioner $450, engineer $600, clerk of markets $300, sexton $80, chief fire engineer $175, treasurer four per cent. on current and six per cent. on delinquent receipts, and councilmen $2 each meeting.

On the 22d of May the German Turners had a celebration, procession, address and gymnastic exercises on the military grounds.

The spring had been backward and wet, and on the 10th, 12th and 16th of June there were tremendous thunder storms, resulting in a sudden and high freshet in White river and other streams in the State.

A brilliant comet appeared in the western sky in the latter part of June.

The Fourth of July was celebrated by the Sabbath-schools only, the firemen not parading, and the Guards were at Lexington attending the Clay monument dedication. This celebration was notable only as the last general one held by the schools.

Meetings were held in July by the business men to encourage the establishment of exclusively wholesale dry goods and notion houses. A committee appointed by the meeting reported that though there were seventy-five establishments and thirty-two manufactories which did a wholesale business to a greater or less extent, there was but one exclusively wholesale dry goods house in the place. Blake,

Wright & Co., started a dry goods house in response to the demand of the meeting; but the enterprise was short lived.

There were two riots in July in which the firemen were prominent actors, attacking houses of ill fame in the western part of the city, destroying the furniture and injuring the buildings. Several affairs of this kind occurred afterward in this and the following years, the firemen being principal actors in all of them.

The county fair this year was a failure on account of unfavorable weather, but the State fair was the most successful ever held here, there being over three thousand seven hundred entries of articles for exhibition, and the gate receipts amounting to nearly $14,000. A vast crowd was in attendance during the three leading days. A grand parade of our fire department, with visiting companies from New Albany and Dayton, was held during the fair.

A negro was arrested here in December under the fugitive slave law. The arrest caused much excitement, and being favored by the crowd, he escaped, but was recaptured after a long chase in the north part of the city, and remanded to his master in Kentucky, being convoyed thither by a large squad of heavily armed deputy marshals.

Dodworth's New York band, ninety in number, gave a concert on the 30th of June on the military grounds, under contract with H. Stone, of Cleveland, in his gift concert enterprise. They also gave a concert at night in Masonic hall, for their own benefit; but neither of the performances was largely patronized.

Edward Everett delivered his Mt. Vernon lecture on the 4th of May at Masonic hall. Thalberg, Parodi and Mollenhauer gave a concert May 7th at the hall. Dudley Tyng, Horace Greeley, Ex-Gov. Boutwell and others lectured during the fall and winter for the Young Men's Christian Association. Mr. Kunz and his daughters gave a series of German theatrical performances, during June and July, at the Apollo Gardens. Stetson & Wood opened the Atheneum September 5th, with Mr. and Mrs. Harry Chapman and an indifferent company, closing November 2d.

The Indianapolis Daily Citizen was started May 14th, 1857, by Cameron & Mc-Neely, at their office, 10 east Pearl street. It was regularly issued by them till June, 1858, when it was discontinued. It was republican in politics, and well conducted. The Western Presage, a literary and political weekly paper, was first issued by Bidwell Bros. at 84 east Washington street, January 3d, 1857. It was the exponent of advanced republican ideas, was issued

in expensive style, resulting in the failure of the firm and the discontinuance of the paper in April. It deserved a longer life and better fate.

Much building was done in 1857. The block opposite the court-house, the Episcopal, and Third and Fourth Presbyterian churches, the United States post-office, Metropolitan Theatre and many other prominent buildings being in progress.

1858. The question as to the constitutionality of the free school tax was decided in January by the Supreme Court, against the tax. The citizens of each ward were requested by the city council to meet and, if possible, devise means by which the system could be maintained. The meetings were held January 20th. It was resolved to continue the schools, and one thousand one hundred scholarships, amounting to $3,000, were subscribed to keep them going for the current quarter. At the end of that time they stopped, the teachers left, the system was broken up, and the houses were closed. Some effort was made to re-establish private schools, and the free schools were opened each year for a short time under the State law.

Three thousand, three hundred and forty-three votes were polled at the May election, the republicans electing the entire ticket and a majority of the councilmen. The council elected Samuel Lefever chief of police, and the fire association having presented the name of Jos. W. Davis for chief fire engineer, he was elected to that office on the 22d of May. Much dissatisfaction arose among the firemen at his election, and from this date, till November, 1859, when it was disbanded, the efficiency of the department was much impaired. The opposition to Mr. Davis was mainly owing to his imperious manner, for otherwise he was a good executive officer. The assessment of city property for the current year showed a total of $10,475.000, and the increase in buildings over last year was $600,000.

The spring of 1857 had been unusually wet, and the spring and early summer of this year were still more so. Constant and heavy rains fell from early in April to the middle of June. Great storms occurred on the 11th of April, the 11th and 12th of May and about the 10th of June. Pogue's run completely flooded its valley on the 12th of April. Several street bridges were swept off; the Central railroad bridge giving way as a locomotive was passing over, throwing it into the creek. The culvert under the canal was also carried off. White river was over the bottoms repeatedly during the spring, and on the 14th of June reached a point but little below the flood-mark of 1847. causing great loss in fencing to the farmers along the valley. The wet season was succeeded by very hot. dry weather, and on the 26th of June eight cases of sunstroke occurred, five of them being fatal. Several cases happened the next day, and for two or three days afterward all persons kept in the shade as much as possible.

A brilliant comet, which passed very near the earth in its course, was visible in the western heavens in September and October, its train bending like a bow.

A Bible investigating class was originated during the summer or fall, holding meetings every Sunday at the court house, for investigation of the authenticity of the Scriptures, or the meaning of disputed passages. Atheists, Deists and members of all orthodox churches participated in the discussions, which were often keen and searching, sometimes acrimonious. The meetings were kept up during this and the next year, were well attended, excited much interest, and if they did no other good, at least caused more study of the Bible by some persons than they otherwise ever would have given it.

Four or five miles of mains were laid by the Gas Company during the summer and fall, and several miles of streets were lighted. Much building and street improvement also were undertaken. Blackford's block, the Ætna building, Metropolitan Theater and the Washington street culvert over Pogue's run were built.

The 4th of July happening on Sunday, no general celebration took place. The 3d and 5th were devoted to pic-nics by the schools, firemen and Turners, the military companies going to Richmond.

A Jewish church, Rev. T. Weschler, was organized in August, worshipping in Judahs' block till 1856, when the Synagogue on east Market street, built in 1865-6, was completed at a cost of $25,000, and occupied by the congregation.

There was great rejoicing and an extemporised illumination on the night of the 7th of August, over the completion of the Atlantic Cable, and on the 17th a formal celebration of that event took place in the Circle, with a display of fire-works and an oration by Governor Wallace. The National Guards held a three days encampment, in October, on White river, north-west of the city.

The Indianapolis Academy of Science was organized during the summer, R. T. Brown, J. W. Barnitz, and others, being prominent in the matter. A room in Judahs' block was rented, meetings and discussions held, papers read on scientific subjects, and a considerable cabinet of

geological specimens accumulated, but the community not taking sufficient interest in it, the society was suspended in July 1860, and its collections scattered.

Lectures and amusements were not lacking this year. Thomas F. Meagher lectured, February 17th, at Masonic Hall. Ormsby M. Mitchell began a series of astronomical lectures there, October 27th, B. F. Taylor, M. F. Maury, E. L. Youmans, Bayard Taylor, Dr. Holland, and others, lectured during the season before the Young Man's Christian Association. Andrew Jackson Davis, the "Pokepsie seer," gave a series of spiritual lectures there, beginning December 16th. The German singing societies of the State held a convention, June 10th-13th, with a procession and grand concert. A German theatrical troupe appeared at the Athenæum in August, and in January and February there were two German theaters at Washington and Union halls. Sam. and Kate Denin Ryan had appeared with a small company at Washington Hall in April. Harry Chapman during the State Fair, opened the Athenæum, Mrs. Drake and J. K. Mortimer appearing on the boards. It had also been opened for a few nights by strolling companies, several times during the summer.

The dramatic event of the year, however, was the opening of the Metropolitan Theater, the first building specially devoted to amusements here. It was erected by Valentine Butsch in 1857-8, on the northeast corner of Washington and Tennessee streets. The corner stone was laid in August 1857, and the house opened September 27, 1858. The building was eighty-two by one hundred and twenty-five feet, three stories high, of brick stuccoed in imitation of sandstone, and, with the lot, cost when completely fitted up, about $58,-000. The cellars and ground floor are used for business purposes. The dress circle and parquet are well arranged, but the gallery was not well designed for a proper view of the stage. The building will comfortably seat about twelve hundred persons. The interior was neatly frescoed and gilded by artists from Cincinnati, and the scenery was mostly painted by S. W. Gulick.

E. T. Sherlock was the first manager and lessee, opening September 27th, 1858, with a rather indifferent company, and closing Feb'y 29th, 1859. Harry Chapman continued it as manager till March 13, 1859. The Keller troupe, H. W. Gossin, Sallie St. Clair, Hacket, Dora Shaw, the Florences, J. B. Roberts, Mrs. J. W. Wallack, Mrs. Howard, Adah Isaacs Menken, the Cooper opera troupe, Eliza Logan, Mr.

and Mrs. Waller, Mrs. Edwin Forrest, Mr. Sedley and Miss Matilda Heron appeared as stars during the season. George Wood & Co. opened it again for a short time in April. John A. Ellsler opened it in April, 1859, for a two months season; Miss Kimberly, Collins, and Kate and Sam Ryan appearing as stars. He again opened it, October 1st, the season closing March 2d, 1861. The Webb sisters, Miss Ince, Sallie St. Clair, Marion McCarthy, F. A. Vincent, Barras, J. B. Roberts, the Richings and others being the stars. The war having begun, and thousands of men thronging here, the theatre was re-opened by Mr Dutch, as proprietor and manager, on the 25th of April, F. A. Vincent being stage manager, and Miss McCarthy leading lady. A good company was also secured, and from this date until after the close of the war, the enterprise was well supported and profitable. Most of the leading members of the stock company continued here for several successive seasons, and some of them, as Mr. and Mrs. Hodges, and F. C. White, until the theatre was finally closed in the spring of 1868. Vincent continued as stage manager until 1863. William H. Riley then succeeded, holding that position till the spring of 1867. He then removed to the St. Charles theatre, New Orleans, dying shortly after his arrival there. M. V. Lingham became manager for the season of 1867-8, and in the spring of 1868 Charles R. Pope became the last manager, with a good company, and giving the people the most brilliant season ever witnessed there. Edwin Forrest played an engagement of five nights, beginning March 16th, to crowded houses, at double the usual rates of admission. Since April, 1861, nearly all the leading actors and actresses in the country have appeared on the boards of the Metropolitan, and among others, Adelaide Ristori appeared there with her company, under Grau's management, on the 25th March, 1867.

The theatre has not been so well supported since the close of the war. Its position was against it, being too far west. The proprietor, Mr. Butsch, early in 1868, purchased Miller's Hall, (then nearly completed,) on the corner of Illinois and Ohio streets, for about $50,000, and has fitted it up in tasteful style for a theatre and music hall, to be opened in the fall of this year. The building is much larger than the old theatre, and the auditorium will comfortably accommodate a much larger audience. The old theatre will hereafter be used for concerts, lectures, meetings, &c.

1859. Some efforts were made in January, to organize a corporation for a University at this point, and in February an application was made to the Assembly for a lease of University Square for a term of ninety-nine years, as a site for the contemplated buildings, the property to be surrendered to the State at the end of the term. As there was some doubt as to the ownership of the square, between the city and the State, the application was not granted, and the project was dropped. The city terminated the dispute as to ownership in 1860, by taking possession of the square and the military grounds. The old seminary was torn down in August and September, 1860, and the square improved as a park. In 1867–8 the military grounds were fenced, and also improved as a park, at the expense of the city. The ownership and possession of the city will probably be uncontested hereafter.

The gas company had laid a number of miles of mains during 1858, and during this year were still further extending the pipes. Many applications for street lamps had been granted, and others were pending, and as no uniformity existed in the position of the lamps, or their number to the square, and no regulations had yet been adopted on the subject, the Council, on the 12th of February, passed an ordinance prescribing a general plan for lighting the city, fixing the number of lamps at four for each square, and their position, and distance from each other. Under this ordinance several additional miles of streets were lit for the first time, in the fall and winter of this year, Washington street, from Pennsylvania to New Jersey, and Illinois from Washington to North street, being in the number.

Early in 1854 a number of young men had formed a gymnastic association, adopted by-laws, fixed admission fees, dues, &c., and elected officers. The third story of Blake's commercial row was rented, and fitted up with a complete set of apparatus. The gymnasium was popular, and well patronized for two or three months, but as the novelty wore off and the hard work began, the interest rapidly lessened, and but few steadily availed themselves of its advantages for exercise and health. The association declined for want of members, and died in a year or two, after spasmodic efforts to continue it. No further effort was made till March, or April, 1859, when the Indianapolis Gymnastic Association was formed, with Simon Yandes, President, and Thomas H. Bowles, Secretary. A code of rules was adopted, and the third story of the Athe-

neum building rented, and fitted up with gymnastic apparatus, bowling alleys, &c., at a cost of about $1,200, and the room opened for use in June. The older men were also invited to share in the enterprise, and with their aid it did very well for two or three years, the bowling alleys and chess tables largely adding to its attractiveness. The interest gradually diminished, however, and though the ladies were asked to share its advantages, the organization became defunct at the breaking out of the war.

A grand procession and celebration by the Odd Fellows took place on the 26th of April.

In April, Rev. Gibbon Williams bought the house and one and a half acres of ground at the north-west corner of Pennsylvania and Michigan streets, and shortly afterward opened the Indianapolis Female Institute, a school which has increased in importance and prosperity to the present time. The building, (at first small and ill arranged) was greatly enlarged and improved at several subsequent periods, and at present is one of the largest educational structures in the city, having a capacity for nearly two hundred boarding, and three hundred day pupils. Rev. Mr. Williams left in 1863, and was succeeded in the presidency of the institution, by C. W. Hewes. A full corps of able professors are connected with the college, and the number of pupils has steadily increased since its origin.

The city election took place May 3d, the city officers being elected for two years, and the councilmen for four years, under the amended charter adopted by the assembly March 1, 1859. At the same time a proposition was submitted to the general vote of the people to divide the first and seventh wards, so that two new wards should be created, forming the eighth and ninth wards, but the result of the vote was largely against it. The proposition was again submitted to vote in May 1861 and carried by six hundred and twenty-one majority. Councilmen were elected from the new wards, but were refused their seats, and the wards were unrepresented for a year or two afterward.

The city clerk reported the receipts from May 8, 1858 to May 30, 1859, at $71,211, expenditures the same, with a debt of $9,317. The total city assessment for the year was $7,146,677. The treasurer reported the receipts from May 8, 1858 to May 1, 1859 at $59,168. Expenditures $56,442, the leading items being $19,232 for the fire department; gas $4,771; watchman $4,582. The salaries of the city officers were raised in May and June. The

bouldering of Washington street, between Illinois and Meridian streets, (the first done here,) had been ordered in April and was done in May, and further street improvements were designed. The council, in view of the probable expenditures, fixed the tax levy at 'sixty cents, which so aroused the tax-payers that they held a public meeting June 22d, to protest against it. They little knew what was in store for them in the future.

A proposition was entertained by the council, during the spring, to build a City Hall on the lot south of the Journal office on Meridian street, but no final action was taken. The city offices and council room were located in the Odd Fellows Hall where they remained till May, 1862, when a lease, for ten years, was secured of the upper stories of Glenns' block. Efforts have often been made to secure the erection of a City Hall and prison, but without success.

The General Assembly of the Old School Presbyterian church met in the basement room of the Third Presbyterian church, May 18th, continuing in session till the 2d of June. The eminent men of the church were in attendance, and the debates between Dr. McMasters and N. L. Rice, and others, on the establishment of theological schools and the policy of the church on the slavery question, excited great interest and attracted crowded audiences.

The national anniversary was celebrated with unusual display. The City Council appropriated $500 for the purpose, and large subscriptions were made by individuals. The procession comprised the artillery, cavalry and infantry companies, three bands, Turners, Butchers, Fenians, Catholic societies, Madison firemen and our own fire department, seven companies with eight engines, reels, hook and ladder wagons and a long line of carriages. The engines were beautifully decorated. The procession, which was nearly two miles in length, marched through the principal streets to the old fair ground, where the usual exercises occurred, Caleb B. Smith delivering the address. A great pic-nic dinner was spread, after which the military were reviewed by Governor Hammond. A grand fantastic parade took place in the evening, and a fine display of fire-works at night. Over twenty thousand persons were present at the celebration. It was rumored in the evening that the "Sons of Malta," a mysterious organization, which had rapidly increased in number during the spring, would parade at midnight; their rigid rules preventing public demonstrations at any other hour. The report

caused much excitement, especially among country visitors and the ladies, thousands of whom impatiently awaited the strange display. It proved to be all that fancy painted it, and the procession was accompanied through its midnight march by a multitude of half crazy spectators, though the gravity of the puissant Knights and reverend prelates was sadly disturbed by the noisy advice of the street boys, "go faster old tin-head," "step up brass mounted man."

On the 23d of August, Adam Deitz drank eight gallons of lager beer together with a bottle of brandy, inside of twelve hours, attaining a wide notoriety thereby and winning a wager.

Much improvement took place during the summer and fall, and a number of good business houses were erected. Yohns', Rays' and Glenns' blocks being among them.

The Daily Atlas was first issued by John D. Defrees as editor and publisher, in July, from an office in Van Blaricum's block, on south Meridian street. The presses were run by a small Ericsson hot air engine, (the only one ever used here,) which attracted many visitors. The paper was regularly issued till about the end of March 1861, and then discontinued, the material and subscription list being sold to the Journal office. Several other newspaper enterprises have been started here before and since the Citizen and Atlas were established. The Brookville American was transferred to this point by the editor and proprietor, Thomas A. Goodwin, in 1857. It was afterward sold to Downey & Co., who issued it as a daily for a short period, and then sold the establishment to Jordan & Burnet. They changed the name to the Evening Gazette. Dr. Jordan afterward issued it till the spring of 1863, when he sold it to Smith & Co. They afterward sold it to Macauley, Shurtleff & Co., and they sold the office and list, in May or June 1867, to the Journal Co. The Gazette was issued most of the time from an office in Hubbard's block, and latterly from the Sentinel office on Pearl and Meridian streets. It was well conducted during a part of its existence, and attained a considerable circulation during the war.

The Daily Telegraph, the only German daily in the city, was issued by the Free Press Co., in 1866, and has continued to the present time. The office is on west Maryland street.

The Evening Commercial was established in 1867 by Dynes & Co., and issued from Downey & Brouse's Publishing House in the Sentinel building on Pearl street. It was subsequently moved with their of-

fice to the old Journal building, on Circle and Meridian streets, and is now published by M. G. Lee.

The year 1859 was dull so far as lectures, concerts and amusements were concerned. Geo. D. Prentice lectured at the hall on the 6th of February, and Henry S. Foote, of Mississippi, at Roberts' chapel, December 2d. Dr. Boynton delivered a series of geological lectures, at the hall, in December and January, 1860. Miss Laura Melrose sang there March 24, and the Cooper opera troupe April 1st.

The coming political contest began to excite attention. Gov. Corwin addressed a large serenading party at the American House, on the 6th of July. Abraham Lincoln visited the city for the first time, and addressed a large audience at Masonic Hall, on the 19th of September. He was personally unknown to the great mass of the citizens, and considerable curiosity was manifested to hear the man who had so gallantly struggled with Senator Douglass, then at the zenith of his power.

Richard Cobden, of England, then on a visit to this country, reached the city on the 5th of May, but remained a few hours only, passing on to the north-west. The year closed with excessively cold weather.

1860. The military grounds being thought too small to properly accommodate the visitors and exhibitors, at the State fairs, the agricultural board determined in 1859 to secure a large tract for the purpose, and locate the fair permanently at this point. Proposals were invited in the fall of 1859, and an unsuccessful effort was shortly after made here to form an association to buy the grounds for the board. An appropriation of $5,000 was then asked from the city, and the proposition being submitted in February to a vote of the people, it was authorized. A question arising, however, as to the legality of such an appropriation, it was not made. The railways and the board finally made an arrangement for the purchase of the grounds, and after much competition between the advocates of various sites, the Otis grove, of forty acres, north of the city, was bought in the spring of 1860. Extensive and costly improvements were made during the summer, and the fair held there, October 15th to 21st. It was not as successful as had been desired. $11,900 only were realized, and a part only of the awarded premiums were paid. The board was seriously embarrassed for several years afterward, but is now getting out of debt.

In April a Mr. Bell, of Rochester, New York, submitted a plan for water works to the council. The project was discussed at a number of meetings. Estimates were made, but no definite action was finally taken. It was again broached by the central canal company in July, 1864. They proposed to furnish water from their ditch. This project was also considered, and committees appointed who reported on it, but the subject was finally dropped without definite results. In October, 1865, the Mayor again brought up the subject by a message, urging the building of such works, and recommending Crown Hill as the point for a reservoir. The council passed a resolution declaring it expedient that such works be built, and that it was inexpedient for the city to undertake them. This action was intended to invite proposals from private companies, but had no immediate effect. In May, 1866, the Mayor again brought the subject before the council, introducing questions propounded by him to James B. Cunningham, civil engineer, and the answers and estimates made by that gentleman in reply. The subject was again brought up October 15, 1855, on a proposition by R. B. Catherwood and his associates to build water-works if a liberal charter was granted them. The council thereupon by resolution declared it expedient that water works be built, and inexpedient for the city to build them. A committee on the subject was appointed.— It reported an ordinance on the 22d of October, authorizing R. B. Catherwood & Co. as the Indianapolis water works company, to build such works, and furnish the city and people with water for fifty years. The ordinance, after various amendments, was finally passed, November 3, 1866. It gave the company the right, for fifty years, to furnish the people and city with pure water, to be taken from White river or its tributaries, several miles above the city.— To use the streets and alleys for pipes, the company to repair the streets when torn up. The city reserved the right to buy the works after twenty-five years; required operations to be commenced within one year, and a given sum to be expended within two years. Hydrants and fire-plugs were to be located where desired, and the city was to pay from $40 down to $25, according to the number ultimately erected. The amount of capital was specified, and the amount of profit on it limited to fifteen per cent., water rates to be placed as low, from time to time, as practicable. The company was organized under the charter, with R. B. Catherwood, president, Jno. S. Tarkington, secretary, and accepted the ordinance, November 5, 1866, filing it with the mayor, who, on the 6th of November, issued his proclamation, stating that fact, and publishing the ordinance. The company, within the year, and to save their

charter, nominally began operations by laying about fifty feet of pipe on North street. Nothing has since been done with the work.

So far as a convenient an I plentiful supply of water is concerned, the works will doubtless be of great benefit, but no surface water will ever equal in purity and healthfulness the water now drawn from wells sunk in the great gravel and sandbeds underneath the city, and if surface drainage was carefully prevented, no deterioration in its purity will occur for scores of years. No artificial filters can equal those nature has given us, and the phosphates and carbonates dissolved by the water in its passage through the sand are those most needed in the human system.

By the treasurer's report in May, the receipts for the past year were $87,262, expenditures $80,172, balance $7,090, debt $11,553. The leading items were for fire department $11,253, bridges $13,915, street improvements $14,875, police $5,960, gas $6,445. The city duplicate showed an assessment amounting to $10,700,000.

Street railroads in the city were first proposed in November of this year, and an unsuccessful attempt was made to form a company to build them. No further action was taken in regard to them until June 5th, 1863, when a number of our citizens formed a company under the general law, electing Thomas A Morris president, Wm. Y. Wiley, secretary, and Wm. O. Rockwood, treasurer. They filed an application with the council on the 24th of August, setting forth their organization, and asking a charter from the city. The application was referred to a committee, who prepared an ordinance and submitted it for the consideration of the council. Amendments were proposed, and while the ordinance was still pending, R. B. Catherwood, of New York, associated with several of our own citizens, formed the Citizens' Street Railroad Company, with John A. Bridgland as president, and proposed more favorable terms to the council, agreeing to begin the construction of the lines at once, and finish a greater number of miles in a given time. The competition between the two companies grew warm. It was charged that the Citizens' company was not responsible or able to fulfill their offers. They responded to this by paying down nearly $80,000 of their capital, and offering bond of $200,000 to fulfill all their agreements. The council finally decided the contest in favor of the Indianapolis company, granting them a charter on the 11th of December, 1863. They declined to accept it on the 28th of December; and the mayor having telegraphed that fact to

Mr. Catherwood, at Brooklyn, New York, he immediately answered that he would accept the charter, re-organize the company, and begin the work. On the 18th of January, 1864, the council passed an ordinance giving the Citizens' Street Railroad Company, (which had re-organized, with R. B. Catherwood, president, E. C. Catherwood, secretary, and H. H. Catherwood, superintendent,) the right to lay single or double tracks of railway on all the streets and alleys of the city, or its future extensions. Horse-cars were to be used only for transportation of passengers and baggage. The council retained the right to govern speed and time. The tracks were to conform to the street grades, and the company were to boulder between the tracks and two feet each side. The tracks were to be laid in the center of the street, or, if double, on each side of the center, and not nearer the side-walks than twelve feet. Fares on any route were not to exceed five cents. The company was to repair all damage to the streets, relay tracks when the street grades are changed, and be liable to private parties for all damages they might sustain. They were to return annually, on the first of January, a full statement of all property for taxation; but each separate line was to be exempt from taxation for two years from its completion. Rules were prescribed for the running and management of the cars, and the cars were given right of way against all other vehicles. The charter was given for thirty years, subject to the following conditions: Three miles were to be built and fully equipped by October 1, 1864, two additional miles by October 1, 1865, two additional miles by December 25th 1866, unless a further extension of time was granted by the council, otherwise all rights, &c., under the charter were to be forfeited. The council reserved the right to order additional lines constructed after the first seven miles were finished; and in case of failure, the company was to forfeit the right to that particular street or route. If, after ten years, the company had not built and fully equipped ten miles of track in the best style, the council might order an appraisement and pay the company therefor, or transfer the property and franchise to another company. The ordinance was to be in force after two weeks publication in the weekly Journal.

The company accepted the charter, and immediately began preparations for building lines. Materials were collected during the spring, cars ordered, and property secured for stables and car-houses. Their operations were somewhat delayed, and the iron and cars detained by the use of

the railways by government. But on application, the council, on tne 27th of August, 1864, extended the time for sixty days, and no forfeiture of their franchise occurred. Track-laying began on Illinois street at the Union depot, and the line was finished on that street to North street within the year. Tracks were also laid on Washington from Pennsylvania to West streets, and thence to the military ground, in time for the State fair in October. The line on Illinois street had been opened for travel in June, 1864—the mayor driving the first car on the first trip, accompanied by the council, city officers and officers of the company. In the fall of 1864 the citizens along Virginia avenue, having subscribed from $25,000 to $30,000 for a bonus, the company built a single-track road from Washington street to the end of the avenue, making the route along the avenue and Washington street (which had a double track from Illinois to Pennsylvania street,) to West street. The route was afterward limited to the avenue alone, causing much dissatisfaction, and the company subsequently changed to the old route, limiting it to the avenue and Tennessee street. In March, April and May, 1865 the Massachusetts avenue line, (which had a double track,) was laid from Washington street up Pennsylvania, Massachusets avenue and New Jersey street to St. Clair street. In June, 1867, one of one of the tracks on New Jersey street was taken up and used to extend the line on Ft-Wayne avenue, and thence east on Christian avenue to College street. In October, 1865, the Washington street line was extended on Washington street and the National road, (which had been adopted by the council, September 18th, as one of the city streets,) to the White river bridge— the line to military ground having been taken up in 1864 after the fair. The council also gave the company the right to lay tracks on all new streets. In the spring or summer of 1866 the Washington street line was extended east by single track to the culvert over Pogue's run. The Illinois street line was extended to Tinker street in June and July, 1866, and the line to Crown Hill, (built by a separate company,) was begun in the fall of 1866, and opened for travel in April or May, 1866.

In the spring of 1868, a new line was laid from Washington street down Kentucky avenue and Tennessee street, and east on Louisiana to Illinois street, being opened for travel in April. The first stables and car house were built on Tennessee and Louisiana streets, in October, 1864, and extended and improved in the summer of 1867. After the first lines were built and

opened, the company placed about thirty two horse cars upon them, and continued using them with drivers and conductors till April, 1868. At one time an effort was made to dispense with conductors, but after trial for some days, the company resolved to adopt a different car. Thirty or thirty-two one-horse cars, requiring a driver only, were procured during the spring of 1868, and placed on the different lines on the 3rd of April. The driver now merely furnishes change, the passengers themselves place the fare in safety boxes. The cars are turned on turn-tables at each end of the route, and trips are made at greater speed than under the old system. The old cars are used only on the Crown Hill route, or in case of pic-nics, or unusual demands on the rolling stock of the company. A portion of them have been sold, eighteen or twenty only being left at the present time. Mules are now almost exclusively used by the company. No bouldering has been done by the company on their tracks, except where they run along bouldered streets, as it is claimed that bouldered streets injured and crippled the animals.

Five hundred and fifty round trips are run, and four thousand passengers carried over the lines daily.

At present, including the Crown Hill line from Tinker street, and including side and double tracks, the company have about fifteen miles of finished and equipped road, costing $458,000. They also own fifty cars, employ sixty-four men, and one hundred and fifty mules and horses. The enterprise has not been as profitable as it was expected to be, but with the future increase of the city, its success will be assured.

R. B. Catherwood in September or October 1865, sold the controlling interest in the company to Messrs. English, Alvord and others. A reorganization took place, E. S. Alvord becoming President, R. F. Fletcher, Secretary, W. H. English, Treasurer, and H. H. Catherwood, Superintendent. J. S. Alvord is the present Secretary, and R. F. Fletcher, Superintendent.

A tornado swept across the State from west to east in the afternoon of May 29th, 1860, passing just south-east of this city, between 5 and 6 o'clock, p. m. It was a rapidly moving, whirling cloud, of small diameter, described by those who witnessed it, as hanging from or cutting through the clouds above and around it, swaying about like an elephant's trunk, rising and falling as it sped forward. Considerable damage was done to houses, timber, gardens and fences in its path. The residence of Gardner Goldsmith, at the end of Virginia avenue, was thrown from its foundation and partially destroyed, and Goldsmith was

seriously injured. It was much more destructive both east and west, however, than near this city.

Great preparations were made for the celebration of the fourth of July, the people feeling that it might perhaps be the last under a united government. The procession included five bands, the entire fire department with beautifully decorated engines and reels, three military companies, the butchers, gardeners, various societies, and a long line of carriages. The usual exercises took place at the fair grounds. A very large frame building had just been completed on University square, by Mr. Perrine, and in the afternoon the military companies drilled there for a prize of $100. A balloon ascension by J. C. Bellman, took place at 4 o'clock, p. m. He rose to a great hight, and landed ten miles from the city. The best display of fire works ever given here took place at night in the enclosure. The "Coliseum"—as it was termed—could accommodate fifteen or twenty thousand persons, being, perhaps, the largest structure of the kind ever built in this country. It was torn down some weeks after.

The political struggle of this year was unprecedented in its interest and bitterness, each party holding repeated monster conventions and torch-light processions; every effort being made by each to surpass the last display by the opposite party. The democrats held a great meeting at the State house yard on the 8th of July, George E. Pugh and C. L. Vallandigham being the leading speakers. The republicans far surpassed this demonstration on the 29th of August, at the old fair ground, Corwin, Blair, Stanton, Lane, Morton and others being the speakers. A great procession marched thither in the day time, and at night a torch-light procession, which included several thousand Wide Awakes, formed on University square, and filed through the principal streets, saluted along its line of march with a constant blaze of fire works and illuminations. This demonstration was equalled if not surpassed by the democrats on the 28th of September. Much money had been spent by them in tasteful arches and other decorations, and the display was a very grand one. Douglass, H. V. Johnson, and other leaders of the party were present, and delivered addresses at the fair ground. There was a grand torch-light procession at night, and the fire works and illuminations equalled if they did not surpass the display by the republicans. The crowds in attendance at these conventions were to be measured only by the acre, and sufficiently demonstrated the perfection and extent of our

railway system. At no other place in the country could such immense throngs have been concentrated or dispersed so readily as at this point.

The first rope-walking exhibition here was given in September, by Theodore Price, in the presence of an immense crowd, the rope being stretched from the roof of the Palmer house to that of the Bates house. Several subsequent exhibitions have occurred, the most notable and dangerous one occurring in the summer of 1865, on a rope stretched from the roof of Blackford's block to that of Yohn's block.

The Escott and Miranda Opera Troupe sang at the theatre in January. A musical convention was held at Masonic Hall in September. Bayard Taylor and Henry J. Raymond lectured there in February. Lola Montez lectured there for several nights, beginning February 28. In the fall and winter, Bayard Taylor, Prof. Youmans, J. B. Gough, Dr. Robt. J. Breckinridge, G. W. Winship and others, lectured before the Young Men's Christian Association. Sallie St. Clair appeared at the Metropolitan for a few nights in February.

In view of the threatening aspect assumed by the southern States, and the lack of patriotism displayed by them, it was deemed proper by the assembly to unfurl the American flag from the State House dome, and the ceremony was fixed for the 22d of January, 1861. A flag staff and large flag were prepared. Extensive arrangements were made, the military, the firemen, city and State authorities, and citizens paraded. The preliminary exercises were concluded, and the flag was started up in presence of a vast and expectant crowd, when the staff broke, and, with the flag, tumbled down the dome to the roof. The crowd dispersed silently, deeming the event ominous of coming trouble. A new staff however was afterward procured, and the flag successfully raised, but with less display and enthusiasm.

1861-8. The First Baptist church, on the corner of Maryland and Meridian streets, was burned during a great snow storm, on the night of January 27th, 1861, presenting a sad but magnificent spectacle as the flames burst from the roof, and wrapped round the spire, which soon toppled and plunged downward through the roof. The fire was supposed to have caught from a defective flue. The loss was a serious blow to the church. The first building occupied by the congregation was a small one-story brick structure, on the same site, built in 1829 or 1830, and holding two hundred and fifty or three hundred persons. The small bell then used was

placed in a separate frame tower at one
end of the house. This building was torn
away, and the house which was now just
destroyed was built there in 1851 or 1852.
The first spire was built in the telescopic
form usual in country towns, the upper
portion being finished inside of the lower,
and hoisted by tackle to its proper elevation. It had just been hoisted to its place
during a hot summer afternoon, and the
workmen were still on it, when a sudden
thunder gust came up, and the spire being
insufficiently stayed, the guy ropes parted
and it turned a somersault, coming point
down on the pavement in front of the
building, narrowly missing a team and
wagon, and shattering itself into splinters.
The men at work on it had barely time
enough to get off before it went over. Another spire was afterward built, but in a
different way.

The congregation, after the destruction
of the church, sold the lot (which is now
occupied by Schnull's block,) and purchased the lot on the north-east corner of
Pennsylvania and New York streets, and
in 1862 erected the present large brick edifice upon it.

President Lincoln arrived here on the
12th of February, 1861, on his way to the
national capital, and was received as the
guest of the city and State, being met at
the State line, and escorted thither by a
committee. He left the Lafayette train at
Washington street, and was escorted to the
Bates House by the military companies, fire
department, State authorities, and a vast
crowd of citizens. In a short speech from
the balcony of the Bates House, he out-
lined his future policy with regard to the
rebellion, and held a reception during the
evening, leaving for the east next morning.

Several meetings of conservative republicans were held at the court house in February and March, to urge a compromise of
the existing political differences, and the
settlement of the controversy by making
concessions to the South. The sessions
were stormy, in consequence of the attendance of the more radical men, who felt
that the time for all compromise had passed, and before any definite action or
course was decided on by the meetings,
the acts of the rebels transferred the discussion from the forum to the field. There
was then no further talk of compromise,
and those who had urged it became earnest
and active in the war.

It can scarcely be expected that a full
history of the part taken by this city in
the war can be given in the limits of an
article like this. It could only be properly
dealt with in a volume. But a brief out-

line at least may be presented of the leading events.

The news of the attack upon Fort Sumter reached the city April 12th, and at
once produced the profoundest feeling.—
Business was suspended, and every one
eager for the latest intelligence. During
the afternoon a handbill was posted calling
a meeting at the court house, and at the
appointed hour the room was thronged.—
An adjournment was voted to Masonic
Hall, and the excited crowd, now momen-
tarily augmenting, rolled down Washington street. The hall was at once filled, as
well as the theatre and the intervening
street. The American flag was produced,
and greeted with deafening cheers. Speeches were made at the several meetings, bitter resolutions were adopted, and volunteering at once begun. The throng dispersed at a late hour, excited and enraged
over the news that the Fort had been surrendered. On the following day the Greys,
Guards, Independent Zouaves, Zouave
Guards, and a light artillery company began recruiting. Flags were everywhere
displayed, and the fife and drum heard at
every corner. The president's proclamation
for seventy-five thousand men appeared
on the 15th, and the governor's call for
six regiments from this State, on the 16th.

The State fair ground was chosen as the
rendesvous. It was named Camp Morton,
and on the 16th and 17th the city companies moved there, having meanwhile been
quartered in the public halls of the city.
Companies from abroad were also hourly
arriving, greeted by cheers and the firing
of cannon, and were sworn in at the State
House and sent to camp. In a few days
eight or ten thousand men had reported
for duty. Had sixty, instead of six, regiments been demanded, the call would have
been almost as readily filled. Our own
companies were full and others forming.
Home guards were organized for each
ward. Every one was anxious to contrib-
ute, and blankets, food and clothing were
collected by the wagon load for the men
so suddenly collected with no provision
for their comfort. The ladies formed societies and materially assisted in this
work. The enthusiasm was wonderful:
The zeal, faith and courage, sublime. The
material and men were superabundant,
and the excess made the labor of the authorities all the more difficult. Everything
had to be learned by a people unacquain-
ted with war, and for some time confusion
reigned supreme. Order, however, was
gradually restored, the six regiments were
organized and brigaded, and the work of
drilling and equipping them began.

On the 24th of April Stephen A. Doug-

lass visited the city and made a speech. He went to Camp Morton, visiting the troops and arousing great enthusiasm among them.

Some feeling arising concerning the support of the families of soldiers during their absence, the City Council, on the 20th of April, voted an appropriation of $10,-000 for their maintenance.

Seven companies were formed here under this call, the most of them being in the eleventh regiment under Col. Lew Wallace. They were moved in a few days to the old Bellefontaine depot, uniformed soon after and persistently drilled. Stands of colors were presented to them at the State House on behalf of the ladies, and feeling like old troops they clamored for service. They were accordingly sent to Evansville, (ostensibly to guard the border,) on the 9th of May. The excess of troops reporting here, over the six regiments called for by the Government, were organized under State authority in six one year regiments for the State service, but were soon after re-enlisted, (except one regiment of one year men,) for three years and all transferred to the Federal service. The six regiments of troops under the first call were reviewed by General G. B. McClellan in the fields north-west of the military grounds, (then occupied by the State troops and known as Camp Sullivan,) on the 24th of May. He shortly after ordered them into active service in West Virginia, where they participated actively and effectively in the campaign. The eleventh regiment, meanwhile, was left at Evansville, but growing tired of their position, an order was obtained from Washington transferring them to Cumberland, Maryland. They afterward joined Patterson's army, participating in the movements of that force prior and subsequent to the battle of Bull run. The three months regiments were discharged, returned home, but shortly afterward were again rendezvoused here to re-enter the three years service. Their old organizations were maintained, although the regiments were mostly composed of new recruits. The State troops, meanwhile, had been transferred to the Federal service and sent to the field, and the additional regiments afterward called for by the Government were gathering here and elsewhere. The nineteenth Regular regiment, added with others to the army by President Lincoln, rendesvoused here and was gradually growing in strength. It remained here till the fall of 1862, when its head-quarters were transferred to Detroit.

After the first flurry arising from the sudden concentration of the three months

volunteers and the State troops at this point was over, and they had gone to the field, the work progressed more quietly and methodically. The anxiety to enter to the service was greater than the demand for troops, and some trouble was experienced in securing permission to raise additional regiments. After the three months troops were re-organized as three years men, however, additional regiments were demanded, and recruits for the first organizations were constantly called for. They were very readily obtained without local bounties, for business had been very dull since the preceding winter, and hundreds of men were out of work. This stagnation in general business continued here until the winter of 1862 and spring of 1863, when, from the Government demand for various articles, and the scarcity of workmen, high wages began to be demanded, and volunteering decreased. Uniforms had been scarce on the streets after the first regiments left. They afterward began to multiply, and from the capture of Ft. Donelson till after the close of the war they constantly became more numerous, until the city at last was a heavily garrisoned post. During the late fall and winter of 1861, however, the skeleton nineteenth Regular regiment constituted the main force here, and their perfect discipline and fine dress parades, with the added attraction of their full regimental band, drew crowds of admiring spectators.

The twentieth regiment and several batteries were rendesvoused here and camped on the commons north-west of Camp Sullivan. The twenty-sixth and thirty-third and other regiments subsequently occupied Camp Sullivan. The drafted men were also placed there in 1862-3. The fifty-seventh regiment occupied a camp on the canal west of the Lafayette depot, and later organizations, recruits and drafted men were sent to Camp Carrington. In August 1862 a further call for troops was made. Bragg and Kirby Smith were advancing on Louisville. Great efforts were made to fill the quota, and good bounties offered for recruits. A draft was ordered and the preparatory enrollment was made, but before it took place the requisition was filled. The seventieth and seventy-ninth regiments were raised at that time, mainly in this district, and hurried to Louisville. They served to the close of the war, participating in Sherman's campaign against Atlanta and the march to the sea. No unusual war excitement disturbed the city from this date until early in July 1863.

It was then announced by the papers that John Morgan had crossed the Ohio

river, and later in the day news came that
he was rapidly moving toward this city, to
release the prisoners. The fire bells were
rung, and a vast crowd collected at the
Bates house. The governor announced the
news, and recommended the immediate cessation of business, and the formation of
military companies. It was resolved to
form companies in each ward, and recruiting at once began. Dispatches were sent
elsewhere calling for aid. The next morning martial law was declared, business
ceased, the ward companies were sworn into the State legion, and a regiment twelve
hundred strong organized under Colonel
Rugg, armed, equipped and constantly
drilled. It met that night on University
square, to receive blankets, accoutrements
and ammunition, and was ordered to march
next day. During this and the two following days, companies and regiments were
coming by rail from all parts of the State,
and a considerable army was extemporized.
The excitement and enthusiasm increased
hourly, surpassing any thing seen during
the war. Other regiments were organized
and sent to meet the enemy, but the city
regiment was persistently marched and
drilled on University square and elsewhere, attaining very creditable proficiency
in forty-eight hours. Signals were established by the fire bells, for the regiment to
start on the campaign, and they were thus
called together about twice a day. The
warriors parted so frequently from their
wives and sweethearts that they grew
tired of it, and finally left for the seat of
war on University square at each alarm,
without a thought of those they left be-
hind. The artillery and cavalry wings of
the regiment meanwhile were executing
various manoeuvres not laid down in any
system of tactics, sometimes putting the
infantry in great bodily fear. Morgan
soon turned eastward, but the regiment
continued its martial exercises for several
days afterward, and rapidly attained celer-
ity and precision in marching and in the
manual of arms. The organization was
continued for two or three months, and
in September an effort was made to uniform it and the police guards at the expense of the city, but it failed, and the
force disbanded shortly afterward. Its
services in the Morgan raid were afterward paid for by the State. The sudden
organization of, and the immediate proficiency attained by this regiment conclu-
sively proved that the people can be fully
relied on in any emergency.

Recruiting went on steadily from this
date, the city's quota always being supplied
with reasonable promptness, but late in
the fall another draft was expected, and

the citizens held a meeting on the 11th of
December, asking the council to appropriate a sufficient sum to pay $50 of boun-
ty to each recruit who might be credited to
the township. On the 14th of December
the council accordingly appropriated $25,-
000 for that object, ordering the sale of
bonds to that amount to raise the money.
The bonds were prepared and sold in a few
days, and recruiting went on with more
activity. Committees were appointed, and
funds raised in each ward to add to the
bounty, and the required number of men
was soon obtained.

During the winter of 1863-'64, and the
following summer, the old veteran regiments were returning on thirty day fur-
loughs for recreation and recruiting, before
re-entering the service. One or more of
them arrived every week, and were suitably received by the State and city authorities, the council having appropriated money for that purpose. Many recruits were
obtained here for their ranks, and the
Seventeenth Regiment re-enlisted and were
credited, in a body, to this city. On learn-
ing that our quota had been filled, they
confirmed their action regardless of bounty,
but on the 8th of March Colonel Wilder
asked the council to grant it to them. A
committee reported against it, but the council, after further consideration of the subject, passed an ordinance on the 14th of
March, appropriating $5,355 in bounties to
the regiment. An attempt was afterward
made to have this sum increased, but without success.

The campaign against Atlanta having
begun, and the governors of Illinois, Indiana and Ohio having tendered a heavy
force of one hundred day men to guard the
lines of communication, a call was issued
for troops for that term. The response not
being very prompt, ward meetings were
held, asking the council to appropriate
bounties to those who might enlist under
the call, and on the 9th of May $5,000 were
appropriated for the maintenance of the
families of one hundred day men, the sum
to be disbursed by the Soldier's Aid Committee. Recruiting was actively prosecuted, and the city regiment was shortly
raised, equipped and sent to Alabama under Colonel Vance, Lt.-Colonel Cramer and
Major Bates. It was assigned to duty
along the line of communication, and after
the expiration of its term was sent home,
discharged and paid off.

From this date recruiting became more
difficult, and larger bounties were required.
The demand for labor had increased the
rates of wages, and few persons were out
of work. Five hundred thousand more
men were called for, and as the response

was not satisfactory, preparations were made for a draft. The enrollment in June, 1864, showed seven thousand five hundred and seventy-three men subject to draft in the city, and the quota was fixed at one thousand two hundred and fifty-nine. Efforts to fill it by recruiting were made, and meetings were held in the wards and in the tabernacle on Court square, to secure subscriptions to pay bounties. Forty or fifty thousand dollars were subscribed and paid to recruits, but the required number was not obtained in time, and the draft took place September 25th, for about four hundred and fifty men. Drafted men's meetings were repeatedly held afterward, and great efforts made to raise money. Sixty or seventy thousand dollars more being subscribed by them, the council on the 28th of September, appropriated $22,000 to assist them, and on the 3d of October $10,000 more were appropriated. The city clerk was directed to collect the subscriptions of the citizens. Mayor Caven used every means to assist the work and by strenuous exertions the required number of volunteers were secured in October and November, and the drafted men relieved at a cost of nearly $180,000. Much complaint had been made prior and subsequent to the draft, of the incorrect enrollment on which it was made, and that the city and township were drafted together, compelling the city to expend $20,000 beyond its proportion, to relieve the township. The council on the 12th of December, appointed a committee to revise and correct the lists, and secure a correct enrollment.

The President, on the 20th of December, again called for three hundred thousand men, directing a draft if it was not filled by volunteers. Mayor Caven, on the 28th, recommended the Council to appropriate $90,000 for bounties, at $150 each, for recruits. The Council, after consideration of the subject, ordered the balance of the appropriation, $2,500, to be paid, and appropriated $20,000 in addition for the same purpose. On the 2d of January, 1865, the Mayor again urged an appropriation to pay $150 bounty for volunteers, and the appointment of ward committees to sell orders and raise funds. He also urged the correction of the enrollment lists, and that the city be drafted separately by wards. The Council at once responded, by appropriating $125,000, to be paid in $150 bounties and $10 premium for recruits. On the 5th of January they authorized the bounties to be increased to $200, and sent Hon. John Coburn to Washington to secure a draft by wards. He succeeded in his mission, and the draft was afterward so made. Commit-

tees were also appointed for each ward, to sell city orders, or warrants. On the 10th special committees were appointed to see if the bounties could be increased in amount, and to urge the Legislature to so amend the charter that loans might be made directly to pay bounties. On the 17th committees were appointed to superintend recruiting and assign the men pro rata to each ward. The time fixed for the draft was rapidly approaching, the quota was large and unfilled, and the citizens grew excited, and many of them turned their attention to recruiting. In February the Council appropriated $400 to each man who might be drafted, provided he had purchased a $50 order before the draft. After the draft occurred they confirmed the grant, ordering the money to be paid at once to those who furnished substitutes, and in installments to those who were compelled to serve. The Council had furnished twelve hundred cords of wool to soldiers families in August, 1864, and now gave $3,500 more for the same purpose. On the 20th of February, three thousand six hundred citizens petitioned the Council to effect a loan sufficient to pay all orders, bounties, &c. The petition was deferred for more names, and on the 22d, seven hundred and seventy-two more were reported. A resolution offered by Mayor Caven was adopted, authorizing a loan of $400,000 in bonds of $50, $100, $500 and $1,000 each, signed by the Mayor and Clerk, at such rate of interest semi-annually, as might be lawful where the bonds were payable. A special tax levy was to be made to pay interest and form a sinking fund to meet the principal. Messrs. Brown, Coburn and Jamison were appointed a committee to prepare and negotiate the bonds. They did so. The bonds were sent to New York, where they remained unsold for several months, and were then recalled, cancelled, and the committee discharged.

The quota not being filled, the draft took place, by wards, on the 25th of February. The Council at once ordered the loan committee to borrow $100,000 from the banks, at one per cent., at four months, with privilege of renewal, depositing orders at sixty cents on the dollar as security, the orders to be sold by the banks on ten days notice, if the debt was not paid. On the 6th of March this was reconsidered, and the Treasurer ordered to borrow $100,000 from the banks, at one per cent., for four months, with privilege of renewal, depositing bonds and orders at seventy-five cents on the dollar, as security, giving the banks the privilege of selling at ten days notice, if the debt was not paid.

The loan was taken by Fletcher's, Harrisons', the Citizens' National, First National and Indianapolis National Banks, $20,000 from each, and the money thus realized was appropriated at once to bounties. The drafted men were now very active in securing recruits. Offices were opened in the Council chamber and elsewhere, $100 bounties were paid, a number of substitutes were furnished, and the quota was nearly filled, when it was announced that on a revisal of the lists of credits, the quota was entirely filled, and with several hundred to spare. Bounties at once fell from $400 to $100, but the work was stopped; and $25,000 to $30,000 of the fund saved. All felt, however, that the lists should have been revised before the draft was made, and a heavy expenditure thus avoided. The war ended four weeks afterward, and no further recruits were needed. The city and citizens had spent about $700,000 in the past ten months, in bounties for troops, and expenses connected with the war.

The government immediately began the reduction of the army. Sick and convalescent troops, new recruits, drafted men, Quarter-masters' employees and others were at once discharged. The rebel prisoners were released and sent home. The veteran regiments rapidly returned and were mustered out. The veteran reserve corps dwindled to a skeleton organization, and by the close of the year the ninth regiment of Hancock's corps constituted almost the entire force stationed in the city. The camps were abandoned and the property sold. The houses were removed elsewhere, and by the summer of 1866 a uniform was rarely seen on the streets. The return of the veteran troops kept up the excitement for some time, and caused great activity in trade, but as the great floating population of the past three years dwindled in number, and the government demand for supplies ceased, the difference in the throng on the streets was soon perceptible, and the town grew dull.

Extensive camps, hospitals, barracks, stables and other structures were built by the government during the war; the most prominent of these may be mentioned here.

Camps Morton and Sullivan had been occupied by the three-months men and State troops while organizing and preparing for the field, and the last named camp had afterward been sufficient for the regiments subsequently organized, Camp Morton being unused; but after the capture of Fort Donelson, when several thousand rebel prisoners were sent to this point, additional troops and camps were at once needed. Camp Morton was then fitted up as a prison camp. It was surrounded with a high, tight fence and sentry walk; additional buildings were added from time to time, and the defenses strengthened, until at last it was as complete in its appointments as any other in the country. More than five thousand prisoners were occasionally confined in it, and many thousands during the war. Among its inmates were the greater part of Morgan's men, captured after their celebrated raid through Indiana and Ohio. Toward the close of the war many of these men, becoming convinced that their cause was lost, enlisted in the Union army for service against the Indians; others took the oath of allegiance and were discharged, and several thousand were released and sent home after the war ended.

The prisoners were guarded at first by the Nineteenth regulars, but other troops were afterward detailed to that duty, and some regiments were raised for that special service. Temporary camps for the guards were at first established near the prison; but after the invalid corps (afterward the veteran reserve,) were detailed to guard duty, camps of a more permanent character were built, requiring many thousands of feet of lumber. Camp Burnside, just south of the prison, grew into a large, populous, well arranged and well built village by the end of the war. The veteran corps guarding the rebels occupied this camp—many of the officers and men having their families with them. Camp Carrington, formerly a temporary affair, and afterward one of the best arranged and constructed camps near the city, was mostly built in 1864. It was at a considerable distance to the west of the prison, near the Lafayette road, and was mostly occupied by recruits, new regiments and drafted men. Camp Sullivan, on the military grounds, was not so extensive, well built or arranged as the two former. It had been occupied by the State troops, and afterward by new regiments, transient troops and drafted men.

As the war progressed and this point became more important as a depot of supplies, troops and prisoners, all these camps, with others in and around the city, were constantly occupied. Among other important establishments the Soldiers' Home founded in 1862, for the accommodation of transient soldiers, soon became prominent, and was greatly enlarged before the war ended. It was in charge of the veteran reserve corps at first, and afterward in that of the Ninth regiment of Hancock's corps. Single soldiers, squads, detachments, and regiments of troops, passing

through or temporarily stopping in the city, were accommodated with lodging and cooked food in this establishment, and it was of great service when the veteran regiments were returning on furlough during the war, and at its close, when they returned for discharge.

In addition to camps Carrington, Burnside, Sullivan and the Soldiers' Home, a cavalry camp was established near the city; and when the negro regiment was authorized late in the fall of 1863, Camp Fremont was temporarily established in Fletcher's woods, south-east of the city. The government, in 1864, took the old Bellefontaine depot, in the north part of the ninth ward, and fitted it up as an extensive stable to accommodate the thousands of artillery, cavalry and wagon horses, bought and brought to this point; and for the storage, also, of the necessary grain and forage. Barracks were also added for the many teamsters and quarter-masters' employees in service here.

It was proposed early in 1865 to abandon all the government camps, prisons, stables and hospitals then in use in and around the city, and construct new, more extensive and better arranged ones several miles out in the country. The site was selected, the plan approved by the authorities at Washington, and the order prepared, but before it was issued, the war terminated, and the new buildings were not needed.

When the war first began and the three-months troops collected here, but few arms and still less ammunition could be supplied. It was evident that ammunition would have to be fabricated, and Herman Sturm applied to the Governor for authority to manufacture it for the State. Permission was granted in May, and with one or two assistants, he immediately began making musket balls and cartridges at McLaughlin's gun-shop, on east Washington street. The demand soon extended the business, and a small frame structure was erected in July and occupied in August, north of the State-house. Additional buildings were soon erected and the number of workmen increased; but the facilities were not equal to the rapidly growing demand, and a removal took place to Ott's building, on Washington street, south of the State-house. It remained there some time, and was then removed to buildings especially designed for it east of the city. It had grown from a small beginning to great proportions; several hundreds of persons were employed, and vast amounts of artillery and small-arm ammunition were daily fabricated—the armies of the west being largely supplied by it. It filled

a pressing want early in the war; but the government having established an arsenal here, and ammunition being largely manufactured elsewhere, the State institution was discontinued in 1864.

The national government in 1861 determined to found a number of arsenals in the west, one of them being located here. Eighty acres of ground were bought north-east of and adjoining the city, plans adopted for the buildings and improvements, and Captain Jas. M. Whittemore, of the regular army, appointed commandant and superintendent. The improvements, consisting of buildings for the storage of small arms and accouterments, artillery and wagons, officers' quarters, magazines, barracks, fencing, grading, &c., were begun in 1862, and have been prosecuted to the present time, and are now nearly completed, at a cost of several hundred thousand dollars. The buildings are large, well planned and perfectly constructed. All the improvements are of the best design, materials, and finish. Large amounts of arms artillery, ammunition, and other government property, are now stored there. The Wallace building, on Delaware and Maryland streets, was used during the war as the U. S. Arsenal and storehouse. Wm. Y. Wiley was appointed military store-keeper. Capt. Whittemore served as commander and superintendent till the close of the war, being then relieved by brevet Col. W. H. Harris, the present commander. An arsenal guard of about thirty men was enlisted for that special duty in 1864, and is now stationed there.

The financial condition of the city was greatly influenced by the war, and it is best, perhaps, to consider it in connection with our war history; though, in doing so, many facts already given in the statement of the war movements will necessarily be repeated.

It is now impossible, from loss of records, to give a certain statement concerning the early financial condition of the corporation. The old books yet in existence are in such shape that no clear idea can be drawn from them. It is only within a few years that a system has been adopted showing the condition of the finances at any given time. Such facts for former years as were published at the time are given below.

The valuation of real and personal property in 1847 was about $1,000,000. In 1850 it had risen to $2,326,185: in 1853, to $5,131,582; in 1856,to $7,149,670; in 1858, to $10,475,000; in 1860, to $10,700,000: in 1862, to $10,250,000; in 1863, $10,750,000; in 1864, $13,250,000; in 1865. $20,144,447; in 1866, $24,231,750; in 1867, it sunk to

$21,943,605, and rose in 1858 to $23,593,-619. These figures show the steady growth of the place, as well as the temporary checks it has experienced. The listed polls in 1847 were about 400; in 1853, 1,460; in 1857, 1,862; in 1860, 2,200; in 1863, 3,200; in 1865, 5,160; in 1867, 5,300; in 1868, 5,780.

Taxation under the charter of 1847, for general purposes, was limited to 15 cents on the $100; but special taxes to any amount could be levied, if authorized by the general vote. Repeated efforts were made, from 1847 to 1853, to induce the citizens to vote special taxes for various objects; but with the exception of taxes for schools, clock, cisterns and to pay debts, the movements were generally defeated, and the entire levy did not exceed 45 cents on the $100. To avoid the trouble in regard to special taxes, the council, in 1853, adopted the general incorporation act as the city charter; and though the taxing power was thereby increased, they hesitated, in view of the general opposition of the taxpayers, to materially advance the rate, and it did not usually go beyond 60 or 80 cents before the war. After the war began, a different policy was necessarily adopted, and the people have since become acquainted with heavier rates on vastly increased valuations.

The receipts and expenditures for all purposes, (other than schools,) are given as published at the time, giving generally the actual current receipts without including balances. The levy for 1847, (including $805 of delinquencies from former years,) amounted to $4,226, nearly $4,000 being realized therefrom, and the expenditures considerably exceeded the receipts. In 1850 the receipts were $9,327, expenditures $7,554. In 1851, receipts $10,515, expenses over that sum. In 1853, receipts $10,906, expenses $7,030, $2,908 being devoted to cisterns and the fire department. In 1854 receipts $20,500, expenses nearly the same. In 1856 receipts $27,889, expenses $46,105. In 1857 receipts $32,697, expenses $31,003. In 1859 receipts $59,-168, expenses 50,412; $19,232, being spent on the fire department cisterns. $4,882 for police and $4,771 for gas. In 1860 the receipts were $87,262, expenses $80,172; leading items being for street improvements, repairs and bridges. $28,700; fire department and cisterns, $11,858; police, $5,986; gas expenditures, $6,445. The actual current receipts and expenditures, (not including balances from former years,) and the leading items of expenditure, as nearly as they can be obtained from the reports from 1861 to 1868, are given as follows:

	Receipts.	Expenses.	Street Improvements, repairs, Cleaning and Bridges.	Fire Department and Cisterns.	Police and Detectives.	Salaries, Fees & Per Centage.	Gas Expenditures, lighting tax, &c.	Jail Expenses.	Bounties and all War Expenses.
1861	$84,503	$84,503	15,653	16,249	$6,300	10,180	$7,618		
1862	79,132	79,132	2,744	12,510	9,653	10,062	8,876		
1863	97,119	95,487	18,809	12,063	10,687	11,524	10,984		$5,010
1864	125,071	156,444	33,522	21,822	18,473	12,010	12,555	$2,842	35,155
1865	597,831	851,390	20,240	21,612	27,990	14,618	15,220	5,509	715,179
1866	409,704	404,713	33,380	20,332	23,416	9,638	3,051	7,636	151,197
1867	445,253	381,525	52,186	27,207	37,511	17,452	38,164	11,113	70,575
1868	431,004	224,941	56,018	23,040	27,509	27,528	37,100	8,116	
								6,336	

The old corporation authorities had incurred a debt of a thousand or fifteen hundred dollars at the time the city charter was adopted. The street improvements then undertaken by the city government soon increased it to nearly $5,000, and in 1849 a tax of ten cents on the $100 was authorized by vote of the citizens to pay it. The proceeds of the levy almost extinguished it in 1850, but in 1851 it again swelled to $5,400. The increased receipts, however, enabled the treasury to meet current expenses and diminished the debt to $557 in 1854. The employment in that year of a police force, together with the increased current expenses, enlarged the debt to $11,000 in the spring of 1855, and to $15,800 in the spring of 1856. Orders were selling at a heavy discount, and the reputation of the city suffered. The Council determined to effect a loan of $25,000 to meet expenses and fund the debt, and having prepared the bonds, sent Jeremiah D. Skeen to New York City, in August 1856, as their agent to negotiate them. He succeeded in hypothecating them for $5,000, which he applied to his own use, and after much trouble and several years delay, they were recovered by the city on payment of that sum with interest. Skeen and his sureties were sued by the city, and judgment finally obtained in January

1868, for the principal and interest of the defalcation. This unfortunate effort to sell bonds still further injured the city credit, and the debt increased, in 1857, to $23,740. A change in the charter and city officers took place that year, and a general tax of sixty cents was levied to meet expenses and debts: until that date the entire tax had not exceeded forty-five or fifty cents on the $100. The debt was reduced to $9,300 in 1859, but swelled to $11,500 in 1860, and to nearly $25,000 when the war began. A considerable part of it was in short-time bonds issued to the makers of the three steam fire engines purchased in 1860, the bonds being the first that were negotiated and sold. The floating debt had not materially increased, but the growing expenditures for gas light and for the police department prevented any reduction in its amount. The salaries and fees of the city officers were also increased in May 1861, and the current expenses then enlarged.

Immediately after volunteering began for the three months service, a demand was made for municipal assistance for the families of soldiers, and on the 20th of April, $10,000 were appropriated to that object, and a committee appointed to supervise its distribution. From this time till the close of the war, many appropriations were made for this purpose, in buying wood and supplying money, and the aggregate sum thus expended was very large. Doubts existed whether bounties could be directly given by the city, and they were generally voted as appropriations to the soldier's families. The various war expenditures early in 1861, soon raised the floating and bonded debt to about $15,000, but the current receipts enabled the authorities to meet expenses, and make payments on outstanding liabilities, until they were reduced in May, 1862, to about $16,500. Recruiting becoming slack in the fall of 1862, bounties were first paid, a small appropriation being made therefor, and about $5,000 were spent in that way by May, 1863. Over $5,000 of the engine bonds had been paid in the meantime, and the debt reduced in May, 1863, to $11,250. This amount was practically paid off soon after, and a close calculation of the finances of the city would have shown her free of debt in the summer of 1863.

A rapid advance in the values of articles, and work, began in the spring of 1863. The officer's salaries, and the policemen and firemen's wages were raised; current expenses increased, large appropriations were made to the poor, and a house of refuge undertaken. To this increased expenditure was added the expense connected with the city regiment in the Morgan raid, and on the 11th of December, in response to the request of the citizens, the council appropriated $25,000, to be paid in $50 bounties to the families of recruits credited to the several wards. The ordinance was amended and re-passed on the 14th of December, and six per cent city bonds to the amount of $25,000, due in fifteen months, were prepared and sold within a week, and the money expended. No further bounty appropriations were made till May 9th, 1864, when $5,000 were given to families of one hundred day men: the money to be paid out by the Soldier's Aid Committee. By these appropriations and the largely increased current expenses for street improvements, salaries, police, gas, &c., amounting to $116,000, the debt had risen in July, to about $80,000, the war expenses amounting to about $40,000. The tax levy for 1864-'65, was fixed at $1 for general purposes, 50 cents for specific objects, and 25 cents for soldier's families.

The President called for 500,000 men during the summer, ordering a draft if the call was not filled by volunteers. The response was not as prompt as had been expected, and the draft took place in September. The mayor in August had recommended appropriations be made for bounties to volunteers to fill the city quota, but no definite action was taken at the time in regard to it. On the 28th of September, however, the council appropriated $92,000 in aid of the drafted men; the sum to be added to that subscribed by the citizens prior to the draft, and to such sums as the drafted men might raise. Twelve hundred cords of wood were also purchased at an expense of $8,000 for the soldiers families. On the 3d of October, $10,000 were appropriated in addition to the former sums in aid of the drafted men, and the city clerk was directed to collect the citizens subscriptions. During October and November, four hundred volunteers were secured at an expense to the city and citizens of about $170,000, and the entire cost of relieving the city from the September draft amounted to about $180,000.

Another call for 300,000 men was made December 20th, 1864, and a draft ordered in sixty days, if the call was unfilled. The mayor on the 28th recommended an appropriation of $90,000, to be paid in $150 bounties. The council appropriated $20,000, together with an unexpended balance of $2,500 of former appropriations.

The Mayor, on the 2d of January, 1865, again urged appropriations for $150 bounties, and suggested the correction of the enrollment lists, and the draft of the city by wards. The Council at once gave

$125,000, increased the bounty to $200, and sent John Coburn to Washington to secure a ward draft. In the meantime the competition for recruits forced bounties beyond $200, and the Council, on the 17th of January, increased them to $400. The Legislature was urged to amend the incorporation law so as to authorize bounty loans. Committees were appointed to sell war warrants, to oversee recruiting, and assign the men pro rata to the wards. Four hundred dollars were to be given each man who bought a $50 order and was subsequently drafted.

On the 20th of February the Council received a petition from three thousand seven hundred tax-payers, asking a loan to pay bounties and fund all orders, which were now selling at twenty to thirty cents discount. It was laid over for additional signatures, and seven hundred and seventy-two more being reported on the 22d, the Council authorized a loan of $400,000 on twenty year coupon bonds, signed by the Mayor and Clerk, with interest semi-annually, payable in New York, and pledged a tax levy to pay interest and sink the principal. The bonds were drawn, signed, sent to New York, where they remained unsold for several months, and were finally recalled and cancelled. The sale of war warrants and the work of recruiting actively went on in the meantime, but the draft took place, February 25th, for nearly five hundred men.

The Council then confirmed the gift of $400 to each drafted man who had bought $50 in war warrants, ordering it paid down to those who furnished substitutes, and in instalments to those who served. A loan of $100,000 was at once ordered from the banks, and on the 6th of March the Treasurer was directed to borrow $100,000, at one per cent., for four months, renewable if necessary, depositing orders and bonds at seventy-five cents as security, the banks having the right to sell them at ten days notice if the loan was not met. The loan was at once taken by the First National, Citizens National, Indianapolis National, and Fletcher's and Harrisons' banks, $20,000 each, and the money applied to bounties. A committee was appointed on the 6th of March to examine and report whether, under the new law, one-fourth of the amount of the war debt and bonds could be added as special tax upon the duplicate. The Mayor on the 3d of April, submitted an opinion by James Morrison, that the city could fund her debt by bonds under the existing law. The strictly war expenditures (except interest) of the city, in the way of bounties, ended with the February draft, the war

ceasing in less than four weeks after the quota was declared to be filled. Nearly $155,000 in war warrants were sold and in the hands of the people. The entire war expenses for the year. from May, 1864, to May, 1865, had reached $718,179.

The city war expenditure for the last three years of the rebellion approximated $1,000,000, and the municipal debt reached $368,000 at its close; $100,000 of this sum was in the shape of a bank loan, at 12 per cent., secured by deposit of warrants at seventy-five cents; the remainder consisted of six per cent. warrants, part of which were applicable on the payment of taxes for 1865, the rest in 1866-7. These orders were selling at twenty and thirty cents discount, and as the discount was added in all bills against the city, the depreciation was largely augmenting current expenses. The Council, therefore, levied a tax of $1 for general purposes, and fifty cents to pay the debt. The bank loan was renewed as it fell due, and in October an ordinance passed to renew it for a year. The unsold war bonds in New York were recalled and cancelled. The finance committee recommended the election of a city Auditor, and John G. Waters was accordingly chosen by the Council, in January, 1866, for two years; the office was discontinued at the expiration of his term. On the 11th of September, 1865, the Council authorized the funding of war orders in six per cent. three year bonds, and about $27,000 were so converted by May, 1866. The current redemption of orders in the mean time in taxes was large, amounting to $397,000 at the close of the fiscal year, and the debt had decreased from $368,000 to about $217,000, $151,000 being paid off. In May, 1866, a tax of $1.50 was levied for general purposes, and twenty-five cents for payment of debt, but in November, at the Mayor's suggestion, the outstanding six per cent. orders were funded to the extent of $82,000, in ten per cent. warrants running eighteen months, and the twenty-five cent tax was struck from the duplicate, materially lessening the burthen for that year. The actual current receipts (excluding former balance) for 1866-7, were $627,700. The expenditures (excluding bank loan,) $200,700. The total debt on three year bonds, ten per cent. warrants, and to the banks, amounted to $200,000, and $122,929 of a balance was left in the treasury. The debt had been reduced $105,757 during the year. The Council, in May, 1867, voted a general tax for the year, of $1.25, and the actual current receipts on it during the fiscal year, 1867-8, (not in-

cluding the balance from 1857) were $231,660, the actual expenses, $225,000. The bank bond and warrant debt, in May, 1868, was estimated at $252,000, and the balance left in the treasury amounted to $210,657. The bond and warrant debt has since been paid at its maturity, and the debt now amounts to about $200,000. The levy for the current year was fixed at $1.10 for general purposes, and fifteen cents for sewerage.

The war brought many rowdies here, and in the summer of 1861 scarcely a day passed without affrays in which weapons were used. The police were kept busy in preserving order. Affairs grew still worse in the fall of 1863, and military aid was invoked. A strong guard was detailed, with its headquarters at the Police office, and until after the war the soldiery assisted in keeping the peace. The convenient position of the place, midway between the large western cities, made it a favorite rendezvous for rascals of all grades, and when large bounties were offered in 1864, hundreds of thieves and bounty-jumpers flocked here. They were soon arrested or scattered by the authorities, and three of them being tried by court martial, and shot, near Camp Morton, as deserters, the rest hurriedly left the place.

For some time after the war began little or no political excitement existed, but at the democratic county convention in Court Square, on the 2d of September, several of the speakers indulged in indiscreet expressions; equally indiscreet retorts were made by parties in the crowd; a personal difficulty occurred, weapons were drawn, and the convention was dispersed by soldiers and others. The leaders were pursued to their homes and compelled to take the oath of allegiance. For sometime a serious outbreak was threatened, and the Sentinel office was in danger. Order was finally re-tored by the military and police. The affair was discreditable to the city and to all engaged in it.

On the 8th of April 1862, Parson Brownlow, of Tennessee, having just been sent north by the rebels, reached this city, and in company with General Carey, of Cincinnati, appeared before our people at the Metropolitan Theater, where both made bitter speeches. Brownlow visited the city again just after the Philadelphia convention, and made one of his characteristic speeches to a large audience in the Circle.

In 1863 the democrats held a State mass convention in the State House yard, mustering in heavy force and generally armed. Anticipating an outbreak the authorities

had taken measures to prevent it. Guards were stationed on the streets, artillery was held in readiness, and the seventy-first regiment put under arms. No trouble occurred, further than the arrest and fining of many persons for carrying concealed weapons. As the delegates were leaving, however, they began random firing from the cars. The Lafayette train got off, but those on the Central, Cincinnati and other roads were at once pursued by the military, the police and citizens. The trains were brought back, the passengers put under arrest and disarmed. They were permitted to leave after a detention of some hours and the confiscation of their revolvers, a large number of which were turned over to the military.

In August 1864, it was discovered that large quantities of arms and ammunition were being secretly imported into the State, and a seizure of four hundred navy revolvers and many boxes of fixed ammunition was made in H. H. Dodd's office in the old Sentinel building. Papers also were found disclosing the existence of a secret military organization opposed to the Government, and implicating prominent parties in the movement. Arrests of a number of them followed shortly afterward, and a military commission was convened here for their trial. After full investigation they were found guilty of treason and sentenced to be hung. The finding was approved and the day fixed for execution, but President Lincoln reprieved them. President Johnson afterward ordered their execution, but subsequently commuted the punishment to imprisonment in the Ohio Penitentiary, from which they were afterterward discharged under a decision of the Supreme Court. During the pendency of the trial H. H. Dodd, one of the leaders in the scheme, made his escape from the third story of the post-office building and succeeded in reaching Canada.

The political canvass of 1864 was earnestly and enthusiastically conducted by the republicans, and the vote for Mr. Lincoln—about twelve thousand—was the heaviest ever cast in this township, probably over ten thousand five hundred voters being residents of the city and suburbs. The meetings were held in the tabernacle, a large frame structure erected on the Washington street front of Court Square, and capable of accommodating several thousand persons. This building remained there for a year or more, and was frequently used for meetings, concerts, lectures, etc. A similar tabernacle had been built for the campaign of 1860, in the south-west corner of the square, and used in the canvass of that year. It, also,

remained standing about a year before its removal. Both buildings were used after the elections for shows and concerts.

The threatened political troubles had seriously contracted business enterprizes here for several months before the war began, and except the temporary activity imparted at intervals by the arrival and equipment of the different regiments, no general improvement took place until late in the winter of 1862-3. Until that time many men were out of work, and from that cause volunteering was steady and recruits easily obtained. After the city was made a prison depot and garrisoned post, the government demand for articles and labor steadily increased, and as operations in the south grew in magnitude, the advantageous position of the city as a supply depot became more evident. This fact attracted general attention and caused a rapid emigration hither, not only from all parts of the north, but thousands of southern refugees also made this their temporary home. The current constantly augmented during 1863-4. Houses could not be provided fast enough for the increasing throng, and cellars, garrets, and stables were crowded. Several families often shared the same tenement, and many persons who came here to settle were compelled to leave, for want of shelter for their families. Rents increased enormously for business houses and dwellings, prices being limited only by the landlord's conscience, or the bonus a former tenant would accept for his lease. House hunting became a serious business, and any tenement was gladly accepted. Many shanties paid fifty per cent. per annum on their prime cost, and the same remark could be truthfully made of some business rooms.— Work was found however for all comers.— Business in all lines was brisk. Every one had money, and fortunes were made in two or three years, apparently without effort or skill. The influx of parties from abroad continued till the close of the war, and counting all persons, permanent residents, soldiers, prisoners, and the miscellaneous floating population in and around the city, it would be safe, perhaps, to estimate the population in March, 1865, at eighty thousand.

Building though vigorously prosecuted during 1863-4 and 5, was greatly limited by the scarcity and high price of materials, and the good wages asked and received by workmen. Little material was on hand when the war began, and the demand being very limited for the first two years, only a small amount of it was collected, and it was not till the early spring of 1863 that the manufacture and importation

of lumber and other materials began on a large scale. Prices then rapidly advanced, doubling within the year. The demand grew faster than the price. Heavy importations of pine lumber from the lakes to this point, were first made in 1863, and for nearly a year the stock was comparatively unsaleable, from the high price asked, and the ignorance of our people with regard to the lumber. It had never been used here to any extent before that year, except in doors and sash brought from Dayton. Brick, stone and lime, also quickly rose in price, and with the rapid increase in wages, contractors lost money on the houses they erected. Many persons desirous of building were prevented from doing so by the fear that the improvement when finished would not be worth half what it cost; at least that was the excuse given by capitalists when urged to aid in the improvement of the city, and by building houses, afford homes, work, and business positions to those who were anxious to come here.

The settled limits of the city were largely extended in 1862-6, but the greatest improvement was effected in filling up vacant lots with houses, and crowding population more closely on the original plat. A rapid change also occurred in business localities. Washington street had thus far been the choice location for the heavier houses, the small retail groceries being thinly scattered elsewhere over the city, but with the rapid increase and concentration of population, came the concentration of this retail trade at subordinate centers, a half-mile from the street. Meat store, tin and shoe shops, drug stores, and doctors offices, collected in such centers, and the retail trade was so far diverted from Washington street that most of the grocery men left it. The wholesale trade also generally went to Meridian street, leaving Washington to the dry goods, boot and shoe and clothing houses, nearly a score of the latter being located along two or three squares.

The sudden and unexpected termination of the war closed many lines of business connected with it, and thousands were at once deprived of their usual employment. To these were soon added the discharged soldiers. Many of those thus left adrift were anxious to remain here, and would have done so had any chance been opened to them, but the general distrust regarding the future caused a rapid contraction in business, and the great mass were compelled to go elsewhere in search of employment. In a few months the unaccustomed sight of vacant dwellings greeted the eye, and shortly after, store rooms were to let. Rents grew less firm, then shaky,

then had a downward tendency, and finally reached a living point; averaging at present about half the war rates.

All parties were inexpressibly shocked by the assassination of President Lincoln, the news being first made known at market on the morning of the 15th of April, and immediately afterward by the tolling of the central alarm bell, calling out the fire department and citizens. Business, which had begun for the day, at once ceased; manufactories closed, stores were shut, and without any concerted action, the people began draping their houses. Men with grief stricken faces gathered on the street, discussing the event. A notice calling a meeting at the State House was at once posted, and by nine o'clock thousands were assembled there. The troops stationed here were paraded, and marched with muffled drums and draped colors to the spot. The assassination and death of the President were officially made known, by the Governor, to the excited throng. Speeches were made in eulogy of the dead President by leaders of both parties, and resolutions adopted, pledging the support of the people to the government and incoming administration. The effect of the shock was so great that business did not recover its former tone and volume for several days afterward.

Toward the middle of April it was announced that the President's body would be brought through this city on its way to Springfield. Meetings were held, and arrangements made to give a suitable expression of the respect entertained by the people for his memory. The city Council endorsed the movement on the 17th of April, invited the authorities of Cincinnati and Louisville, and voted to defray the expenses. Many arches, beautifully decorated and draped, were thrown across the streets on the line of the contemplated procession. Festoons of black, bound with wreaths of evergreens and immortelles, were stretched at regular intervals across the streets, and from house to house. Many thousand yards of black and white fabrics, and car loads of evergreens, were thus used on the streets, and on the State House and other public buildings. All business houses and nearly all the dwellings in the city were more or less draped and ornamented, many of the decorations being very beautiful. Pictures and busts of the dead President, furled and draped flags, wreaths of evergreens, mottoes and shields, were displayed everywhere, until the appearance of the city was startlingly transformed. The State House, under the rotunda of

which the remains were to lie in state, was profusely and tastefully decorated, being wreathed with black and white, trimmed with evergreens and flowers, inside and out. The hall was lined with black, relieved by stars, flower wreaths, pictures, busts and flags. The gate entrance was occupied by a beautiful quadruple arch, profusely draped and covered with mottoes. The fence all round the square was covered with festoons of evergreens and flowers. It was said by parties accompanying the cortege, that the decorations here were more extensive and beautiful than those at any other place on the route.

The arrangements were completed late at night on the 29th of April, and the funeral cortege arrived by special train early on the 30th. A great civic and military funeral procession had been arranged, and extensive preparations made for the visitors from other parts of the State, who were to come by special trains. These arrangements were defeated, and the crowd greatly lessened, by a cold, heavy rain, beginning on the night of the 29th and lasting all the next day. The President's remains, removed from the train early in the morning, and placed on a large funeral car built for the purpose, were taken under military escort to the State House, where, during this and a part of the next day, they were visited by many thousand persons, who, regardless of the driving storm, patiently waited their turn for hours, in long lines before the building.

The decorations, though badly injured by the rain, were allowed to remain standing for nearly a month, when they were removed, and the materials sold by order of the Council.

The war having closed the people desired the great commanders who had become prominent in it to visit the place, and in response to their invitations Generals Sherman and Grant visited the city in 1865. General Sherman arrived on the 25th of July, and was conducted through the principal streets by a great civic and military procession to the State House yard, where he made an able speech to the people counselling peace, and earnest efforts to repair the damages caused by the war. He held a reception and attended a banquet at Military Hall given by the former officers and soldiers of his command. General Grant arrived in September, and was received by the State and city authorities and military forces with the honors accorded to the Commander-in-Chief of the American army. A great military and civic procession conducted

him to the State House yard, where he was welcomed in fitting terms by the Governor, and bowed his acknowledgments with a few well chosen words to the public. He held a reception in the evening and attended the banquet at the Bates House at night.

Amusements were numerous and constant in the period intervening from 1861 to 1866. Nearly all the leading actors of the country appeared at the theater, which was open the greater part of each year, and constantly crowded by soldiers and strangers sojourning in the city. From 1864 to 1866 a museum was kept by Madame English in the Kinder building on east Washington street, and largely patronized by the rural population and soldiers. Shows and circuses appeared regularly each summer to reap a full harvest, and negro minstrel bands and panoramas drew crowded houses. Sleight of hand and ledgerdemain were illustrated at Masonic Hall, by Herman and Heller, the great masters in the art, exciting the wonder and adding to the enjoyment of their audiences. Concerts, operas and lectures had their full share of votaries, and fairs were revived for church and charitable purposes. A great fair was held in September, 1864, on the military grounds for the benefit of the Sanitary Commission, lasting one week, and realizing a large sum of money. Since the war ended amusements have been fewer and less well patronized, the hard times telling seriously upon them.

The leading event in the musical line since the war was the annual German Sængerfest, held about the middle of September, 1867, lasting three or four days. The programme included processions, addresses, vocal and instrumental concerts, a ball, displays of fireworks, etc. The arrangements were made by a committee under direction of the Männerchor of this city. A two story frame building, ninety or one hundred feet wide and one hundred and eighty feet long, was erected on the south east corner of Court Square. The floor was closely seated and wide galleries ran round three sides of the house, the whole affording accommodations for three or four thousand spectators. The north end was occupied by a wide raised platform for the orchestra and singers, and the whole interior was profusely decorated with pictures, wreaths, flags, mottoes, gas jets, etc. The exterior was also fully decorated and the roof surmounted with the flags of all nations. Many buildings in the city were finely decorated with flags and evergreens. The expenses were met by individual subscriptions, and an appropriation of $1,500 from the city treasury.

The Fest was very successful pecuniarily and otherwise, a considerable sum being left on hand, and devoted afterward to charitable purposes. Thousands of visitors were in attendance.

It has been stated heretofore that the four acre tract on the river bank southwest of the town, set aside for burial purposes by Judge Harrison, in 1821, was for years the only cemetery, and that at subsequent periods two or three adjoining tracts were platted as cemeteries by different parties. These were rapidly filling up as the city increased in size, and it became evident that some further provision must be made for cemeteries at a greater distance from the city. With this object in view, a number of gentlemen held a preliminary meeting on the 12th of September, 1863, to consult regarding the matter, and on the 25th of September, an association was formed, with James M. Ray, President, Theodore P. Haughey, Secretary, S. A. Fletcher, Jr., Treasurer, and with seven directors. S. A. Fletcher, Sr., offered to loan the necessary funds to purchase grounds, and a committee being appointed to select a site, soon after reported in favor of purchasing the farm and nursery of Martin Williams, three miles north-west of the city, on the Michigan road, together with several smaller adjoining tracts. The report was accepted, and the purchases made in the fall of 1863, and January, 1864, at prices ranging from $125 to $300 per acre, two hundred and fifty acres in all being secured at a cost of about $51,500. The money was loaned to the association by Mr. Fletcher, with additional amounts to begin the improvements. A survey was ordered and plats made in October and November, and Mr. F. W. Chislett selected as Superintendent. He began the improvements in the spring of 1864. The large trees were cut into logs, which were sawed by a portable mill on the grounds, into lumber and fencing, with which the tract was enclosed. A gate lodge was built at the western entrance near the Michigan road, and in 1867, a large cottage residence for the Superintendent, was erected on the southern part of the grounds. The improvement of the carriage ways and footpaths began in the spring of 1864, lots, irregular in plan and of various sizes, ranging from a few square feet to half an acre or more, were laid out. The grounds were dedicated in May or June, 1864, Albert S. White, delivering the oration. The first lot sale took place June 8, by auction, the price of lots being fixed at twenty-five cents per square foot as a minimum. The price has been advanced several times at subsequent dates.

Rules and regulations were adopted for the government of the association and cemetery, June 4, 1864. Each lot-holder is interested in the capital of the association to the value of his lot. The lot-holders choose the officers. No profits or dividends are allowed, and after payment for the ground, (which has been fully made, the loan being repaid to Mr. Fletcher,) all receipts are expended in the care and improvement of the cemetery. No fences or enclosures of lots are permitted, and the erection of great monuments is very properly discouraged. Notwithstanding this rule, the cemetery already shows too much marble for a strictly pleasing effect.

The improvements, consisting of gate lodges, superintendent's cottage, enclosing fences, carriage and foot ways, grading, sodding, grubbing, &c., have been rapidly forwarded since the spring of 1864, covering forty or fifty acres near the hill, and already the cemetery compares well with older ones near other cities. The hill itself—formerly called Sand hill, and now known as Crown hill, giving name to the cemetery—covers a base of twelve or fifteen acres, and is over one hundred feet high. It is yet unimproved, and it is proposed to use it as the site for the receiving reservoir in the contemplated system of water-works. Water is an excellent absorbent of gases arising from the decomposition of decaying bodies, and water consumers would be constantly reminded of their departed ancestors, by the taste and smell of their daily beverage.

A line of omnibuses was established to the grounds in 1864, but the facilities for reaching the spot were not thought sufficient, and in the spring of 1866, propositions were made to extend the street railroad from the terminus at the north end of Illinois street, to the cemetery. The residents in the neighborhood, the cemetery board of directors, and the street railroad company finally made the necessary arrangements, and the line was completed during the fall of 1866 and spring of 1867, and opened for travel in April or May.

In May, 1866, the board dedicated a tract of ground to the government, for the interment of the Union soldiers buried in the vicinity of the city. The grant was accepted, and during the fall and following spring, the transfer of the bodies was effected under the direction of the government authorities, and the spot dedicated with appropriate ceremonies. On the 30th of May, 1868, under a general order issued by Gen. Logan, commander of the Grand Army of the Republic, a grand ovation was paid to the memory of the Union dead. Arrangements had been made by appro-

priate committees. The ladies labored zealously in preparing the floral tributes. A procession marched to the grounds, which were thronged by several thousand spectators, and after an address, singing and other preliminary exercises, each grave was wreathed and strewed with flowers by young ladies, and orphans of deceased soldiers. The demonstration was a grand success, the only drawback being the difficulty experienced by many in reaching and returning from the grounds. Business was generally suspended, and the day observed as a holiday. It is probable that the ceremony will be continued annually hereafter.

This article may close with a rapid and brief mention of the more important acts of the city government from 1861 to 1867.

The mayor, in May 1862, called the attention of the Council to the number of abandoned women incarcerated in the jail, and the bad results arising from such a course toward them. He recommended the erection of a house of refuge to which they could be sent, and in which a reformatory treatment could be pursued. Nothing, however, was done at the time with the project. On the 27th of July, 1863, S. A. Fletcher, Sr., submitted a proposition to the Council, offering to give seven or eight acres of ground south of the city as a site, provided the city would agree to erect the buildings. Estimates, by D. A. Bohlen, architect, were also filed, fixing the cost of the house at $8,000, and a Citizens Committee, at the same time, asked that the proposed enterprise should be committed to the care of the Sisters of the Good Shepherd. The donation was accepted by the Council August 10th; $5,000 were appropriated toward the house, which was to be used partly as a house of refuge for abandoned and drunken women, and partly as a city prison for females. Plans were submitted and adopted on the 24th of August. The house was put in charge of the building committee, and a board of three trustees provided for. Contracts were let in the fall, and during the next year the basement story was finished in good style. The rapid advance in material and labor caused great loss to the contractor, and difficulty ensued between him and the city. The work stopped and has ever since been suspended. The entire cost thus far being about $8,000. Good faith to the generous donor of the site, and charity to the class provided for by the enterprise demand the speedy completion of the buildings.

A society for the amelioration of the condition of fallen women was formed in 1866, with a board of trustees and direc-

tors and a list of officers. Aid was also to be extended to worthy and friendless females. A house was rented in the north part of the second ward as a home for the friendless, and a home for those wishing to escape the life of infamy to which they seemed condemned. It was placed in charge of Mrs. Sarah Smith as matron, and has since sheltered many of this unfortunate class. Some have been entirely reclaimed, and the institution seems destined to effect much good. Material aid has recently been asked from the Council, and it is not improbable that to the society will be given the charge of the house of refuge when that building is completed.

The city ordinance required parties building houses to obtain special permission before obstructing the streets with materials. These applications consumed much time in the council, and to avoid further trouble from this source, an ordinance establishing a board of public improvements was introduced in the fall of 1863. It remained pending for several months, and on the 19th of April, 1864, another ordinance was substituted and passed, creating a board of public improvements, to be composed of three members annually selected from the council. They were to choose one of their number president, and the city clerk was to be their secretary. All projects connected with the public buildings, market houses, bridges, culverts, sewers, drains, cisterns, street improvements, parks, gas lighting, waterworks, &c., were to be referred to them for examination, and all work was to be executed under their direction. They were to report their action in all cases to the council. Persons intending to build, repair or remove houses, were to get permits from the board, giving the location, cost, &c., of the proposed work, and a register was to be kept and reported of the permits.

The board made no annual report for 1864, and the extent and value of the improvements for that year can not be given; but in 1865 they reported that one hundred and fifty houses costing $200,000, were built in the Additions, and one thousand four hundred and seventy-one permits issued for buildings and repairs in the city, costing $1,850,000. Nine miles of streets and eighteen miles of side-walks were graded and graveled; one mile of street was bouldered, and four miles of side-walk paved; three miles of streets were lighted. In 1866 permits for one thousand one hundred and twelve houses, costing $1,065,000, were issued; eight and one-half miles of streets and sixteen miles of side-walks graded and graveled; three and a half squares of streets bouldered, and two miles of side-walks paved; three miles were lighted. In 1867 one hundred and ninety-five houses, costing $770,470, were built, and five hundred and fifty-two permits for repairs, costing $132,050 were issued; four and one-half miles of streets and nine of side-walks were graded and graveled; four squares were bouldered, and twenty-two squares of side-walks paved; four and one-half miles of streets were lighted. The members of the board receive pay for the time actually employed, and the clerk receives fees for the permits issued.

Under the provisions of the incoporation act, the council, on the 1st of October, 1864. nominated L. Vanlandingham, A. Naltner, James Sulgrove, D. S. Beatty and D. V. Culley as a board of city commissioners, to assess damages and benefits from the opening of new streets or alleys, or the cutting of sewers or new channels for streams. The nominations were confirmed soon after by the common pleas court, and applications of that nature have since been referred to that board.

The many troops and prisoners stationed here had caused uneasiness among medical men for fear of sudden epidemics. The prevalence of measles, small pox and cholera had been prevented by care and prompt attention—small pox cases being treated in a small building on the hospital grounds. In January, 1864, however, cases of small pox became quite numerous not only among the troops, but in different parts of the city; and in February, the government and city authorities rented ground and built a pest house on the river, two miles north-west of town. Further cases were promptly sent there, and the spread of the disease was soon checked. After the war the government turned the house over to the city, and the ground was afterward bought and deeded to the city, December 23d, 1865.

Repeated complaints of the inefficient drainage on Illinois street and elsewhere, and of the damage caused by Virginia river, Pogue's run and Lake McCarty, had been made to the council. Various plans for improving the drainage at small expense, had been proposed and considered at different times without result, and sewers had been advocated on particular streets. The council in July, 1865, selected James W. Brown, F. Stein and L. B. Wilson as a board of engineers to take levels on all the streets, and devise a general system of sewers for the city. Money was appropriated for the work, and the survey and profile was made during the fall. The expense involved had hitherto prevented the building of any regular sewers, but a tax of fifteen cents was levied in May, 1868,

for a sewerage fund, and the council is now considering the propriety of building sewers to drain Lake McCarty and provide against floods in Virginia river. The res idents in the seventh and eighth wards along the course of the last named bayou have been repeatedly drowned out. The trouble is increasing every year with the rapid settlement and improvement in that section, and large claims for damages are now pending against the city, with the prospect of many more in future. Some of them have already been decided against the city by the courts.

A large number of additions adjoining the corporation limits had been thickly settled, and the parties who lived in them were doing business in the city, and had the advantages of the city government and improvements without contributing by taxation to the city finances. It was proposed in 1865 to annex them to the city, under the provisions of the incorporation act, and an ordinance to include the additions on the north line of the city was introduced in the council, but while it was pending a remonstrance from the parties interested was presented against the measure, demanding that all the additions should be included. A new ordinance, therefore, was drawn up and introduced in December, 1865, providing for the annexation by name of forty-five separate additions adjoining the city on the north, east and south sides. The measure was resisted by the people of the additions, and the council, after consideration of the expense involved for police and other items for the new territory, let the matter drop for the time.

During 1865, several former railway enterprizes, suspended by hard times or by the war, were revived, and in May, 1866, petitions, largely signed by the citizens, were presented to the council, asking a subscription by the city to the Vincennes, Indiana & Illinois Central, and Crawfordsville lines, to enable them to construct their roads. The petitions being laid over for additional signatures, they were soon obtained by committees, and on the 21st of May, the council voted to issue $154,000 in twenty year bonds, in sums of $1,000 each, to be divided as follows: $60,000 to the Vincennes road, $45,000 to each of the other lines, and at a subsequent date the same amount was voted to the Junction road. The companies were first to finish forty miles of road inside of three years, favor the city in freights, and comply with other conditions. Work was afterward begun, and has been actively prosecuted on all except the Indiana and Illinois Central, the Junction road being completed, and

the Vincennes well advanced at the present time.

Several serious accidents having occurred by collisions between street cars and other vehicles, with trains on the Union track, the council on the 5th of February, 1866, ordered the employment of flagmen by the railroad company at each crossing; it being their duty to constantly watch the trains, and warn all parties of their approach. The company at once complied with the ordinance, and since that time few or no accidents have happened.

During the summer of 1866, to get rid of the heavy charges made for boarding city prisoners in the county jail, the council determined to build a station house, and after examining various sites, bought a lot in September, on Maryland, between Pennsylvania and Meridian, at $4,000. No subsequent effort has been made to build the house. Propositions were made at about the same time to rent buildings for the city offices, or sell lots for the site of a city hall. The Second Presbyterian church was offered at $15,000, in bonds. The Journal company offered to build a block next their office, and Andrew Wallace tendered his building. The council declined all these proposals, and resolved not to build a hall till the debt was paid.

On the 29th of October, 1866, the council passed the eight hour law. The question arose, (but was ignored,) whether it applied to the officers and police. It was applied by the street commissioner in his department, but as he reduced the wages in the same proportion, trouble ensued with the employees, who resisted the reduction in their pay. The commissioner applied to the council for instructions, but was advised to use his own discretion in the matter. The ten hour system has since been restored.

The names of the streets were ordered to be put on the lamps in November, 1866. In December, propositions for an alarm telegraph were received from several parties, but declined, and the arrangement was finally completed in 1867-'68, as stated in the history of the fire department. In February, 1867, the Vincennes railroad and Indianapolis Furnace company, were authorized to lay tracks on Kentucky avenue. The corner stone of the Catholic Cathedral, on Tennessee street, was laid with appropriate ceremonies, on the 20th of July, 1867, in presence of a vast audience. The building will be of brick, with white stone facings, and is in the regular gothic style, with nave, transept, center and side aisles, high altar, and great eastern window. It is about 56 by 195 feet, will be very solidly built, and is to have the high-

est spire in the country. The walls are now being constructed, but several years will elapse before its completion. The estimated cost is over $300,000. It will be the largest religious edifice in the State.

The author regrets that he has failed to procure the facts connected with the organization of the several Catholic churches, schools, and societies in the city, and will therefore give generally such information as he has obtained.

St. John's Church, on west Georgia street, a small, plain, brick edifice, built about 1850, is the oldest one here. It has a large number of communicants, and is in charge of Rev. August Bessonies, who succeeded Rev. Daniel Maloney. St. Mary's Church, under Rev. Simon Seigri-t, was built in 1858, on east Maryland street, near Delaware, and has many communicants, mostly Germans. St Peter's Church, on Dougherty street, near Virginia avenue, was built about 1865, and is in charge of Rev. Joseph Petit. Flourishing Sabbath schools are attached to each of these churches, and a number of church and charitable societies are also directly or indirectly connected with them.

St. John's Academy for girls, in charge of the Sisters of Providence, is situated on Georgia and Tennessee streets, adjoining the Cathedral and St. John's Church. The buildings, (erected about 1860,) are well designed, and the school is large, well conducted and prosperous. St John's Academy for boys, east of St. John's church, is in the care of Rev. August Bessonies. St. Mary's Academy for boys, on the alley south of St Mary's church, is of brick, and three stories high. A school for young children in charge of Mrs Keating, is supported by the St. Peter's church congregation.

The writer neglected to state in its proper place, the fact that a very large and flourishing private German school has been conducted for ten or eleven years past, on east Maryland street, between Delaware and Alabama streets. The school-house, (originally small,) was much enlarged, and improved in its arrangements two or three years since. Several hundred pupils are in attendance.

The Saturday Evening Mirror, a literary weekly journal, was first issued December 22d, 1867, from an office in Schnull's building, by Harding & Henry: George C. Harding, the former noted war correspondent of the Cincinnati Commercial, and the local editor of the Journal and of the Sentinel, at subsequent periods, being editor. It was published on Sunday for a short time, but the Sentinel beginning the issue of a Sunday paper, the publication day of the Mirror was changed to Saturday. J. R. Morton subsequently bought Henry's interest, the office was removed to Tilford's building, on Circle street, and the paper is now issued by Harding & Morton, with G. C. Harding and W. B. Vicke.., as editors. It has been much enlarged, is well conducted, and has steadily advanced in public favor.

The commissioners in the original survey made no provision for a public park, and with the exception of the squares or parts o: squares, reserved for State, County, Hospital, University and Market purposes, no public square was designated. So long as the town was openly built, and the wide streets properly shaded, the want of public grounds was unfelt, but in recent years, with the crowding of population and the paving of the streets, the increased noise, dust and heat, drew attention to a want formerly unconsidered. The city took possession of the Circle, University square, and military grounds, in 1860, and since that date has expended considerable sums in the improvement and planting of each as public grounds, but the limited area afforded by these tracts will not supply the future demand for a properly constructed and ornamented park. To supply in some measure this public want, and as a memorial of Calvin Fletcher, Sr., the heirs of that gentleman, in the spring of 1868, offered to donate thirty acres in a triangular form, adjoining the Bellefontaine railway at the north-east corner of the city, for a public park; the city in case of acceptance, to expend the sum of $30,000 on it in improvements within a given period. The offer was at first favorably considered by the council, but unexpected opposition arose, partly on account of the location, partly on account of the expenditure to be incurred, and partly from the jealousy of the sections not thus favored. After long consideration, the city council coupled other conditions with the acceptance of the donation, and the offer was withdrawn. This result is to be regretted, for such tracts will ultimately be needed, not only in that neighborhood, but elsewhere, and they should be secured while the ground is comparatively cheap.

A brief statement of the facts connected with the formation of the leading libraries in the city may be given here. First in importance, both for the variety and number of volumes it contains, is the collection made by the State, now placed in the lower rooms of the State house. Its formation began shortly after the organization of the State government, though but little had been achieved until after the erection of the State house. The few books prior to

that date had been kept in the Court house and Circle building. It has since gradually increased, by donations. exchanges and purchases, (a small appropriation being annually made for the purpose,) until it now numbers between twenty-five and thirty-thousand volumes. Many of these are in foreign languages, gifts from foreign governments. The library was at first used both for reference and circulation The State officers, legislators, judiciary, attorneys and professional men only being entitled to take books out, though any one could use them for reference at the library room The circulating feature was afterward abandoned, it being found that valuable sets were broken, and many books annually lost. The library is well supplied with works in the several departments, and contains some rare and valuable books. Though in better condition now than in former years, it has never been as well arranged and catalogued as it should be. The several rooms on the west side of the State house are now occupied by the library, and by the trophies and flags collected and returned by Indiana regiments in the Mexican war, and war of the rebellion.

B. F. Foster, Gordon Tanner, S. D. Lyon, R. D. Brown, Nathaniel Bolton, J hn B. Dillon, John Cook and others, have been the librarians

The collection of books for the County library began shortly after the organization of the county, two per cent. of the lot-fund sales being set apart for that purpose, and though many of the original books have been lost or worn out, the library has slowly and constantly increased until it now numbers over two thousand volumes It has been located in the upper room of Court house for many years, and has been in charge of James A. Hamilton. John W. Hamilton, Calvin Taylor, John Caven and others, as librarians. Seventy-five cents fee per year is charged for the use of books, and the library, which is well selected and valuable, is largely patronized, but it deserves even more attention than it receives.

The township library, formerly kept in the upper rooms of the Court house, but more recently in the third story of Herreth's block, was formed under the law of 1852, providing for the formation of such collections, and levying taxes for their purchase and maintenance. It numbered about two thousand volumes of generally well selected works, but many of the volumes have since been lost and destroyed, and not over twelve or fourteen hundred are now retained. It is free to all readers, who can take out books if they choose, and is very well patronized.

The Indianapolis Library Society, the first private library association here, was formed in 1827, and collected by donation, subscription and purchase, a considerable number of good books, which were located the greater part of the time the organization existed, in the Circle building, and used by the members. Obed Foote, Sr, was the librarian. The greater part of the volumes were lost, and the rest divided, and the organization died after seven or eight years.

The next private library was collected by the Union Literary Society, formed in 1835, and existing till 1851. This collection consisted of several hundred books, for the use of the members, and after the death of the society, was handed over to the Young Men's Christian Association.

The Young Men's Christian Association formed in 1854, soon afterward began the collection of a library, receiving the books of the Union Literary Society, and adding thereto until about 1,500 volumes are now found in their rooms, under charge of Rev. Mr. Armstrong, librarian.

The Young Men's Library Association, formed in 1863, shortly thereafter established a reading room in the third story of Hubbard's block, gave annual courses of lectures, and began the formation of a library, which at present includes about two hundred volumes, mostly current magazine literature. The annual fee required of members is $5, entitling the holder to the use of the library and reading room, and attendance during the annual course of lectures. John Caven, has been president of the association since its origin.

The Ames Institute, a literary, lecture and library society, formed in 1860, has since accumulated a library of about five hundred volumes, now stored at the society room in Wesley Chapel. Carl Hamlin is president of the organization.

The writer has now briefly considered the leading events in the progress of the city from its first settlement to the present time. This consideration has shown that it has passed through four separate periods of development. The first began in the temporary reputation and prosperity enjoyed by the town when selected in 1820, as the seat of government. The location immediately drawing a relatively large population here, when the surrounding county was a complete wilderness. The slow development of a region so heavily timbered, the sickness among the early settlers, the delay in establishing the government here, and the want of communication with the outside world, put a stop to this speedy advance, and though the Capital was afterward removed here, very little improve-

ment in the prospects of the town took place. The Internal Improvement scheme in 1836, began the second era, and for the time completely changed the aspect of affairs. Another sudden advance occurred. A marked increase in trade, in population, and in wealth, was visible, and the town was assuming an important rank, when the failure and suspension of the public works cut short its career. Its subsequent growth was very slow, being governed by the development of the surrounding territory, and it remained a country village of the better class, till October, 1847. The completion of the Madison railroad in that month and year, began the third era, giving the town an outlet, and making it a center for the surplus products of the surrounding region. From that time till the war of the rebellion, its growth was steady, rapid and solid, and the foundation gradually laid for its future trade, but it still remained subordinate to other business centers. The fourth period began with the war in 1861, the place being at first stopped in its development, but soon advancing with a rapidity astounding to those who had been educated only by their early experiences here, and who constantly predicted a downfall The war growth, though so rapid, was a healthy one. It was the direct result of a large trade, and the fact that a greater scope of territory was made tributary to the city, and had manufacturing been largely commenced at the close of the war, no permanent cessation of the trade and growth of the place would have occurred. The four periods of development in the history of the city show that just as facilities for trade and travel have been increased, just so certain and constant has been its subsequent growth. Merchants and manufacturers should apply the lesson, and not only aid every effort to open new channels, but go before, and interest themselves in the trade and products of the region to be traversed by them. A great trading and manufacturing center may be created here by proper effort, and the destiny of the city rests directly in the hands now controlling its active business. On the merchants, bankers and manufacturers, rests the responsibility for its future growth or decadence and they can not escape it by waiting for citizens of other sections to do that which so clearly devolves upon them.

This sketch is now ended. No apology is needed for the effort to write it, but one is due for the manner in which the task has been executed. When the writer consented to undertake it, he intended to give merely a general review of the progress of the city from its first settlement, (revising, correcting and extending an article he had prepared for the Directory of 1857,) and limiting the sketch to forty-eight pages. The material collected soon compelled an enlargement of the work, and finally much care was needed to prevent its expansion to a volume. All attempt at embellishment by personal sketches or anecdote, was abandoned, and the author's sole aim was to crowd the greatest number of facts, important or unimportant, into the fewest words, the object being to perpetuate matter that would soon be irrecoverably lost. To this cause must be ascribed the careless style, the paragraphic character of the contents, and the repetition of the same facts in different connections. Many of these repetitions were necessary, but others, especially in the last half of the work, arose from the fact that several compositors were constantly wanting "copy," and as fast as the manuscript was prepared, it went to the printer, and not being again seen by the writer, some repetitions unavoidably occurred. The collection of material and its preparation for the press, has been done at night, or in leisure moments, amid the press of other matters. It has involved much rapid and exhausting labor, and though errors have doubtless been committed, the author trusts he has recovered so much that was almost lost, that crudities in style and inaccuracies in statement will be forgiven.

The author would return his thanks to the old citizens who assisted him by their personal statement of facts, and especially to the heirs of the late Calvin Fletcher, for the use of the files of papers collected and left by that gentleman, from which, far more than from any other source, the facts were secured on which this article is founded.

IGNATIUS BROWN.

www.ingramcontent.com/pod-product-compliance
Lightning Source LLC
Chambersburg PA
CBHW030831270326
41928CB00007B/1005